Thomas Stiverd Livius

Mary in the Epistles

The implicit teaching of the apostles concerning the Blessed Virgin contained in

their writings

Thomas Stiverd Livius

Mary in the Epistles
The implicit teaching of the apostles concerning the Blessed Virgin contained in their writings

ISBN/EAN: 9783337163815

Printed in Europe, USA, Canada, Australia, Japan

Cover: Foto ©Lupo / pixelio.de

More available books at **www.hansebooks.com**

MARY IN THE EPISTLES

OR

The Implicit Teaching of the Apostles concerning the Blessed Virgin

CONTAINED IN THEIR WRITINGS

Illustrated from the Fathers and other Authors

WITH

INTRODUCTORY CHAPTERS

BY THE

Rev. THOMAS LIVIUS, C.SS.R.

M.A., Oriel College, Oxford

LONDON: BURNS & OATES, Ld.
NEW YORK: CATHOLIC PUBLICATION SOCIETY CO.
1891

PREFACE

It would be a mistake to infer from the Title given to this volume that everything which has been applied in it to the Blessed Virgin is held to be actually contained in the Apostolic writings. On the contrary I am well aware that some of the applications, whether of texts from the Epistles or from saints and theologians, have been made rather by way of pious accommodation or illustration. But after making all necessary deductions, I hold that enough remains fully to sustain my thesis as explained in the *Introductory Chapters*, viz., that there is a considerable amount of teaching on our Lady implicitly contained in the Canonical Epistles; and I show by the quotations adduced that this view is borne out by the Fathers and ecclesiastical writers.

If I cite at times passages which some may deem irrelevant, or of purely accommodated application, I do so for the purpose of showing that my method is not novel, but was familiar to saints and theologians, and is entirely consonant with the traditional teaching of the Catholic Church; even though the whole ground that I occupy has not perhaps been before entered upon *ex professo*.

The aim of my work is positive, rather than controversial: its treatment devotional, rather than scientific; being set forth in what might be called, *Devout Comments*.

At the end of the volume will be found an alphabetical list of the Authors cited, and their date, with a reference to the page in which the several quotations appear; and also an analytical Index of the principal subjects, together with the places where they are treated.

T. LIVIUS, C.SS.R.

Feast of the Presentation of the B.V. Mary,
    21*st November*, 1890.

CONTENTS.

	PAGE
Preface, ...	v

MARY IN THE EPISTLES.
INTRODUCTORY CHAPTERS.

CHAPTER I.
The Fallacy of the Argument of Silence in the Epistles, illustrated by Sunday Observance, and Administration of Baptism, ...   3

CHAPTER II.
On the little that is said about the Blessed Virgin in the Gospels, ...   20

CHAPTER III.
The Oral Teaching of the Apostles on the Blessed Virgin in their General Preaching and Catechetical Instructions, ...   42

CHAPTER IV.
Reasons for the Silence of the Apostles on the Blessed Virgin in their Epistles, ...   65

CHAPTER V.
The Implicit Teaching of the Apostles on the Blessed Virgin in their Epistles, ...   80

CHAPTER VI.
The Catholic View of the Blessed Virgin as an Ideal of all Christian Perfection, ...   87

COMMENTS ON THE EPISTLES.

The Epistle of S. Paul to the Romans,	97
The First Epistle of S. Paul to the Corinthians,	133
The Second Epistle of S. Paul to the Corinthians,	155
The Epistle of S. Paul to the Galatians,	171
The Epistle of S. Paul to the Ephesians,	181
The Epistle of S. Paul to the Philippians,	196
The Epistle of S. Paul to the Colossians,	203
The First Epistle of S. Paul to the Thessalonians,	208
The Second Epistle of S. Paul to the Thessalonians,	210
The First Epistle of S. Paul to Timothy,	212
The Second Epistle of S. Paul to Timothy,	218
The Epistle of S. Paul to Titus,	220
The Epistle of S. Paul to Philemon,	221
The Epistle of S. Paul to the Hebrews,	222
The Catholic Epistle of S. James,	240
The First Epistle of S. Peter,	248
The Second Epistle of S. Peter,	254
The First Epistle of S. John,	256
The Catholic Epistle of S. Jude,	263
The Apocalypse of S. John,	264
Note A,	275
Note B,	279
List of Authors, quoted or referred to on the pages indicated,	281
Analytical Index of Subjects,	286

INTRODUCTORY CHAPTERS.

CHAPTER I.

THE FALLACY OF THE ARGUMENT OF SILENCE IN THE EPISTLES ILLUSTRATED BY SUNDAY OBSERVANCE, AND ADMINISTRATION OF BAPTISM.

WERE a candid and earnest Protestant asked what was the principal difficulty that prevented him from joining in the praises and honours which the Catholic Church offers to the Blessed Virgin Mary, he would reply, if we mistake not, that it was founded on the utter silence of S. Paul and the other Apostles regarding Our Lady in their numerous Epistles.

They enter, he would say, into such minute details concerning the whole spiritual life, and give so many precepts and exhortations on every virtue, that had " devotion to the Blessed Virgin" held the place in their minds that it did later on, and does still amongst Catholics, they could not possibly have left it, as we find they do, entirely unnoticed, without making to it even some distant allusion.

It would be useless to quote passages from Protestant writers insisting on this objection. They are innumerable. But the objection scarcely requires development. Its meaning is sufficiently clear at a glance : and we cannot deny that it has an apparent force. It is one, moreover, that presents itself to some

Catholics, especially to converts to the faith in the early days of their conversion. Hence it is an objection that justly claims some explanation at the hands of Catholics.

To solve the objection entirely would demand a lengthened treatise on the formation and scope of Holy Scripture—particularly of the Epistles, which form so large a part of the New Testament—as well as a full explanation of the relations between Scripture and Tradition. Such a treatise is quite beyond our present purpose. We shall, however, treat cursorily on these topics, so far as their immediate application to the matter which we have in hand may seem to demand.

Our main object in these introductory chapters is first—after giving some reasons why the Evangelists say comparatively so little on our Blessed Lady in the Gospel—to account for the silence which the Apostles preserve regarding her both in their public preaching as recorded by S. Luke and also in their Epistles: and secondly to examine into the nature of this silence; when we shall endeavour to show that devotion to Mary indirectly, but inevitably, flows from principles laid down in every page of the Apostolic writings.

Here, for the moment, we shall content ourselves with a general answer to the following question: What is the force of the argument drawn from the silence of the Apostles regarding devotion to the Blessed Virgin; and does it prove that such devotion was unknown to them, was untaught, or forbidden by them? If so, then we urge that the same argument of their silence must hold good with regard to other matters also, and will, in particular, henceforth abrogate Sunday observance as a Christian duty, and show that the ordinary mode of administering Baptism is quite indefensible.

First, as regards the observance of Sunday.

We are not now referring to the change, adopted by Protestants from the Catholic Church, of the seventh day of the week to the first: but what we mean is, that the objection made against our devotion to the Blessed Virgin on the ground of Apostolic silence, would prove that no day whatever in the week should be observed beyond the rest, or what would be almost the same thing, that there should be no week at all.

We may fairly retort his own argument on the Protestant in this manner:

We find amongst you that the Sunday, or the Lord's Day, or the Sabbath, is held to be an institution of the greatest religious importance. It affects the whole of your spiritual life in a very marked manner. Your apologists abound in treatises on the duty and advantages of observing the Sabbath, while your preachers and moralists and tract-writers often enough inveigh against the sin and evil consequences of sabbath-breaking.

Now, after carefully examining all the Epistles which have come down from the Apostles, and the history of their Acts, we find no allusion whatsoever to any such practice as Sunday observance existing as a Christian duty in their time amongst their disciples.[1] We read,

[1] We readily allow that the mention of the "first day of the week" in a few places of the New Testament may tend to confirm an already-formed conviction that the Christian Sabbath was an Apostolic ordinance. But such casual mention is far too slight and indefinite to serve for proof of the fact, or of any obligation for Christians to keep the Sunday, and could avail

indeed, of S. Paul preaching on the Sabbath day in the synagogues of the Jews, but this only proves that *they*
for corroboration with those only who had already accepted the observance as Apostolic on other grounds.

The following are the passages referred to :—

Matt. xxviii. 1.   *Mark* xvi. 2, 9.   *Luke* xxiv. 1.   *John* xx. 19. Where "the first day of the week" is recorded as that of our Lord's Resurrection, and *John* xx. 26, of one of His appearances to His disciples : "After eight days again," that is, on the following first day of the week.

Acts xx. 7. Where S. Luke writes : "We came to Troas . . . and on the first day of the week, when we were assembled to break bread, Paul discoursed with them."

1 *Cor.* xvi. 2. Where S. Paul gives order that "on the first day of the week every one put apart with himself, laying up what it shall please him," so that the collection of alms be ready when he should come to Corinth.

Apoc. i. 10. Where S. John writes: "I was in the spirit on the Lord's day."

Protestants, on their side, should not here forget that though the New Testament is silent on the practice in the Church of devotion to Our Lady, still Catholics can appeal for its justification and support to certain plain passages in the Gospel that bear with far more importance on that devotion, than do these passing allusions to the first day of the week on Sunday observance. We mean where S. Luke records how the Archangel Gabriel was sent by God Himself to the Virgin of Nazareth, how reverently he saluted her, and with what words of praise he addressed her; how Elizabeth, under the inspiration of the Holy Ghost, broke forth in benediction of Mary, humbled and amazed at the too great honour that the Mother of her Lord had done her in deigning to visit her; how the Baptist, yet unborn, rejoiced at her presence, and was sanctified at the voice of her salutation; how the humble Virgin herself uttered her inspired prophecy, proclaiming that thenceforth and for ever all the generations of God's faithful should unite in ascribing to her blessing and praise.

observed it, and that he took advantage of the occasion. The Apostle preached, for that matter, wherever and whenever he could find hearers, whether on the Sabbaths in the synagogues, or to the heathen on Areopagus, or every day of the week, as at Ephesus for two whole years in the School of Tyrannus, or at Rome in his own hired lodgings.[1] But when S. Paul is writing to Christians he never exhorts them to observe the Sabbath, and nowhere mentions sabbath-breaking among the sins to be avoided. We should remark too that whereas all the other commandments of the decalogue are to be found in the Epistles, either in their formal or equivalent statement, the commandment to keep holy the Sabbath day, on which Protestants lay such special stress, is the one alone to which no allusion is ever made.

Nay, we might go even further than this, and show that the Apostle seems to speak of the observance of one day rather than another as something that may, indeed, be tolerated among those who are so weak as to attach importance to it, but must be positively resisted, if it is sought to elevate such observance into a duty.

Thus, writing to the Romans in favour of mutual charity and forbearance, he says :—" One judgeth between day and day, and another judgeth every day: let every man abound in his own sense."[2] Whereas, writing to the Galatians against those who wished to impose the Jewish law on Christians, he says :—" You observe days and months, and times, and years ; I am

---

[1] *Acts* xix. 9, 10. xxviii. 30, 31.   [2] *Rom.* xiv. 5.

afraid of you, lest perhaps I have laboured in vain among you." [1]

Hence we would ask a fair-minded Protestant to consider whether there is not as little in favour of the observance of the Sabbath in the Epistles, as there is in favour of devotion to the Blessed Virgin; or, as we might rather put it, whether, from what is actually said in the Epistles about Sabbath observance, there is not more in apparent opposition to *his* practice, than he can thence allege to be in apparent opposition to ours.

The passage which, perhaps, above all others, a Protestant would bring forward from the Epistles, as most in direct opposition to devotion to the Blessed Virgin, is the following:—" Let no man seduce you willing in humility, and religion of angels " [2] — or, as it is in the Protestant version:—" Let no man rob you of your prize by a voluntary humility [or, *of his own mere will, by humility.* Marg.] and worshipping of the angels."

Protestants interpret these words as condemnatory of all invocation of Angels and Saints. But they should bear in mind that the warning conveyed in them is immediately preceded by another regarding Sabbath observance:—" Let no man judge you in respect of a festival day, or of the new moon, or of the sabbaths." [3]

But were an objector to quote these last words against keeping the Sunday, as Protestants quote the

[1] *Gal.* iv. 10, 11.   [2] *Col.* ii. 18.
[3] *Ib.*, v. 16.

words that follow against the invocation of Saints, what would be the answer?

Probably, that the institution of the Christian Sabbath, though in some respects similar, was very different from that of the Jews; that the Apostle was condemning the latter, not the former; that he could not intend to blame the setting apart one day in the week for a more direct and perfect worship of God, and attention to our souls, since such a custom is both innocent and useful, and even necessary, considering what men are; and the like.

Now we make a similar reply regarding "the religion of angels." Supposing that the phrase means the invocation of created spirits—which is a disputed point both among Catholics and Protestants[1]—still, we reply, the Apostle is not condemning such invocation as the Catholic Church sanctions, but what was being taught by certain philosophers and ancient heretics.[2] And to prove what we say, we point to the

---

[1] It is wonderful how any "text" will serve the purpose of those who are determined to "have a hit" at Catholics. Melancthon took "the religion of angels" to be celibacy, because our Lord declares the angels to be unmarried, and, therefore, the doctors of the Church call celibacy, "the angelic life." On the other hand, the late Dr. Cumming, who had Popery on the brain, interprets S. Paul's words to Timothy:—" In the last times some shall depart from the faith giving heed to doctrines of devils," in this way: " doctrines about $\delta\alpha\iota\mu o\nu\epsilon\varsigma\ daimons$, i.e., intercessors, or canonised men."—*Voices of the Day*, p. 428. So it is all the same, angels or devils, if only the Church can be attacked.

[2] The Apostle had already bid the Colossians beware of such false philosophy and erroneous teaching in v. 8.

words that next follow:—" Not holding the Head, from which the whole body, by joints and bands being supplied with nourishment and compacted, groweth unto the increase of God."

The invocation of Saints (it is thus we argue) is certainly not an abandonment of the Head, but a most emphatic recognition of Him. To say, " Holy guardian angel, pray to Jesus for me," is not a denial that Jesus is the Head and Source of grace; but it is simply to recognise the angel as a " joint or band," and to seek for a supply of nourishment and strength through that band from the Head.

We might go on to show that prayers offered to the Saints are most innocent and salutary, and that devotion to the Blessed Virgin—not as to the Head, but as to the neck, so to say, which connects the body to the head, and as being the principal of those joints or bands of which the Apostle speaks—is a devotion full of holy influences and spiritual profit.[1]

---

[1] MARIOLATRY.

Sir,—People see things very differently. I should be exceedingly sorry to back my mere opinion against any body of Churchmen infinitely better read and more deeply acquainted with Theology than I should ever dream of professing to be; still but comparatively few of your readers have for years been Roman Catholics, but few have known high and low, rich and poor, in that communion as I have, and yet, as you know, I have, like Ffoulkes, Capes, and others, had my own mental troubles and uncertainties on the questions in dispute between Canterbury and Rome.

There is, however, one point on which never, for a single moment, have I ever had one moment's doubt—and that is, that the veneration and invocation of the Blessed Virgin is produc-

SO TOO IS DEVOTION TO MARY.

A Protestant, then, who finds it difficult to conceive that invocation of Saints and devotion to the Blessed Virgin could have existed in Apostolic times, because no direct allusion is made thereto in Apostolic writings, must not at once cry victory, as though he had already gained his point, and made out his case against Catholics. Before claiming such silence as a triumph, he should, if he is honest, and would be consistent with his principles, well consider first his own position. He holds firmly the observance of Sunday to be a very important religious duty, that it was in practice amongst Christians from the earliest times,

tive of good, not ill, in those who practise it. Fully and heartily do I re-echo the words of two such thorough Englishmen as Newman and Faber, the latter a relation of my own. The former, when he says, " He who charges us with making Mary a divinity, is thereby denying the divinity of Jesus ; " the latter, when he says, " Jesus is obscured, because Mary is kept in the background."

It may be said we are the creatures of habit—possibly it is so, but whether habit or not habit, all I know is that, as a lad in my teens, I learned ever in my prayers to add the " Hail Mary " to the " Our Father," and now a man between forty and fifty, I do not think a night or morning has ever gone by without the same old boyhood prayer being offered. Certainly my *adoration* of Jesus has not been impaired by my *veneration* of His Immaculate Mother. This is rather an opening of the closet of one's soul to the jeers of a general public ; but I feel intensely that the adoration of Jesus as God can never be complete if the intense veneration of His Mother is not part of the devotional system of the worshipper.

W. PROBYN-NEVINS.

Oxford.

—*Church Times*, Dec. 13, 1889.

and yet the entire silence of the Apostles concerning it does not militate against or shake his belief. For it is admitted on all hands, both by Catholics and Protestants, that the Christian observance of a Sabbath was taught by the Apostles as a duty, and practised in their days, though not the least trace or hint of this appears in the Apostolic Epistles.

Hence, we see that the mere argument of silence is very fallacious, and has of itself no conclusive force to determine the truth of questions in dispute.

We will now apply the same argument to another matter of religious observance common amongst Christians, viz., the almost universal mode of administering the Sacrament of Baptism, on which the Epistles are equally silent.

Protestants have for the most part, adopted the practice which has come down from the Catholic Church, of Infant baptism, and of baptism by affusion. They regard it as a Christian duty to have their infants baptised, and hold that baptism by aspersion, in place of immersion, is perfectly lawful. Consequently they must deem that such baptism is in accordance with the institution of Christ and the teaching of His Apostles. And yet neither in the Gospels, nor in the writings of the Apostles, nor in the history of their Acts, can any express warrant be found for this practice, nor any instance of such baptism be adduced, nor any direct trace of such custom be shown to have existed in Apostolic times. Nay, all that is said of baptism in the New Testament would seem to show the other way.

ON THE BAPTISM OF INFANTS.

And first as regards Infant baptism :[1]
Any one who had only his Bible to go by would, we think, naturally suppose that baptism was in-

---

[1] It will perhaps seem superfluous for us here to remark that the Catholic Church teaches that infant baptism is not only in entire conformity with the doctrine and practice of the Apostles, but also that this may be *inferred* from certain passages in the New Testament. On this subject we will quote the words of the Catechism of the Council of Trent : " *Infants are by all means to be baptised.* That this law (of baptism) is to be understood, not only of adults, but also of infants, and that the Church has received this its interpretation from Apostolic tradition, is confirmed by the concurrent doctrine of the Fathers. Besides, it must be believed that Christ our Lord was unwilling that the sacrament and grace of baptism should be denied to children of whom he said—" Suffer the little children, and forbid them not to come to me, for the kingdom of heaven is for such "— (*Matt.* xix. 14)—to children whom He embraced, on whom He imposed hands, whom He blessed.—(*Mark* x. 16.) Moreover, when we read that some entire family was baptised by Paul, children, who are included in their number, must, it is sufficiently obvious, have also been cleansed in the salutary font. Circumcision, too, which was a figure of baptism, affords a strong argument in favour of this practice. But children were circumcised on the eighth day, everyone knows.—(*Gen.* xxi. 4, *Lev.* xii. 3, *Luke* i. 59, ii. 21.) If, then, circumcision, ' made by hand, in the despoiling of the body of the flesh ' (*Coloss.* ii. 11) was profitable to children, it is clear that baptism, which is the circumcision of Christ, not made by hand, is also profitable to them. Finally, as the Apostle teaches, ' if by one man's offence, death reigned through one ; much more they, who receive abundance of grace, and of the gift, and of justice, shall reign in life through one, Jesus Christ.'—(*Rom.* v. 17.) If then through the sin of Adam children contract original guilt, with still greater reason may they attain grace and justice through Christ our Lord, to reign

tended only for adults. For whenever in the New Testament baptism is spoken of, or its administration is recorded, we find that certain moral dispositions are required for its reception, and personal acts attributed to the baptised, of which responsible adults could alone be capable. Such, for example, as hearing and accepting the word preached, believing, repenting, and receiving instruction in the faith.[1] Hence were the express statements of Holy Scripture on baptism our only source of information, we

in life, which cannot be effected otherwise than by baptism. (Conc. Trid. Sess. 5, decret. de Peccat. Orig., et Sess. 7 de Bapt. cap. 12, 13, 14.) Wherefore pastors will teach that infants are by all means to be baptised. . . . " (*Catec. Rom.* Pars ii. *De Bapt. Sacram.* n., 32.)

The teaching of the Catholic Church on the validity and lawfulness of baptism otherwise than by immersion is shown from the same Catechism, as follows: " As in the administration of this sacrament, it is also necessary to observe the legitimate mode of ablution (legitimæ ablutionis rationem), the pastor will deliver the doctrine on this point also, and will briefly explain that, by the common custom and practice of the Church, there are three ways of administering baptism—immersion, affusion, and aspersion, and that, administered in any of these three ways, it is to be held true and valid baptism; for in baptism water is used to signify the washing of the soul, which it accomplishes; whence baptism is called by the Apostle a laver. But ablution is not more really accomplished by immersion, which was long in use from the earliest times of the Church, than by affusion, which we now see to be the general practice, or aspersion, the manner in which there is reason to believe Peter administered baptism, when on one day he converted and baptised three thousand persons."—*Acts* ii. 41,—*Ib.* 17.

[1] *Acts* ii. 38, 41; viii. 36-38; ix. 18; x. 34-48; xviii. 8; xix. 5; xxii. 16. *Matt.* xxviii. 19. *Mark* xvi. 16.

should conclude that infants were inadmissible to the sacrament.

As regards the Epistles in particular, there is nothing whatever to be found in them, if we regard only their letter, that would lead us to suppose that the baptism of infants was practised in Apostolic times, nor is a single word there said by the Apostles on what is now almost universally held to be the duty of Christian parents in this matter. Indeed, we should gather from the very words of S. Paul, in the passages of his Epistles, where he speaks of baptism, that he is directly contemplating the baptism only of adults, since the effects of the sacrament which he there describes cannot meet with their adequate realisation, save in adults. Such effects are the death of the baptised to sin and to sinful works, together with their rising to the new life of holiness;[1] their hearts being cleansed from an evil conscience, as their bodies are washed in the clean water;[2] their being washed from their past actual sins, and their personal sanctification.[3]

Then, again, with regard to the *mode* of baptism.

If we are to go exclusively by what we find expressly written in the New Testament, we should have to conclude that baptism must be by immersion alone: For this is the only mode of baptism there spoken of, and,

---

[1] *Rom.* vi. 3-14.

[2] *Heb.* x. 22. Compare also *1 Peter* iii. 21.

[3] *1 Cor.* vi. 9-11. Compare v. 11, "But you are washed,"with *Acts* xxii. 16, "Rise up, and be baptised, and wash away thy sins."

so far, at least, as their own words imply, the only mode contemplated by the Sacred Writers.

The baptism of John, which was a preparation and figure of Christian baptism, was by immersion.[1] It was in this way that Jesus Christ Himself, the Head of the Church, was baptised.[2] Thus, too, we read in the Acts, the first Christians were baptised. So obviously was this the ordinary and recognised mode of baptism in Apostolic times, that it at once suggested itself to the Ethiopian eunuch on his accepting the preaching of Jesus, by Philip. "As they went on their way," writes S. Luke, " they came to a certain water, and the eunuch said: See here is water, what doth hinder me from being baptised? And Philip said: If thou believest with all thy heart, thou mayest. And he, answering, said: I believe that Jesus Christ is the Son of God. And he commanded the chariot to stand still: and they went down into the water, both Philip and the eunuch; and he baptised him. And when they were come up out of the water," etc.[3] So, again, in the account of the conversion of Lydia, through the preaching of S. Paul at Philippi, it is expressly mentioned that this took place by the river side, as though to indicate that the consequent baptism of herself and of her household, recorded in the same narrative, was in the waters of that river.[4]

As regards the Epistles: S. Paul calls baptism the "bath of regeneration," and, again, "the bath of

---

[1] *Mark* i. 5.   *Acts* xix. 4.   [2] *Matt.* iii. 16.
[3] *Acts* viii. 35-39.   [4] *Acts* xvi. 13-15.

water;"[1] and the very notion of a bath implies immersion. Moreover, all the symbolism and figures which the Apostle makes use of in his teaching on this sacrament are drawn from baptism by immersion, and in that mode alone can find their full and proper verification. It is because Christians had been immersed in the baptismal water, that S. Paul can speak of them as having mystically died, and been buried with Christ in His death, through the laver or bath of regeneration, and of their having risen thence with Christ to the new life of grace and sanctification;[2] of their having in baptism put off the garment of the old Adam, and put on that of the New, and of their being clothed with Christ.[3]

Notwithstanding, then, this objection of silence, and other difficulties of a more positive nature in the New Testament, which appear, at first sight, to weigh against Infant baptism, and baptising otherwise than by immersion—still Protestants, for the most part, recognise, with Catholics, the baptism of their infants to be a Christian duty, and agree that immersion is not obligatory, but that baptism by affusion, or even aspersion, is sufficient and lawful. They must consequently hold that such baptism—in this twofold as-

[1] λουτρὸν, lavacrum. *Tit.* iii. 5. *Eph.* v. 26.
[2] *Rom.* vi. 3-11. *Col.* ii. 12.
[3] *Gal.* iii. 27. We do not deny that the Apostle's symbolism finds its expression, to some extent, in baptism by affusion and aspersion, but not so fully or precisely as in that by immersion. We might say, indeed, that the former modes derive their significance from their association in our thoughts with the more general use in primitive times of immersion.

pect—is, in no sense, opposed, but wholly conformable to the institution of Christ, and to the teaching of His Apostles.

Hence it is clear from the principles and practice of Protestants themselves, that a doctrine, or a religious observance is not to be condemned as not Apostolic, false or wrong, simply on the ground that no mention of it is made in the written word, or even because certain objections therein may seem to be against it, and cannot be fully cleared up from that word alone. For the observance may find its justification by an appeal to reasons drawn from other sources. And such a doctrine or practice may justly be held to be in entire accord with the faith delivered by Christ to His Apostles, to have formed a part of their own teaching and practice, and rightfully to claim, as a religious duty, the assent and obedience of all Christians.

Thus we have applied the argument of silence to two most important matters of the Christian life, viz., Sunday observance, and the Sacrament of Baptism, as ordinarily administered amongst Christians, and have seen that whatever objection or difficulty such silence presents is over-ruled on other grounds, as being alone by itself, of no real force either against the lawfulness, or even the obligation of these religious usages; but that, on the contrary, their constant recognition by almost universal Christendom, forms a conclusive proof that they have been ever held, though on grounds independent of Scripture, to have had the sanction of the Apostles in their teaching, and to have been practised by their disciples in their own days.

We claim, then, that the same line of reasoning

holds good also with regard to Catholic devotion to the Blessed Virgin, and that the mere silence of the Apostles on this matter in their Epistles, has no force to disprove the existence of such devotion in their times, and affords no solid argument against believing that they themselves taught and practised this devotion, and inculcated it on their disciples.

CHAPTER II.

ON THE LITTLE THAT IS SAID ABOUT THE BLESSED VIRGIN IN THE GOSPELS.

IN reading the holy Gospels we are at times inclined to marvel, not without feelings of regret, that the Evangelists say so little, or indeed are wholly silent, on certain passages of our Blessed Lord's life on earth, about which we should be greatly interested to have some details.

We may, however, rest assured that the Holy Ghost, who inspired the sacred writers in what they have recorded, directed them also in their silence for the greater profit of the Church.

We have, for example, several circumstances narrated regarding the Conception, Birth, and Infancy of Jesus Christ, until His Presentation in the Temple on the fortieth day; and then for nearly thirty years His life is left without record, save by the mention of the flight of the Holy Family into Egypt, their return to Nazareth, and the incident of their going to the Feast at Jerusalem, and of our Lord's manifestation there in the Temple when twelve years old. Whilst the remaining eighteen years until His Baptism are summed up in those few brief words, which tell us that His days were passed in the practice of humble obedience and holiness before God and men.[1]

Let us now reverently inquire into some of the reasons why the Evangelists have made use of this economy of silence and reserve in their Gospels.

The purpose of God in inspiring the Evangelists to write their Gospels was, that the Church might have them as enduring monuments in testimony to the fulfilment of the prophecies made of old concerning the promised Messiah, through the Incarnation and Birth of Our Lord Jesus Christ, the only-begotten Son of God, made man; who, by His infinite condescension and abasement in taking our human nature, His humility and obedience, has remedied the pride and disobedience, through which man fell, and has thus shown Himself to be the Way whereby he must return to God.

The end proposed in the Gospels was, moreover, to make known Jesus Christ, by means of His holy doctrine and example, as the great Teacher of divine truth, and the giver to man of the more perfect New Law of grace and the Spirit.[2]

And, again, to proclaim Jesus Christ as the Divine Redeemer of the human race and the restorer of men's souls from spiritual death to life, who, by Himself suffering and dying upon the Cross, has made full atonement for our sins by the merits of His Precious Blood, has saved us from death; and by His Resurrection and Ascension into heaven has secured to us the means of attaining to eternal life. Thus is our

---

[1] *Luke* ii. 51, 52.   [2] *John* i. 16, 17.

Lord Jesus Christ revealed to us in the Gospels as the Way, the Truth, and the Life.[1]

It was necessary to attest by some record of facts the fulfilment of prophecy in His Divine Conception and Birth.[2] It was meet to bear witness to the mean and obscure estate of His sacred infancy and childhood by some narration of the poverty and misery that surrounded and the persecutions that accompanied Him. It was meet, too, to give testimony that still that lowly Child was the Only-begotten Son and the Wisdom of God, ever, from the first moment of His Incarnation, doing that Divine Will which He came on earth to accomplish, and occupied "about His Father's business."[3]

All this was fitting. But to sound the exhaustless depths of humiliation wherein the Divine Incarnate Word effaced Himself, shrouding His glory and hiding away all His infinite treasures of wisdom and knowledge—this needed not, but might ill assort with, any narrative in words.[4] What clearer revelation could we

---

[1] *John* xiv. 6.

[2] *Matt.* i. 18-23; ii. 14, 15, 17, 18. *Luke* i., ii.

[3] *Ps.* xxxix. 9; *Heb.* x. 9; *John* iv. 34, v. 30, vi. 38; *Luke* ii. 49.

[4] "Think not that thou hearest small things in hearing of this generation. But lift up thy soul, be straightway astonished and shudder, at hearing that God has come upon earth. For so wondrous and unlooked for was this, that thereat the angels gathered together in choir, offered praise and glory in behalf of the world for the same, and already the Prophets of old were in amazement that God was born on earth and conversed with men (*Baruch* iii. 38). For astounding exceedingly is it to hear that God, ineffable, inexpressible, incomprehensible,

have in truth of this abyss of profound abasement, than that for the greatest part of His time on earth nothing should be recorded of Him; that He should be left out of sight, with no mention made of His name or existence, save that in an obscure, out-of-the-way village He was living a life of humble subjection to His earthly parents, making withal progress in virtue with His growing years, to the approval of those about Him.[1]

St. Matthew alone records the fact of our Lord's being carried in flight to Egypt: of the circumstances of His life in Egypt, and how long He was there he says nothing; but, in mentioning the return of the Holy Family to Nazareth, the Evangelist adds

co-equal with the Father, came by a virginal womb, deigned to be born of a woman, and take for forefathers David and Abraham. But why say I David and Abraham? What is indeed far more astounding—those sinful women of whom we have just now made mention. Hearing these things, raise up thy soul, and have thought of nothing mean and low; but marvel exceedingly at this, that being the Son of God, without beginning, even His own very Son, He endured to be called also the Son of David in order that He might make thee the son of God, and endured to have a slave for His father that He might make the Lord of all a Father for thee the slave. Seest thou at once from the beginning what the Gospels are? But if thou doubtest of what concerns thee, learn then to believe it from what concerns Him? For it were much more hard, according to human reason, that God should become man than that man should be called the son of God. When, then, thou hearest that the Son of God is Son of David and of Abraham, no longer doubt that even thou, too, the son of Adam, will be son of God. For not in vain and to no purpose did He humble Himself so low, but that He intended to lift us up . . ." (S. Chrysost. *in Matt. Hom.* ii. n. 2).

[1] *Luke* ii. 51, 52.

that Jesus Christ dwelt in that town, that He might, as was prophesied of Him, be called a Nazarene[1]—an appellation held at that time in much contempt amongst the Jews[2]—which attached to Him during His life, even until His death of shame, forming part of the title that was affixed to His Cross.

How greatly should we have desired to know something of the occupations, the words, and actions of the Incarnate Word during those long years that He lived in the Holy House at Nazareth, alone with His Blessed Mother and S. Joseph. How much could Mary tell us of that hidden life and of her close companionship with Him. But if S. Luke learnt aught thereof from Mary's lips, his own were sealed. He has disclosed nothing.

This silence of Inspiration that broods over our Lord's Hidden Life is, indeed, more eloquent than many words, and has, doubtless, illumined devout souls in holy meditation with a much clearer knowledge and deeper understanding of the infinite condescension and abasement of God made man than would have done long detailed narration.

It is otherwise with what regards the public life of our Lord as the Divine Exemplar and Teacher. The Evangelist, in giving an account "of all things which

---

[1] *Matt.* ii. 22-23.

[2] "'Can any good thing come from Nazareth?' (*John* i. 46.) For it was a very mean place; and not only such was the place itself, but also the whole region of Galilee. Hence the Pharisees said: 'Search and see that out of Galilee a prophet riseth not' (vii. 52)."—S. Chrys. *Ib. Hom.* 9.

Jesus began to do and to teach,"[1] must needs record many of His works and deeds, His words and discourses. The Prophet had foretold: "Thine eyes shall see thy Teacher."[2] And our Lord Himself says: "For this was I born, and for this came I into the world, that I should give testimony to the truth. Every one that is of the truth heareth My voice;" and "I have given you an example . . ." "Learn of Me . . ."[3]

So, too, was it with His sacred Passion, whereby our Divine Redeemer has shown forth His infinite mercy and love, and has saved the world. "All flesh," it had been prophesied, "shall see the salvation of God."[4] And writes the Apostle, "The grace, the goodness and kindness of God our Saviour have appeared unto all men."[5] Hence it was fitting that the Evangelist should dwell with full detail on the bitter sufferings and Crucifixion of Jesus Christ, thereby to make manifest to all the excess of His infinite charity and the plenteousness of His Redemption.

Again, it was necessary to place on record in the Gospels very clear proofs that our Lord really rose again from the dead, as He had Himself foretold, since on the certainty of this fact rests, as on its foundation, the whole fabric of Christian faith. Here, too, we find the Evangelists multiplying their testimonies with many details. But it should be observed, whilst the

---

[1] *Acts* i. 1.   [2] *Is.* xxx. 20.
[3] *John* xviii. 37, xiii. 15; *Matt.* xi. 29.
[4] *Luke* iii. 6; *Is.* lii. 10; *Ps.* xcv. 2, xcvii. 3.
[5] *Tit.* ii. 11, iii. 4.

sacred writers irrefragably establish the *fact* of Christ's Resurrection, they leave in much obscurity all that surrounds it, and give us no information as to where He was, His manner of life, or what He was doing, during the forty days that He still remained on earth, save on the occasion of His appearances to His disciples which they were inspired to narrate. The same may be said as to their record of the Ascension. In the wisdom of God it was not expedient that we should know more on these matters than is written in the Gospels.

We are thus able to give some account of the silence preserved by the Evangelists on far the greater part of our Lord's life on earth, by showing that such reticence accords with the purpose for which, under Divine inspiration, the Gospels were written.

But if the history of our Divine Saviour is thus veiled in mystery, through the silence of the Evangelists on so many years of His life, how much more should we expect that this would be the case with regard to the Blessed Virgin.

The one central theme of the Gospels is our Lord Jesus Christ; and the principal end of their inspiration is to show Him forth to men. Whatever else they contain is solely subsidiary to this end. If others are brought upon the scene, it is for His sake alone, and to aid in making Him better known.

The Evangelists must needs speak of Mary; but what they say of her is not so much on her own account, as to show the relation that Jesus Christ bears to her. In the mystery of the Incarnation she cannot be separated from Him, nor He from her.

Since she is Mother of the Divine Word made Man, of and from whom He took His flesh. Hence she is clearly set forth as the Woman of prophecy, the Virgin Mother of Emmanuel, in the detailed narration of our Lord's divine Conception and Birth.

But since, as we have already seen, it was the intention of the Holy Spirit that the sacred writers should dwell rather on the abasements than the glories of the Incarnate Word, and for this end preserve so much silence regarding Him, much more would they be reserved and reticent on the greatness of Mary, who was but accessory to Him, and, at the same time, naturally as His Mother, so closely associated in all the humiliations of her Son.

Moreover, she herself preferred to obscure the glories of her divine maternity, and to take the place of "handmaid of the Lord," as being altogether ancillary to Him during the days of His earthly sojourn. The time will come, when He has entered into His glory, for Him to glorify her, to recompense her service, and apportion to her the preeminence due to her dignity in His mystical Body.

We need not marvel, then, at the silence, and what appears at times a mysterious economy of reserve, which we meet with in the Gospels regarding the Blessed Virgin, since all this accords well with the end for which the Evangelists were divinely inspired to write.

Still, though little be recorded concerning Mary in the Gospel page, enough is said to proclaim her divine maternity, and her perpetual virginity, her supreme blessedness above all other creatures, the veneration that is due to her, and her fulness of grace and sanctity; that she is chosen to be the chief channel of grace, whereof Jesus Christ her Son is the meritorious cause and source, to the souls of men;[1] the peculiar love of predilection, the life-long affection, devoted filial piety, honour and submission that Jesus bore to her as her Son; the choice that He made of sole converse with her, and of her sanctification before all others during the thirty years of His hidden life;[2] her tender compassion and anxious care to succour all in any need or distress; her influence and the wondrous power of her intercession with her Son, Who, at her prayer, inaugurated His public ministry with a splendid miracle, whereby He first showed forth His Divine power and glory,[3] so that His disciples believed on Him; her ready, active co-operation in the mysteries of the Incarnation and Redemption; that she was specially given by her dying Son to be the Mother of all His redeemed, to cherish and succour them as her own children, and that they in turn should look to, and cherish her as their spiritual Mother; the willing sacrifice that the love of her maternal heart made for them in assisting at the Death of her Son, when the same sword that laid open His Sacred Heart pierced through her own with bitterest sorrow.[4]

The beloved disciple S. John, to whom Jesus on the Cross commended His Blessed Mother, is himself the Evangelist who narrates the circumstance, and bears

---

[1] *Matt.* i. 18-23; *Luke* i. 26-44; ii. 4-16.
[2] *Luke* ii. 51-52.   [3] *John* ii. 1-11.
[4] *Luke* i. 38; *John* xix. 25-27, 34.

record in his Gospel that from that hour he took Mary, the Mother of his crucified Lord, " to his own " —to his home and to his heart, to cherish her thenceforth as his own Mother. Thus by his word and example he bears witness in the Gospel to that filial love and devotion to the Blessed Virgin Mary, which was to be the special characteristic mark of the Faithful of Christ in all generations to the end of the world. And let us here bear in mind that this was " the disciple whom Jesus loved," the type and model, emphatically, of all whom He loves, and calls to follow in His steps; the disciple who had reclined on His bosom at the Last Supper, and had drunk in, with large draughts, from His Sacred Heart, the spirit and affections of his Master, and with them His own devotion and love to His Most Blessed Mother. Jesus had passed His life in the closest companionship with Mary. And when He left this earth to return to heaven S. John took His place imitating His example. As tradition tells us he now lived with the Mother of Jesus, cherishing her with all the love and care of her adopted son. Her sojourning on earth being in due course ended, she went to heaven, there to be united with Jesus in glory; and the filial services of the disciple to his Mother were no longer needed. After she was gone he had still to tarry long years on earth; but all his thoughts and conversation were already in heaven, whither he followed Jesus His beloved Lord, and Mary his dearest Mother with wistful longings. His love and devotion were recompensed even here below. He was given to see Jesus in His glory, and to receive a vision of Mary in her heavenly splendour. For the honour of Mary and for the consolation of all her children, the redeemed of her Son, the disciple-Evangelist, inspired by the Holy Ghost, thus records his vision: "A great sign appeared in heaven, a woman clothed with the sun, and the moon under her feet, and on her head a crown of twelve stars."[1]

Again; though very few circumstances and incidents of Mary's life are found in the Gospel narrative, and few details are there recorded of the examples she gave and the virtues she practised. Still, from the little that is said, we may discover many traits of her character, and the inner beauties of her soul; her humility, spirit of poverty, modesty, purity of heart, holy reserve and prudence; her spirit of recollection, her habits of retirement, meditation and prayer; her love and esteem for God's word; her charity to her neighbour, forgetfulness of self, and thought of others; her promptitude in following every inspiration of grace and indication of God's Will, her strong faith, unshaken confidence, and ardent charity; her desire for the glory of God alone; her wisdom, and illumination of soul on divine things; her sublime spirit of adoration, thanksgiving, and praise; her perfect obedience to the law of God in minutest details, her abandonment to the providence and holy Will of God; her tender love for her Divine Son, and

[1] *Apoc.* xii. 1. Many of the Fathers interpret the Apocalyptic Vision of our Blessed Lady and her Divine Child: And the Holy Church gives a sanction thereto by introducing it into her Divine Office. See *Fest. Immac. Concept. B. M. V., Respons. ad Lect. vi., Capit. ad Non.,* and *Lect. viii. Die Octava.*

zeal for all His interests, and especially the work of redemption; her heroic patience, courage and fortitude; her meekness and forgiveness of insults and wrongs; her desire to suffer with her Divine Son; her union with His brethren, the Apostles, and first Christians.

We have but to go in spirit to Nazareth and Bethlehem, to Jerusalem and Egypt, and Nazareth again, to Cana, and to return to Jerusalem—we have but to think of Mary at the scenes of the Annunciation, the Visitation, the Nativity, the Purification—the Flight into Egypt, the Loss in the Temple, at the Marriage Feast of Cana; to see her on the hill of Calvary, and in the upper chamber at Pentecost—and we shall recognise in her all the virtues and traits of character which we have just enumerated. For, with a revelation of wondrous fulness, does the little recorded in the Gospels of the words and actions of Mary portray her to those who with faith and love bear impressed on their minds and hearts the image of the Mother of God. If little is said of Mary in Holy Writ, it is that we may meditate the more. Nay, that little is enough, and better than much more, to enable us to contemplate Mary as a created ideal and perfect model of grace and sanctity.

But this very silence in the Gospels on so many passages of Mary's life is of itself most eloquent in her praise. Though the Evangelists wrote under the inspiration of the Holy Ghost, the events they record came to their knowledge by human means. Of these events they were either themselves eye-witnesses, or they learnt them from the sure testimony of others.[1] For the circumstances of our Lord's life during thirty years, the Blessed Virgin must have been the chief, and of many incidents she could have been the only, living witness. From her alone would St. Luke, who has been called our Lady's Evangelist, have obtained the knowledge of what he relates concerning the Annunciation, our Lord's birth, infancy, childhood, exile in Egypt, and hidden life at Nazareth. But how short and fragmentary are the passages recorded of those thirty years. How much more, and how many interesting details might Mary have disclosed of them. In her deep humility and zeal for the glory of God alone, she would have only so much recorded about herself as was necessary for showing forth to the world her Divine Son. She would remain herself in the back-ground, appearing only here and there, and now and then, for His, or for us her children's sake.[2]

---

[1] The Evangelist, St. Luke, tells us this himself at the beginning of his Gospel. (Ch. i. 1-3.) He says that he narrates the facts of our Lord's life, "according as *they* have delivered them unto us, who from the beginning were eye-witnesses and ministers of the word:" and that "having diligently attained to all things from the beginning, it seemed good to him also," though not himself an eye-witness to write his Gospel.

[2] "In treating of the excelling dignity of the Blessed Mother of God and St. Joseph it is to be well remarked that but few things are said of them in the New Testament. And for this the following reason may be fitly assigned, viz., that the whole intention of the Evangelists and Apostles was turned to Christ: for, when He was known, and His faith sufficiently established, the excellence of His true Mother, and of His reputed father,

Before closing this chapter, we would speak more particularly of a case, in which the Evangelists themselves had direct and personal knowledge, and

could not be ignored or hidden: whilst in the few but most weighty words spoken of them, certain chief heads are indicated, that virtually contain all other things that can be said concerning the Blessed Virgin and S. Joseph, which thence flow forth as from their fountains. But if thou askest, why Christ our Lord, Who published the charity of Magdalene, and the praises of John Baptist, never spoke aught like of His Mother nor of His reputed father: I answer first, that this was due to a certain temperance and modesty of Christ: since whatever He should say of them, would seem to refer and belong to Himself. And this He avoided for our edification, saying, 'I seek, not my own glory;' and 'if I glorify myself, my glory is nothing' (*John* viii. 50, 54). Again, too, because Christ our Lord was then especially desirous to teach men His own divine origin; and when this was known, it was easy to understand the excellence of His human Conception, the dignity of His Mother, and the singular prerogative of His reputed father. Most of all, because, since the very facts and deeds, whereby Christ honoured His Mother and Joseph, spoke aloud for themselves, words were not so necessary. And lastly, it was not without special design of the Holy Ghost, that some of the mysteries and privileges of the Blessed Virgin and St. Joseph were neither written nor received by certain tradition, that opportunity might be given to learned and devout faithful for meditating and repeatedly reflecting the more on these mysteries, for discoursing on them, for publicly preaching them, and for committing to writing many things regarding the Virgin and Joseph in a reasoned way, and for drawing inferences from the principles handed down by tradition—as in treating of the Blessed Virgin have taught the learned Canus (L. xii. *De Locis*) and Suarez (tom. ii. in 3 p. in præfatione)." Morales, S. J., In cap. I., *Matt. De Christ. Dom., SS. V. Deip. Mar., ejusq. Virgin. Spons. Joseph.*—L. iii. tr. 7.

where their silence about the Blessed Virgin is the highest praise they could bestow upon her.

It is their narrative of Our Lord's appearances after His Resurrection. Here they say absolutely nothing of His appearing to His Blessed Mother. But this silence serves only to emphasise her singular faith, since all the appearances they record, were made to those who, more or less, had lost faith in His word, doubted of His Resurrection, and were consequently upbraided by Him for their unbelief.

The Evangelists were therefore inspired to narrate in detail our risen Lord's appearances to them; since the testimony of such witnesses would be more convincing for the establishment of the Faith. This, too, is what S. John, after relating our Lord's appearances to the incredulous Thomas, expressly declares: "Many other signs also did Jesus in the sight of His disciples which are not written in this book. But these are written that you may believe that Jesus is the Christ, the Son of God: and that believing you may have life in His Name."[1]

To record the appearances of Our Lord to His Holy Mother would, then, have been beside the purpose of Inspiration; since what was said to her by Elizabeth at the Incarnation might have been addressed to her at the Resurrection: "Blessed art thou that hast believed."[2] We read of Mary assisting on Calvary at the crucifixion and death of her Son, but she is not found with Magdalene and the other women at the Sepulchre, bringing sweet spices to anoint His body,

---

[1] *John* xx. 30, 31.   [2] *Luke* i. 45.

or seeking the living amongst the dead. Mary had never doubted like the rest, but believed all along with full assurance of faith that He would rise again from the tomb the third day according to His promise. Consequently, and also because she was His Mother, her testimony to His resurrection would seem to be less impartial; and to record Our Lord's appearances to her would not have served the special end the Evangelists had in view.

To infer from the silence in the Gospels that our risen Lord did not appear to His Blessed Mother might seem to be in contradiction with what is said by the Evangelist S. John: that from the hour of her Son's death, " that disciple took her to his own." From which words we should rather gather that where S. John was, there also was Mary, dwelling in the same house, whether in Jerusalem or in Galilee. It is, moreover, mentioned incidentally that even when Our Lord appeared to the eleven Apostles particularly, there were others with them.[1]

And surely it would be out of harmony with all that we know of Our Lord's life, if after His Resurrection He did not visit Mary, His own most blessed Mother, principally, before and beyond all others beside. During thirty years of His earthly sojourn He had chosen to be habitually alone with her: and even during the remaining three years of His public ministry, which was an exceptional time, many considerations would lead us to infer that Mary was in the near company of her Divine Son. It is worthy of

---

[1] *Luke* xxiv. 33.

remark and reflection, that throughout those long years of Our Lord's life, about which the Evangelists are so reticent, one thing at least we know of Him, whether in Egypt or at Nazareth, that He was *with Mary*. And when He had returned from the tomb to tarry still for a short space on earth, before He ascended to His Father in heaven, where should we naturally most expect to find Him, but once more with Mary, in whose company He had chosen, by preference to dwell habitually during His life, and from whom with such words of dutiful love He had last parted at death? *Dominus tecum.—Resurrexi, et adhuc tecum sum, alleluia.*[1]

How, indeed, could we so conceive of the love, filial piety, and honour which Our Lord bore to His holy Mother, as to think that He should not have visited her especially after His Resurrection, to console and compensate her for all that she had suffered with Him, and for His sake? She had taken the chief part with Him in His Passion; and, according to the canon laid down by S. Paul,[2] the part that we have in the sufferings and death of Christ, is to be the measure of the share we shall have in His resurrection. The effect of our risen Lord's appearances to His disciples was to fill their hearts with peace and joy.[3] What then must have been the fulness reserved for Mary?

May we not well believe that those touching and consoling words of Jesus Christ, in His last discourse

---

[1] Introit of Mass for Easter Sunday.—*Statio ad S. Mariam.*
[2] *Rom.* vi. 5-7.   *Phil.* iii. 10, 11.   [3] *John* xx. 19, 20.

to His disciples on the eve of His Passion, had their highest signification and fulfilment in their application to Mary? "A little while, and you shall not see Me; and, again, a little while, and you shall see Me. Amen, amen, I say to you, that you shall lament and weep, but the world shall rejoice; and you shall be made sorrowful, but your sorrow shall be turned into joy. A woman, when she is in labour, hath sorrow, because her hour is come: but, when she hath brought forth the child, she remembereth no more the anguish, for joy that a man is born into the world. So also you now, indeed, have sorrow, but I will see you again, and your heart shall rejoice; and your joy no man shall take from you."[1]

Mary was, doubtless, with the disciples when Our Lord thus spake. And was not she emphatically that Woman then present to His thoughts? Her hour, His own hour also,[2] was now come, when she was to bring forth her Child Jesus again, not as once at Bethlehem with a joyous, painless child-birth, but in labour of bitter sorrow and anguish on Calvary. This dolorous travail past, her Son risen again from death, she will see Him re-born from the tomb to a new and glorious life, "the First begotten of the dead," "the first-fruits of them that sleep,"[3] and seeing Him once more, remembering now no more her anguish, her heart will rejoice, and at sight of Him, exclaim, "According to the multitude of sorrows that were in my heart, Thy consolations have given joy to my soul."[4]

[1] *John* xvi. 19-22.   [2] *John* ii. 4.
[3] *Apoc.* i. 5. *1 Cor.* xv. 20.   [4] *Ps.* xciii. 19.

Mary is celebrated throughout the Church as emphatically "the Blessed Virgin." She was pronounced Blessed by God Himself in the Angelic salutation, and by inspiration of the Holy Ghost.[1] Hence to her belongs pre-eminently the heritage of every blessing. She was blessed, because she bore Jesus Christ in her womb, and suckled Him at her breasts, yet still more blessed, because she heard the word of God and kept it.[2] She was blessed, in seeing her Son risen from the dead, and had also the greater blessing of those who had not seen and yet have believed.[3] Others saw and still doubted.[4] Mary before, and without seeing, firmly believed in His resurrection.

In saying that the Blessed Virgin had the principal share in the joys of Jesus Christ's Resurrection, is implicitly contained the proposition that His first appearance was to her. On this point we shall content ourselves with quoting the words of the learned Suarez:—

"We should unhesitatingly believe, that, after His Resurrection, Christ appeared first of all to His Mother. This opinion, from its very terms, is of itself so credible, that, almost without controversy, it is firmly seated in the minds of all the faithful and Doctors, and is the teaching of all Catholic writers, who have touched upon the question. Hence it seems to have been the constant sense of the Church, since we cannot discover the time when it first began to be taught in the Church. And, although the ancient Fathers do not

---

[1] *Luke* i. 28, 42, 48.
[2] *Luke* xi. 27, 28.
[3] *John* xx. 29.
[4] *Matt.* xxviii. 17.

frequently affirm it, this is not because they held the contrary opinion—for they never denied it—but because they were used to expound only those things that the Evangelists had written. Still we are not altogether without indications and testimonies from antiquity. For S. Ambrose expressly affirms this opinion in the following words:—'Mary saw the Lord's Resurrection, and was the first to see, and believed. Mary Magdalene saw too, though still she doubted.'[1] .... Well does S. Anselm say,[2] that the immensity of joy wherewith the Virgin was whelmed at this appearance of her Son, was admirable to Angels, but unutterable to men. He then asks why the Evangelists did not record that Christ appeared first, and principally to His Mother: He answers first, because to do so might seem superfluous: and, secondly, lest they should seem to put the Queen of heaven and earth on the same level with the rest to whom Christ appeared."

Suarez, commenting further on, on the words of S. Mark:—" He appeared first to Mary Magdalene,"[3] and quoting from Rupert,[4] continues:—" The Evangelists related those appearances only which were made to attest the truth of the Resurrection according to what is written:—' Him God raised up the third day, and gave Him to be made manifest, not to all the people, but to witnesses pre-ordained by God.'[5] For they did not assume the task of writing everything that

---

[1] L. iii., *De Virginit.*, ad init.   [2] *De Excell. Virg.* c. 6.
[3] *Mark* xvi. 9.   [4] L. vii. *De Divin. Off.* c. 25.
[5] *Acts* x. 41.

Christ did, nor all the singular favours He showed to His Mother, but those only that appeared to suffice for confirming and recording the mysteries of faith. When, then, Christ is said to have appeared first to Mary Magdalene, this must be understood to mean, either *first* amongst those who were to be witnesses of the Resurrection, or *first* amongst those to whom Christ appeared, for the confirmation of their faith. Consequently the Blessed Virgin is not included. For neither was she to be a witness of the Resurrection, for she might be suspected of making up some story, out of love for her Son ; nor did she ever waver in her belief of His Resurrection. It was not, therefore, on this account that Christ first appeared to her ; but to offer her the due expression of His love and honour. And hence not only should we look on this favour as granted to the Virgin for her own comfort, but also as an act that was most becoming for Christ Himself to do ; both because, as a Son, He was bound to specially honour His Mother, and also, because, since He was so greatly loved by her, He was bound to show her especial marks of love in return. And consequently, by means of this singular favour, the Virgin's faith, hope, and charity towards Christ must needs have been very greatly increased and confirmed."[1]

The foregoing considerations, which have their source in the page of the New Testament, tend, we think, to show clearly that our risen Lord appeared principally, above all, and consequently, first, to His Blessed

---

[1] Suárez, *De Myst. Vit. Christ.*, Dist. xlix., Sect. 2.

Mother, even though the Evangelists are silent on this point; moreover, that this silence is intelligible, and emphatically eloquent in Mary's praise.

Hence is confirmed the principle which was laid down in the last chapter, that the silence of the inspired writers on some question of doctrine or fact, is of itself no valid argument at all against the existence, truth, and importance of such doctrine or fact.

CHAPTER III.

THE ORAL TEACHING OF THE APOSTLES ON THE BLESSED VIRGIN IN THEIR GENERAL PREACHING AND CATECHETICAL INSTRUCTIONS.

WE have already seen in a former chapter that the silence of the Apostles on devotion to the Blessed Virgin in their Epistles is of no force, as an argument, against the existence of such devotion in their days, and fails to prove that they did not themselves teach and practise it.

Were, indeed, this silence pressed into an argument of conclusive force, it would prove too much, viz., that the Apostles, in teaching the Christian faith, wholly ignored the Blessed Virgin, and did not speak of her at all. This, however, is quite impossible to conceive. For they could not have established the truth of the Messiahship of Jesus Christ, or the mystery of His Incarnation, without speaking explicitly of Mary, His Virgin Mother; and, to explain these truths, and answer objections against them, they must necessarily in their disputations, both with Jews and Gentiles, have entered into many details regarding her.

True it is that this does not appear from their recorded discourses, which S. Luke has given us in abridgment or summary. But here we should take into account the main end that the Evangelist had in writing his narrative, and reporting those particular discourses, as well as the general scope of the Apostles in preaching them.

The chief object of S. Luke in writing his history was to record the first establishment of the Church, and the early diffusion of the Gospel through the preaching of the Apostles. With this view, he selects —to weave them into his narrative—certain of their sermons, as typical of that preaching whereby the faith was propagated both amongst Jews and Gentiles.

If we examine these discourses themselves, they seem intended to serve rather as preludes or preambles to a fuller and more explicit exposition of the truths of Christianity that was to follow. We see that the Apostles make choice in them of such topics and arguments as would most awaken and arrest the attention of their audiences, whether Jews or Gentiles, and would best insinuate motives in their hearers for believing the Gospel which they preached.

Most often, especially amongst the Jews, the topic which they chose for their argument was Our Lord's Resurrection, since this was a patent fact that had so recently taken place in their very midst, and was supported by the strongest testimony—a fact, moreover, so evidently miraculous and of so critical and pregnant a nature that the conviction of its truth bore with it, so to say, the credibility of all the rest of their teaching.[1]

---

[1] *Acts* ii.; iv. 2, 10, 33; v. 30; xiii. 33, 34; xvii. 3, 18, 31, 32.

Not unfrequently their theme was an appeal to the Scriptures, showing the manifest fulfilment of the Old Testament prophecies in Jesus Christ and the insufficiency of the old law.[1]

Sometimes, and more particularly amongst the heathen, the topic dwelt upon in this Apostolic preaching was the universal character of the Christian religion, as coming from the One only God and Father of all men throughout the world.[2]

Besides such like topics and arguments, intended rather to convince the intelligence and reason, the Apostles added in these discourses others of a moral and more practical nature, calculated to awaken the consciences of their hearers to a sense of their sins, strike fear into their hearts, and move them to repentance. Thus they set before them their personal responsibility, and the strict obligation they were under to serve God and keep His law; declaring, on the one hand, the severe judgment that awaited them at death, and at the same time the means afforded for obtaining forgiveness of all their sins and saving their souls if they accepted the religion of Jesus Christ which was preached to them.

It thus appears that what the Apostles had specially in view in these discourses was to propose the grounds of faith and the motives for believing, rather than to set forth explicitly and in detail the doctrines of the faith itself, or, as they are termed, its material objects. We can discover in them, for instance, no allusion to

[1] *Acts* iii.; vii.; viii. 28, 35; xiii. 17, 41; xvii. 2, 3, 11; xxvi. 22, 23.
[2] *Ib.* x. 34, 43; xiii. 46, 48; xiv. 13, 17, 22, 31.

the Trinity, nor any explicit teaching on the Incarnation—the two chief mysteries of the Christian religion. So implicitly, indeed, is the whole faith of Christians expressed in the language of the Acts, that whatsoever at least is essential as belonging to its substance, is there comprised under "believing in the Lord Jesus," or "believing that Jesus Christ is the Son of God."[1] Again, as though all the rest turned on, or was included in, the belief and profession of this single article—as being the central and most distinctive truth of Christianity—those who really were baptised in the explicit Name of the Holy Trinity, are spoken of as "baptised in the Name of the Lord Jesus Christ."[2]

We gather from the Acts that converts to the Faith were in those early days, as the general rule, at once

---

[1] *Acts* xvi. 31; viii. 37.

[2] *Ib.* viii. 16; x. 48; xix. 5. Some few Catholic writers have supposed that there was a time when the Apostles baptised in the Name of our Lord Jesus Christ only—wherein were signified also the Person of the Father by whom, and the Holy Ghost in whom, Jesus Christ was anointed; and that they did so in order, in the infancy of the Church, to proclaim more effectually the glory and divinity of Jesus Christ. If the Apostles ever thus baptised, which is generally considered to be highly improbable, it is certain that they must have done so by an express inspiration of the Holy Ghost. The commonly-received opinion is, that the Apostles never used any other form in baptism than that which our Lord had commanded to be observed, and that baptism "in the Name of Christ" means baptism instituted by Christ, as distinguished from the baptism of John. So S. Paul speaks of being "baptised in Christ" and "putting on Christ" (*Gal.* iii. 27), meaning thereby being baptised in the faith of Christ.

baptised,[1] though, doubtless, the later discipline of catechumens was not long in taking its first beginnings. In any case, the new converts needed more detailed and explicit instruction in the doctrines of the faith and in their duties as Christians than was given them in these general sermons. That such further teaching was supplied by the Apostles, or by others appointed for this purpose, is implied in many places of the Acts. Thus we read that both at Jerusalem and abroad amongst the heathen the Apostles were constantly assembling the first Christians together, for prayer, teaching, and exhortation, in the Temple, in their house to house visitations, in private dwellings,[2] and in the synagogues.[3] They, moreover, ordained priests in all the churches that they founded[4] for the further instruction of the new converts. It is also expressly said that when the Apostles Paul and Barnabas were making a more prolonged stay at Antioch, there were many others also teaching and preaching with them.[5] Again, we find the Apostles, after they had evangelised certain cities, returning after some short time, in order to confirm their converts in Christian faith and practice by fuller instruction and renewed exhortation.[6]

---

[1] *Acts* ii. 4; viii. 12, 15, 38; ix. 18; x. 48; xvi. 14, 15, 33; xviii. 8.

[2] *Ib.* ii. 46; v. 42; vi. 4; xi.; xii. 12; xviii. 7, 8; xx. 7, 8; xxviii. 30, 31.

[3] *Ib.* xiii. 43; xiv. 20, 21; xvi. 40; xix. 8; xx. 20, 35.

[4] *Ib.* xiv. 22; xx. 28.

[5] *Ib.* xv. 35. See also xviii. 26, 27.   [6] *Ib.* xv. 36, 41.

Whilst, however, it is clear from S. Luke's history that the Apostles gave their converts fuller and more explicit instruction in the faith than can be found in their recorded discourses, still we can gain from the sacred narrative itself scarcely any information at all as to the particular matters treated of in this further teaching. But we may be quite sure that the Apostles would explain more fully those primary truths of faith which are the most necessary for every Christian explicitly to know and believe; especially that of the Holy Trinity, in Whose Name they were baptised, and the Incarnation of Jesus Christ, as well as the other articles contained in the Apostles' Creed. They would instruct the converts also in all that was most important for them to know about the Sacraments—those particularly they were about to receive—their nature and effects, as well as the proper dispositions for their reception, whether it were Baptism, or Confirmation, or the Eucharist, or Penance, or Extreme Unction, or Matrimony, since each and all of these bore their part, then as now, in the ordinary life of Christians. They would teach them, too, the sacred character and power of those who were ordained, whether as priests or bishops, to minister to them in spiritual things; the nature of Christian worship, and especially of the Eucharistic Sacrifice. Besides dwelling on these and kindred topics, they would explain to their converts their moral obligations, and point out in detail, as occasion offered, what they must, on the one hand, avoid as forbidden and sinful; and, on the other, the duties and virtues which as Christians they were specially called to practise.

Such oral instruction of the Apostles in the first principles of Christianity may be called Catechetical. To it S. Paul refers in his Epistle to the Hebrews; where, speaking in a tone of reproach, he says: "For whereas for the time you ought to be masters; you have need to be taught again what are the first elements of the words of God; and you are become such as have need of milk, and not of strong meat." He then goes on to enumerate some of these "first elements" which he calls "the word of the beginning of Christ," as follows: "not laying again the foundation of penance from dead works, and of faith towards God, of the doctrine of baptisms,[1] and imposition of hands, and of the resurrection of the dead, and of eternal judgment."[2]

The foregoing cursory review of Apostolic preaching recorded in the Acts discovers to us—what, indeed, is of itself sufficiently obvious—how large must have been the store of Christian teaching imparted orally by the Apostles to their disciples, of which we have no written account—on many points, too, of doctrine and practice to which no direct or explicit reference is made at all in S. Luke's history. This, as we have already remarked, applies especially to the mystery of the Incarnation which may be said to be the centre and substance of the Christian Faith. In

---

[1] We can find mention in the Acts of but one matter only on which it is related this further instruction is given to Christian disciples: and that is "the doctrine of baptisms," the distinction, namely, between the baptism of John and that instituted by Jesus Christ. *Acts* xviii. 24-26; xix. 1-5.

[2] *Heb.* v. 12; vi. 1, 2.

the language of the Acts the preaching of that Faith is summarily described, as "teaching and preaching Christ Jesus;"[1] "teaching in the Name of Jesus;"[2] "preaching that He is the Son of God;"[3] "teaching the things that are of Jesus;"[4] "testifying penance towards God, and faith in our Lord Jesus Christ;" and, "the Gospel of the grace of God."[5] But how much is contained in these implicit terms; and how many things needed to be explained concerning the Divine Person and eternal Godhead of Jesus Christ, as the Only-begotten of the Father, and His true and perfect humanity as Son of Man; how much had to be further said to show that He was in truth the long promised Messiah with the threefold office of Prophet, Priest, and King, who, it was foretold, should arise from the tribe of Juda, and as Son of David be heir to his throne. But here, there was need of much explicit teaching concerning Mary His Virgin Mother: for, to convince their hearers that Jesus Christ was indeed the Son of God and the long expected Messiah, the Apostles must show forth His Mother as that Virgin foretold by the Prophets, who should conceive and give birth to Emmanuel; and to make it "evident that Our Lord sprung out of Juda,"[6] and was Son of David—yet without earthly paternity—they must explain that Mary was the Rod from the root of Jesse which should blossom into flower, and that this figure of prophecy was fulfilled

---

[1] *Acts* v. 42; viii. 5, 35.   [2] *Ib.* iv. 18.
[3] *Ib.* ix. 20.   [4] *Ib.* xxiii. 35.   [5] *Ib.* xx. 21, 24.
[6] *Heb.* vii. 14.

in her Virginal Childbirth.[1] For we should bear in mind that the Incarnation and Birth of Jesus Christ together with all other circumstances of His earthly life, were proposed to the world's belief, not only as supernatural mysteries and doctrines of faith, but also as objective facts, and events that had their place in time; and, as such, depended for their verification and due significance, on positive testimony and historical proof.

Hence, as is evident, this historical aspect of the Gospel, and of all that bore on the life of Jesus Christ, demanded that the Apostles should in their preaching speak explicitly of Mary His Mother, and teach many things in detail as to her ancestry and life, her character, and functions in relation to Him.

But besides this historical aspect of the gospel, there were considerations also of a moral kind, which would lead the Apostles in their preaching to speak explicitly of the Blessed Virgin. Here we must bear in mind how greatly opposed to the supernatural and spiritual character of the new Faith were the generally prevailing associations and ideas of those to whom the gospel was first preached.

The Jews, on the one hand, had for the most part been looking forward to the Messiah as a temporal prince who should restore their nation to its former greatness, and whose reign was to be one of earthly glory. Hence, the apparently mean parentage of Jesus Christ, as well as His obscure and humble condition, would naturally be a subject of difficulty and

[1] *Is.* xi. 1.

scandal even to those Jews who were more favourably inclined to the Apostles' teaching. It was necessary to remove such prejudice and to correct this spirit of worldliness. But compensation must be made at the same time for their disappointed hopes, and for the reversal of their long-cherished ideas by substituting new matters of another and higher order, wherein they might with better reason justly glory, and this would be most effectually done by showing forth—whilst unfolding the divine perfections of Jesus Christ—the sublime dignity, privileges and excellence of His Blessed Mother, in whom, as the elect daughter of the Jewish people, were fulfilled so many glorious prophecies and types of the Old Testament.

A large proportion of the first converts to the faith, on the other hand, were Gentiles. These, we must remember, from having been brought up in the traditions of heathen idolatry, had their religious sense tainted by the impure associations of Pagan mythology and the immoral legends of its anthropomorphic divinities. Obviously, then, one great aim of the Apostles in preaching the Gospel to the Gentiles was to counteract their corrupt tendencies and habits of thought by striving to impress their disciples with the supernatural purity and spirituality of Christianity, and to jealously guard its mysteries, especially that of the Incarnation from any gross and carnal conceptions.

Hence, in proclaiming that mystery, they would be led to dwell—at least to some extent, and with due regard to the various needs and capacity of disciples— upon the perfect and spotless virginity of the Mother of Jesus Christ; on the truth and dignity of her divine maternity, and her sublime graces, virtues, and sanctity, thereby to show that Mary was made by God worthy of His election of her to be the Mother of the Incarnate Word, and deserving, at the same time, of their own deep reverence and loving admiration.

There could, certainly, be no more effectual antidote to the corruption of Paganism, nor would any thing tend more to elevate and refine the moral and religious sense of these Gentile converts, than the contemplation of the Virgin Mother of the Divine Redeemer—herself God's creature, lowly and dependent on Him as all others, and of the same human nature as the rest of mankind—made, through the fulness of grace she received, a perfect type to the world of spotless innocence, purity, holiness and humility.

That this was the view of Mary presented by the Apostles to their more instructed disciples there can be no doubt, for we find it clearly expressed by Fathers who wrote soon after the times of the Apostles, and who most nearly reflected their traditional teaching. S. Justin, S. Irenæus, and Tertullian, when speaking of the Blessed Virgin, unite in giving utterance to this one simple thought, that Mary was the ideal of sanctity, the second Eve, who, by her perfect innocence, faith, and obedience repaired the ruin which the first Eve had brought upon mankind through her unbelief and disobedience; that as Eve took part with Adam in man's Fall, so Mary co-operated with Jesus Christ, her Divine Son, in the work of his Redemption.

But whilst there can be no doubt that the Apostles in their catechetical teaching spoke explicitly about the Blessed Virgin, and said much in her honour that would inspire their hearers with love and veneration to her, still we should not expect that they would all at once develop in full detail their doctrinal teaching regarding the Mother of God, and with all its practical consequences. We should expect, rather, that such early teaching would be for the most part implicit, and given in such measure and sort as would best lead converts, according to their various circumstances and antecedents, to an intelligent knowledge of, and faith in, Jesus Christ and the mystery of the Incarnation.

The end that the Apostles had in view was to lead souls to salvation and eternal life by bringing them to believe the Gospel which they preached. And the substance of that Gospel was, " to know the One true God and Jesus Christ whom He had sent." Here was work enough for them to do in a world beset with the hereditary prejudices of Judaism on the one hand, and the ignorant superstitions of Paganism on the other. They did their work as best they could, bearing with many traditional customs amongst the Jews, and condescending to much weakness amongst the Gentiles, thus making themselves all to all, so that by all means they might save some.[1] From this necessity

---

[1] " Everything in this book," writes S. Chrysostom on the Acts of the Apostles, " is worthy of admiration, but most of all the condescension of the Apostles, which, indeed, the Spirit suggested to them in preparing them to enter upon the word of the economy. Consequently, whilst discoursing so much about Christ, they have said few things concerning His Divinity, but many more about His Humanity, Passion, Resurrection, and Ascension. For what was wanted at that time was, that it should be believed that He rose again and ascended into

laid upon the Apostles, we can well understand how some revealed truths of a secondary order, being subservient to the substance of faith, had to wait their turn, until circumstances of time and opportunity offered a favourable occasion for their explicit and more general teaching.

So, too, would it be with the practical consequences to which the doctrinal teaching concerning Our Lady could not fail to lead. By these we mean all that is comprised in the cultus of the Blessed Virgin, and especially the practice of invoking her and rendering to her acts of religious veneration. The Catholic Church has ever sanctioned this cultus, and declares it

heaven. Just, therefore, as Christ Himself took care most of all to show that He came from the Father, so, too, (the principal matter was to show) that He rose again, and was taken up, and returned to Him from whom He had come. For if this was not first believed, and much more when were added His Resurrection and Assumption, the whole teaching of faith would have seemed incredible to the Jews. Therefore, by degrees, and little by little, He leads them up to matters more sublime. But at Athens Paul simply calls Him a man, saying nothing more (*Acts* xvii. 31), and with reason too. For if they often attempted to stone Christ Himself when discoursing on His equality with the Father, and called Him on that account a blasphemer, hardly would they have received this teaching from fishermen, and when the Cross had gone before.

"And why should I speak of the Jews, when even the disciples themselves, on hearing the more sublime doctrines, were, we know, often troubled and scandalised? Wherefore He said: 'I have many things to say to you, but you cannot bear them now' (*John* xvi. 12). But if they could not bear them who were so long time with Him, participating in such great secrets, and beholding such great miracles, how would men—then first

to be lawful and salutary. It was, consequently, contained in the revealed deposit, formed part of the Apostles' teaching, and in their days, at least in rudimentary form, had a place in the piety of the faithful.

We may here remark that doctrines and principles of a practical tendency, being of themselves purely objective, are capable of being set forth all at once in full and explicit statement; whereas the practice or acts to which they naturally lead must be of gradual growth, showing a development from germ to maturity. The inculcation of such doctrines and principles is like the sowing of seed into the ground. As the seed when sown depends, for its springing up and yielding fruit, on the nature of the soil into which it is cast, on various extrinsic circumstances, and favourable

torn from altars, and idols, and sacrifices, and cats, and crocodiles (for such were the things worshipped by the Gentiles), and from other abominations—have received all at once the sublime words of the doctrines of faith? How, too, could the Jews, who every day were learning and being instructed by the Law, 'Hear, O Israel, the Lord thy God is one Lord, and beside Him there is no other' (*Deut.* vi. 1), who had seen Him nailed to a cross—nay, rather had themselves crucified and buried Him, and had not seen Him risen—should they hear that this same was God, have not at once sprung back and broken away altogether? Wherefore they lead them on gently, and step by step, and make much use of the economy of condescension. But they enjoy more abundantly the grace of the Spirit, and work in His Name greater things than He had done, in order to raise up from both sides those lying on the ground and to make their preaching of the Resurrection believed. For this book is principally a showing forth of the Resurrection; and if this is believed, the rest easily follows. This then, to sum up, is above all the argument and whole scope of the book" (*In Act. Apost. Hom.* i. 1, 2).

influences, so is it, our Lord tells us, with the preaching of God's word.[1] The Apostles sowed, as seed, in the minds and hearts of their disciples the divine truths and doctrines that were contained in the revealed deposit. These doctrines, handed down in their integrity from age to age, are the principles whence have arisen whatever developments the Church, under the infallible guidance of the Holy Ghost, has at any time sanctioned in Christian faith and practice. In the explicit teaching of the Apostles were contained the principles of the Church's divine constitution, of her Primacy, of her hierarchical government, of her ecclesiastical discipline, of her Liturgy and ritual, of her religious Orders, of her moral theology, of her pious usages, and devotional practices. But it was impossible that these manifold results should show themselves, all at once from the beginning, in active operation. They would at first be seen in germ; and it would be only by more or less slow and gradual process that they would visibly spring up, and attain their normal development; " bringing forth fruit, first the blade, then the ear, afterwards the full corn in the ear."[2] These results would appear some sooner, others later, some more visible here, others there : since their growth and external manifestation had to depend on a variety of circumstances, of persons, time and place, and other surrounding influences, favourable to their development.

In other words : For principles of objective truth to

---

[1] *Matt.* xiii. 3-8, 18-23 ; *Mark* iv. 3-8, 14-20 ; *Luke* viii. 5-15.
[2] *Mark* iv. 28, 30-32.

become subjective, that is to say, for them to practically energise, and give a form to man's moral action, they must needs go through a certain process of assimilation with the thought and intelligence wherewith they come in contact: and consequently there is required some fitting preparedness of mind and heart in those who receive the principles, together with such extrinsic opportuneness as will call forth their energy into practical working, and make manifest their due and normal effects.

How, for example, could the universal Primacy, conferred by Christ on S. Peter and his successors, appear in its full development and normal exercise during the lifetime of the other Apostles, all of whom were, alike with S. Peter, divinely commissioned to found the Church and govern it in its infancy; and for this end had severally received from our Lord a certain fulness of jurisdiction which was wholly exceptional, and, being given to them personally, was to cease at their death? In this inchoate and provisional state of things, as also in the next age of persecution, when the Church's complete organisation had, so to say, yet to be formed, and its constituent elements but imperfectly cohered, the primacy, it is obvious, had neither adequate subject-matter whereon its whole energy could work, nor a sphere of action proportioned to the plenitude of its jurisdiction, as it showed itself later on; whilst at the same time, the occasions were wanting for calling it into such exercise, as would manifest its powers and prerogatives to their full extent.

As it was with other elements of Christianity, so

also doubtless was the case with the Cultus of the Blessed Virgin; so that what our Lord says of God's visible kingdom on earth, the holy Catholic Church, is applicable to devotion to our Lady in its external manifestation. It was in its beginnings like to the little grain of mustard seed; but ere long it grew up and appeared as a great tree, whose branches have extended throughout the world.[1]

But though devotion to the Blessed Virgin may be affirmed on most solid grounds to have its origin in the times of the Apostles, it was not likely that this would bring her cultus into prominence all at once. The foundations of Christian worship had to be laid: and its primary elements, which belonged to the substance of the Faith, inculcated in the first place; for example, the essential obligation, and the practice of adoring and supplicating the Triune God; rendering divine honour to "the Man Christ Jesus,"[2] our crucified Saviour; offering up the Eucharistic sacrifice of His Body and Blood; and worthy Communion. Other religious practices and observances that may be termed secondary, as being subservient to, and complemental of, what were primary, had necessarily to wait until opportune time and occasion should bring them more fully to view.

But apart from this necessity of order, there were also, we conceive, special reasons of prudence, which would lead the Apostles to use much reserve and caution in setting forth popularly the cultus of the Blessed Virgin in the first age of Christianity. Large

---

[1] *Matt.* xiii. 31, 32; *Mark* iv. 30-32.   [2] 1 *Tim.* ii. 5.

numbers of the earlier converts to the Faith had been brought up amongst the superstitions of an idolatrous paganism, and were still surrounded by heathen influences.

Hence, before they were solidly grounded in the doctrines of the Faith, and more thoroughly imbued with the spirituality of the Gospel, and until the society in which they lived had become more generally infused with Christian principles—there might be serious danger lest some of them should misinterpret the cultus of the Blessed Virgin, as well as of Angels and Saints, and regard it as a sort of substitution for their former heathen worship of heroes or demigods. That such was the tendency of Gentiles favourably disposed to the Apostles' preaching appears from the conduct of the people of Lystra, who, on hearing the eloquence of S. Paul, and witnessing a miracle of healing that he wrought, conceived such admiration and veneration for him and S. Barnabas, that they called them by the names of their gods, and sought to pay them divine honours.[1] That there was real danger lest the cultus of our Lady and the Saints might in those earlier times be perverted by some to a wrong sense, appears again from the special warning given by S. Paul to the Colossians against a depraved religion, or worship of angels, which was at that time being taught by heretics.[2]

We know, too, that in the first ages of the Church prevailed what was called the *Discipline of the Secret* (Disciplina arcani), according to which great reserve

---

[1] *ts* xiv. 7-17.   [2] *Col.* ii. 18.

was used in popular teaching with regard to certain points of Christian doctrine and practice, so that these were purposely veiled or kept back altogether from the view of the general public. Even catechumens were not, as a rule, fully initiated into all the mysteries of the Faith until they had been well proved, and had passed through their complete course of instruction.

This reserve was exercised to prevent the doctrines and practices of the Faith from becoming, through prejudice, imperfect apprehension, or misunderstanding, a subject of scandal, and to guard Christian truths and mysteries from being profaned by unbelievers. There is evidence in the Epistles that the Apostles used this economy of reserve on several points, and we have given reasons for thinking that they would do so particularly as regards the cultus of the Blessed Virgin.

We will conclude this chapter with some passages from the fathers on this economy of silence and reserve in the New Testament, which have special reference to the Blessed Virgin.

S. Chrysostom, in answer to the question, Why the genealogy of Joseph, and not of Mary, is recorded in the Gospels—after the reason he had given in his second Homily on S. Matthew—goes on thus to expose in the third Homily another reason, which, he says, is more mystical and hidden :—

" What is it? you ask. It is because God was unwilling it should be known, even at the time of the Nativity, that Christ was born of a Virgin. Be not, however, troubled at so unexpected an answer. For what I say is, of a truth, not my word, but that of our fathers, men admirable and renowned. For if Christ at the beginning spoke much that was obscure, calling Himself the Son of Man, and did not on all occasions clearly reveal His equality with the Father, why dost thou marvel if He put this truth, too (of His Mother's virginity), in the back-ground, thereby making use of a great and wonderful economy?

"But, thou wilt say, what is it precisely that is wonderful here? I answer, the conduct of Divine Providence thus to save the Virgin, and to free her from evil suspicions. Since, had the Jews heard of this from the first they would have put a malicious construction on the Virgin Mother, and stoned her, condemning her as an adulteress. For if even on other occasions, of which they had similar examples in the Old Testament, their conduct was so outrageous; if, for instance, when our Lord cast out devils, they called Him a demoniac, and because He wrought cures on the Sabbath—though the Sabbath had been often broken before—they charged Him with being an enemy of God, what would they not say if it came to their ears that His Mother was a Virgin? Since here they had on their side the whole history of the past, in which nothing at all like was ever known. Again, if after all His numerous miracles, they still called Him the son of Joseph, how before these miracles would they ever have believed Him to be the son of a Virgin? For this reason, then, was the genealogy of Joseph drawn out, and he espoused the Virgin. Now, if even Joseph, a man so just and admirable, needed many arguments to bring himself to accept what took place, *e.g.*, the assurance of the angel, the vision during sleep, and the testimony of the prophets, how would the Jews, who were perverse and corrupt, and so hostile to our Lord, have received such a notion? For anything so strange and novel would certainly have been made only fresh matter of difficulty and scandal, since nothing of the kind had ever happened in the time of their forefathers. But, if anyone believed once for all that Jesus Christ was the Son of God, he would have no further ground for doubt about this other matter; whereas, if he held Him to be only an impostor and an enemy of God, would he not at hearing of His being born of a Virgin be all the more scandalised rather than induced to believe in its truth?

"For the same reason the Apostles also do not speak of it straightway at the beginning; whereas we find them discoursing much and often about the Resurrection, since of this there were examples in past times, though, indeed, they were dissimilar. But they are uniformly ($συνεχῶς$) silent as to His being born of a Virgin, and not even did His Mother herself venture to utter it. For, observe what the Virgin says even to Himself: 'Behold, I and Thy father have been seeking Thee.' Since had there been any suspicion here, He would not have been held to be really even the son of David, and were this not held many other further evil consequences would have arisen. For like cause, too, even the angels do not affirm it, save to Mary alone, and to Joseph, and when proclaiming the glad tidings of what had happened they altogether refrain from adding it."[1]

---

[1] *In Matt. Hom.* iii.

S. Jerome, on the words, "When His Mother Mary was espoused to Joseph" (*Matt.* i. 18), writes as follows:—

"Why is He conceived not of a simple Virgin, but of one espoused? First, that by means of the genealogy of Joseph, might be shown the origin of Mary. Secondly, lest she should be stoned by the Jews as an adulteress. Thirdly, that, in her flight to Egypt, she might have the solace of a husband. Ignatius, the martyr, added also a fourth reason, why He was conceived of one espoused; that His birth, he says, might be concealed from the devil, by his supposing Him to be the offspring not of a virgin, but of a wife, and, therefore, that He was not the true Messias foretold by the Prophets."

It seems, however, that S. Jerome here does not quote directly from S. Ignatius, but from Origen; for we cannot find any such express statement in the writings of that Saint, though it may, in some sense, be gathered from his Epistle to the Ephesians, towards the close.

The following is the passage of Origen:—

"Hence it is admirably said, as I have found in the Epistle of a certain martyr, I mean Ignatius, the second bishop of Antioch after Peter, who, in the persecution, fought with beasts at Rome: The Virginity of Mary was hidden from the prince of this world. It was hidden by reason of Joseph. It was hidden by reason of the nuptials. It was hidden, because she was supposed to have a husband. For, if she had not had a spouse, and, as was supposed, a husband, it could not, by any means, have been concealed from the prince of this world. For, at once, the devil's silent thought would have stealthily crept along: How is she, who has not known man, pregnant? This conception must be divine, it must be something more sublime than human nature. Our Saviour, on the other hand, had so disposed, that the devil should not know His dispensation, and His taking to Himself a body: and hence even, in His generation, He concealed it; and afterwards charged His disciples not to make Him known. And, when He was being tempted by the devil himself, He nowhere confessed that He was the Son of God, but only answered:—'It is not right that I should adore thee, or that I should make these stones bread, or that I should cast Myself down from on high.'[1] And, in thus speaking, He always refrained from saying that He was the Son of God. Look, too, in another Scripture, and thou wilt find that it was Christ's will, that the devil should not know the coming of the Son of God. For the Apostle, when affirming that the powers of wickedness were ignorant of His Passion, says:—'We speak wisdom among the perfect. But not the wisdom of this world, nor of the princes of this world who come to nought; but we speak the wisdom of God hidden in mystery, which none of the princes of this world knew. For, if they had known it, they would never have crucified the Lord of Glory.'[2] Hence the mystery of the Saviour was hidden from the princes of this world. . . . So much as to why Mary had a spouse."[3]

[1] *Matt.* iv. 3-10.   [2] *1 Cor.* ii. 6-8.
[3] *S. Hieronymi Translatio Homiliarum Origenis in Lucam.* Hom. vi.

CHAPTER IV.

REASONS FOR THE SILENCE OF THE APOSTLES ON THE BLESSED VIRGIN IN THEIR EPISTLES.

IN treating hitherto of the Apostles' teaching on the Blessed Virgin, the record of their preaching in S. Luke's history of their Acts has so far served as the sole field of our investigation.

We now come to that which forms the main and special object of our whole inquiry—viz., an examination of the Epistles, in order to discover what there may be that bears on our Lady in the Apostles' own writings.

We shall, then, first, give reasons for the silence of the Apostles in their Epistles on the Blessed Virgin, and, secondly, we shall inquire into the nature of that silence, which we shall endeavour to show is far from being absolute. By this we mean, that the Apostles do not ignore Mary in their Epistles; but, on the contrary, therein explicitly inculcate those very principles which lie at the root of, and have served to form, the doctrinal teaching and devotional practice of the Catholic Church with regard to the Mother of God in every age; and that in these same principles that teaching and practice are implicitly, albeit latently, contained.

The following words from S. Thomas of Villanova may not be out of place here:—

"Whilst longing with all the desire of my soul to praise, to the best of my mean ability, Mary, the Mother of God, so admirable and surpassing in every virtue, I have been unable to find in the Sacred Scriptures almost any encomium of her that shows us, to the letter, her glory and excellence. For though we read in different places of the Prophets many things mystically said and done relating to her, from which may be shown the greatness of her virtue, yet seldom do we find anything said of her, and much more seldom anything said in her praise, either in the Gospels or in the Apostolic writings. But still, if I confess the truth, she is not given over to silence in such sense, as that the brightness of her virtues fails to shine forth, though it be but by a most slender ray, and by, so to speak, certain little chinks of words. But whence else shall we be better able to conceive of her glory, her virtues, and the gifts of her soul, than from that wondrous colloquy which she had with the Angel. For there, besides her being deservedly proclaimed by the Angel's voice, most full of grace and the first of all women, there arose forth from her own acts and words a whole host of matters for praise too numerous to reckon."[1]

In order to account for the silence on the Blessed Virgin in the Apostolic Epistles we must take some note of their nature and scope. And here we shall make some preliminary remarks on the relation of the

[1] S. Thom. Villan. *Conc.* 2, *De Annunt.*

written to the unwritten word, which have their application to the Epistles in particular.

As we have already said, the great object of the Apostles in their preaching was to establish the grand primary doctrines of the Unity of God in Three Persons, and His essential attributes; to set forth the holy, spiritual, and supernatural character of the Christian religion as opposed to the polytheism, immorality, scepticism, and materialism of the Heathens; to make manifest the Messiahship of Jesus Christ and His two-fold nature as God and Man in One Divine Person; and to publish His work and office as the Saviour of the whole human race, both Jews and Gentiles.

The sacred writers of the Books of the New Testament had no intention of giving, in their several writings, a full account of all the doctrines that belong to the Christian revelation, nor even a summary of the whole Faith. This Faith was supposed to be already known, at least in its primary and most essential points, by the Christians whom the Apostles addressed in their Epistles. It had been delivered to them by oral teaching. And provision had been made for its being preserved amongst them in its integrity and purity through the instruction of the pastors whom the Apostles placed over them, and to whom they had committed, for their guidance, special doctrinal formularies and precepts.[1] Again and again S. Paul

---

[1] *2 Thess.* ii. 14. *1 Tim.* iv. 6, 11, 13, 16; v. 17; vi 3, 14. *2 Tim.* i. 13, 14; ii. 14; iii. 10, 14. *Tit.* i. 9; ii. 1. *Heb.* xiii. 17. *Jude* 3, 17, 20.

admonishes these pastors to avoid all novelties in their teaching.[1]

This oral teaching, or preaching of the unwritten word, we should ever remember, was the essential and normal means ordained by God, for the evangelisation and instruction of the world in the truths of the Christian religion, and for perpetuating the Faith. "It pleased God," writes the Apostle, " by the foolishness of preaching to save them that believe."[2]

That unwritten word, first revealed to the Apostles, was by them deposited in the Church, with which Christ promised Himself always to remain, and on which He sent down the Holy Ghost who should abide with it for ever to guide and preserve it in all truth.

The commission given by our Lord was: "Go ye into the whole world and preach the Gospel to every creature." "Teach ($\mu\alpha\theta\eta\tau\epsilon\acute{\upsilon}\sigma\alpha\tau\epsilon$—make disciples of) all nations, baptising them . . . teaching them to observe all things, whatsoever I have commanded you, and, behold, I am with you all days even to the consummation of the world."[3]

In virtue of this divine charter bestowed by Christ on his Church—and no other has since been given to her—the Apostles " went forth and preached everywhere, the Lord working withal, and confirming the word with signs that followed."[4] In virtue thereof,

---

[1] *1 Tim.* i. 4, 6, 7; iv. 1-3, 7; vi. 20. *2 Tim.* ii. 14; 16-18 23; iv. 3, 4. *Tit.* i. 10, 13, 14; iii. 9.

[2] *1 Cor.* i. 21.   [3] *Mark* xvi. 15.   *Matt.* xxviii. 19.

[4] *Matt.* xxviii. 20.

too, the Catholic Church continues to teach that same revealed word; which she hands down from age to age in its integrity, as she received it from the Apostles.

Moreover, it pleased God in His gracious and all-wise Providence to inspire certain of the Apostles and Evangelists to commit to writing the books of the New Testament, to wit, the four Gospels which narrate circumstances in detail of the life, death and resurrection of the Incarnate Word, and many of His works and words; the Acts of the Apostles, which records the infancy of the Church, and the first preaching of the Faith: the Epistles of St. Paul, and of four of the twelve Apostles, viz., St. James, St. Peter, St. John, and St. Jude, which form so many commentaries or treatises explanatory of certain doctrines of the Faith, and particular points of Christian practice; lastly, the Apocalypse of St. John, wherein is figuratively foretold the history of the Church until the consummation of all things.

It would be impossible to exaggerate, and might appear almost unseemly to expatiate upon, the praises of God's written word in the New Testament, and its inestimable value and importance to the Church, as affording her so direct a witness to, and so authentic an interpreter of her doctrine, as also supplying to her, by means of inspired documents coeval with her birth, such priceless knowledge of so many circumstances and details regarding her Divine Founder, and her own origin, which would otherwise have doubtless been lost. Suffice it to say, that these Scriptures are the oracles of God Himself, directly inspired by the

Holy Ghost; that alongside of the unwritten word, they are equally of Divine authority with it, and, together with it, the fountain of revealed truth to the Church.

Still, priceless as is the value and importance to the Church of God's written word, it cannot be considered equally essential and necessary with His unwritten word. For we should never forget that the Faith was propagated and preserved, souls were saved, numerous Churches were founded and flourished, without the written word: that there passed a considerable time before all the books of the New Testament were received in the various Churches; and that some centuries elapsed before its Canon was definitely settled, and the inspired books were distinctly marked off from other pious Christian writings.

Moreover, the written word could never be an adequate organ by itself for imparting to the people generally the due knowledge of the truths of faith, in the sense that the unwritten word or oral teaching is.

It would be out of place here to go into the many obvious reasons which prove this. It is enough for our present purpose to remark that, whilst the written and the unwritten word, regarded objectively, that is, simply in themselves, are of equal and paramount authority—for both are Divine—yet, regarded subjectively, that is to say, in their application to the minds of men, the latter has the precedence; since the written word must be always interpreted and believed by the faithful, according to the sense of the unwritten word, that is, as the Divine authority of the Church infallibly rules and teaches.[1]

The foregoing observations on Divine Scripture, in general, apply, of course, to the Epistles, of which we shall now treat in particular.

The Apostolic Epistles pre-suppose, as we have already said, in those to whom they were addressed, a general knowledge and the acceptance of the faith through means of previous oral teaching of the unwritten word. They were written, for the most part, with the view of explaining more fully certain points of doctrine and practice with which the faithful in some particular Church had but an implicit and imperfect acquaintance, or which they had not rightly understood. Hence they contain answers to questions, or solutions of objections and difficulties that had arisen on these matters. The Apostles had also for their object in writing their Epistles, to correct certain abuses; to allay prejudices, differences, jealousies, and strifes that had sprung up amongst the brethren; to warn the Christian converts against some prevalent erroneous doctrine and false teachers, or to confirm them in faith and charity, and exhort them to the practice of holiness and virtue.[2]

Most of S. Paul's Epistles were written to the faithful of some particular place; the nine, namely, that

[1] See Franzelin, De Div. Trad. et Script. De Trad., Sect. 3. De relat. int. Div. Trad. et Scripturam.

[2] In several of his Epistles, S. Paul deals at some length with matters personal to himself, or to others, at that time, v.g., his claims to the Apostleship, the special difficulties which beset him, the sufferings and persecution he was enduring, etc.

are addressed to seven Churches which he had either founded himself, or by means of others. Each of these Churches had its own various circumstances and matters of special local interest that gave him the occasion of his Epistle, and suggested, at the same time, the topics on which to write.

Four of S. Paul's Epistles were of a character and scope still more particular, being addressed to individual persons, viz., to Timothy, Titus, and Philemon. Of like nature were the Second and Third Epistles of S. John.

The rest of the Epistles are of a general scope, being addressed to no special Church or person. In these, however, we can detect something definite in their occasion or aim, which gives to each Epistle its leading idea: whether it were to animate the faithful then suffering under persecution to patience and courage; or to counteract the evil influences of some heretical teaching then abroad; or to enforce and develop some particular doctrine which it was desirable at the time to bring into special prominence.

As an illustration of this last motive, we may note the insistence that S. James makes in his Epistle on the necessity of good works as an evidence of living faith. Another example is S. Paul's Epistle to the Hebrews, which may be regarded as a special treatise on the High-priesthood of Jesus Christ: its aim being to prove the pre-eminent excellence of our Lord's priesthood over that of Aaron, and of the New Dispensation over the Old.

Here the seasonable opportuneness of elucidating this topic, for the benefit of recent converts from

Judaism, would seem to be, at once, the immediate occasion, and the main reason, for that Epistle.

The gist of what we have been saying is, that the Apostles wrote their several Epistles on certain definite occasions with the view of meeting the various special circumstances of time and place, nationality, personal character, and condition incidental to the faithful generally at that date, or peculiar to those whom they immediately addressed. These Epistles were mainly intended to convey further instructions or counsels on particular points of faith and practice that had been before orally preached; to correct abuses that had sprung up, and to give answers to certain questions of doctrine, discipline and practice which were then rife amongst the first Christians. These and such like matters were present to the minds of the Apostles, and their immediate and principal object in writing their Epistles was to deal with them.

It would, consequently, be out of all reason for any-one to expect to find every doctrine and practice of the faith treated of in the Apostolic Epistles, since they do not profess, nor were ever meant by their writers to be complete or general exposition of the whole Christian religion. They are, moreover, disconnected, save in a few instances, one from another. The collection of all fails to form together one integral whole. Each Epistle stands alone, apart from the rest, and must be regarded singly by itself. The faithful of a particular church to which an Apostle wrote an Epistle did not necessarily receive all the other Epistles which the Apostles addressed to Christians elsewhere. The Apostles did not contemplate that they should do so; nor, indeed, was this possible, since the Epistles were written at different intervals of time and place. The case of the Epistle to the Colossians seems to be exceptional in this respect, perhaps because Laodicea was at no great distance from Colosse. In any case S. Paul gives special instructions on the matter.[1] True it is that in course of time the several Epistles were communicated to the faithful in other places than those to which they were originally addressed, and thus became generally known all or in part throughout the Church.[2] But still they remain unconnected one with another, and each has to be regarded by itself, independently of the rest. And looking on them in this light, we might as well expect to find every Christian doctrine and practice spoken of in each separate Epistle, as in all of them collectively. Or we might ask with equal right, why some point that has prominent mention in one Epistle is passed over altogether in all the rest. Why, for example, are all the other Epistles silent on the precept given by S. James to anoint the sick, and his teaching as to the effects of such unction? Why, too, are all the other Epistles silent about our Lord's priesthood from Melchisedech, of which the Epistle to the Hebrews is so full? For, to judge from that Epistle alone, and the prominence this doctrine there receives, we might suppose that it was one of the most important points of Christian faith, whereas were we to judge from the silence on it in all the other Epistles we might conclude its non-existence.

This, no doubt, is not a complete account of the

---

[1] *Col.* iv. 16. [2] *2 Pet.* iii. 15-16.

nature and scope of the Epistles, and of why the Apostles were divinely inspired to write them. For, though written primarily for certain occasions and local circumstances, it is certain that in God's providence they were intended for the instruction and guidance of the whole Christian Church in every age and country. And as the Holy Ghost inspired those who wrote them for this general end, all was overruled for universal edification, and hence the particular topics treated of in them have a greater significance and a wider bearing than the occasions which called them forth. But even so; and though we should conceive that, taken collectively, they, in some sense providentially form one harmonious whole, still they do not contain an exposition of all revealed truths and of every Christian practice. Amongst the manifold doctrines, practices, and precepts that are generally accepted as belonging to Christianity, some are passed over altogether in silence, whilst others have no explicit and adequate teaching in the Epistles—viz., the Mystery of the Trinity, the distinct personality of the Holy Ghost, prayer to our Lord Jesus Christ and to the Holy Ghost, infant baptism, and baptism otherwise than by immersion, the obligation of Sunday observance and of monogamy, the lawfulness for Christians to bear arms, to hold slaves, to take oaths, and to go to law with one another in the civil court. There are, moreover, matters which are held to be of great moment that have but one single mention in the Epistles—viz., the duty of public worship,[1] Holy

---

[1] *Heb.* x. 25.

Communion, and Extreme Unction—or only a distant allusion, as the Eucharistic Sacrifice.[1]

It would be interesting to examine what, and how many, Christian doctrines are set forth explicitly in the Epistles. We think that, after all, they would be found to be but few; and, again, to inquire, how many can be only indirectly inferred, or receive more or less confirmation in the Epistles from some passing remark, whilst their positive proof must be obtained from elsewhere. We may here observe that several of the topics which are most dwelt upon and developed in the Epistles have come to be of comparatively much less immediate interest and importance in these later times than they were in the days of the Apostles; or, perhaps, appear to us now so trite and obvious as hardly to have needed such great insistence as is given to them in their writings: as, for example, the insufficiency of the Mosaic law and the non-obligation of its rites; the admission of the Gentiles to the Christian Church

---

[1] It is perhaps superfluous to note—for all Catholics are taught it—that there are many passages in the Epistles which allude to, serve to confirm, and elucidate several of the points here enumerated, and that some of them may be thence logically proved and inferred. But all this is very different from express statement and adequately explicit teaching regarding them. In making such allusions the Apostles suppose in those to whom they write a previous knowledge of these truths through their oral teaching, and without this previous knowledge the first Christians would not have understood these allusions. In the same way, Christians in after ages could never have attained to the definite knowledge, which they have of these mysteries and truths, from the written word alone, and without the traditional teaching of the Church.

and to an equal share with the Jews in all the blessings and privileges of the Gospel; the pre-eminence of Christ's priesthood over the Levitical, and of the New Law over the Old; the proofs of S. Paul's apostleship; and the belief of the near approach of the Last Day. Then, again, matters of minor importance, or which, being only of passing interest, are now quite out of date, are mentioned in the Epistles with more or less prominence, such as the Agapæ, the eating of meats offered to idols, baptism for the dead, the washing of feet, and the religious institution of widows.

On the other hand, we find scarcely any mention in all the Epistles of the birth and life of our Lord Jesus Christ, or of His acts and words, which in the Gospels are recorded with such great care; whilst in several of them hardly any reference is made to the great leading truths and mysteries of the Faith; in some none at all; and in one not only is there no mention of the Name of Jesus Christ, but no allusion whatever is made to Him.

We must not, then, be surprised at the silence on the Blessed Virgin in the Epistles. Besides what we have here urged, all the reasons which we gave for this silence of the Apostles in their general preaching, as recorded by S. Luke, are applicable with still greater force to their writings: since these were mainly intended to be but supplementary comments on their oral teaching.

Those reasons were reducible to a two-fold principle. The first is that of due order in the proposition of revealed truths; whereby those primary truths which are necessary to be explicitly known and believed by all the faithful, are explicitly set forth first, and from the beginning. Whilst secondary truths, not thus necessary, but which serve more fully to explain, and give a more complete and integral knowledge of the Faith—though they may be implicitly contained in the exposition of the primary truths—are not set forth at the beginning so clearly and fully, but with less of set purpose, and only so far as may be needful for the adequate proposition and understanding of the more necessary truths.

The second principle is that of exercising a judicious discrimination, and prudent reserve in imparting the knowledge of the doctrines and practices of Faith to disciples, according to their various capacity, needs, dispositions, and surrounding circumstances of time and place.

As we discovered the recognition of these two principles by the Apostles in their oral teaching, so too may we find it in their writings. Thus S. Paul speaks of some Christian truths as the rudiments or first elements of revelation, forming, so to say, the foundation amongst the objects of faith. These he calls "the beginning of Christ;" and likens to milk which is given to infants, because all the faithful had received a knowledge, more or less, of these truths at their baptism and confirmation. Again, he speaks of himself, as having been careful to lay solidly the foundation, whilst he left it to others to build thereupon, by more fully explaining what he had himself then orally taught, and by imparting a more extensive knowledge of revealed truths, and thus supplying what was wanting to the integral complement of the Christian faith.¹ At the same time, he bids these teachers take heed that they build on the foundation that he had laid, sure and well-approved doctrine.² As the Apostle speaks of some revealed truths as rudimentary and fundamental,³ so he speaks of others as "wisdom," and "things more perfect," distinguishing these from those which were but the first elements. And he calls them "strong meat," which some of his disciples, he says, being still, as though only "little children," and "babes in Christ," still "carnal," unskilful in the word of justice and too weak to hear them, are as yet unable to bear and properly understand. Such teaching, says the Apostle, is reserved for "the perfect," the "spiritual," who have already to some degree themselves become "masters" in spiritual things, "by habitually exercising their senses to the discernment of good and evil."⁴

[1] *1 Thess.* iii. 10. [2] *1 Cor.* iii. 10-15.
[3] *1 Cor* ii. 2, 6 : iii. 11.
[4] *1 Cor.* ii. 6; iii. 1, 2. *Heb.* v. 11-14.

CHAPTER V.

THE IMPLICIT TEACHING OF THE APOSTLES ON THE BLESSED VIRGIN IN THEIR EPISTLES.

We have given reasons for the silence of the Apostles on the Blessed Virgin, and why they did not speak explicitly of her in their Epistles.

We have now to deal with what is more positive. And it remains for us to show that notwithstanding this silence, there lies hidden beneath the surface of the Apostolic writings a large amount of implicit teaching on our Lady, which we propose to bring in detail to view. But we must first claim as incontrovertible what we have before observed, viz., that the Apostles could not have deigned by their silence to ignore the Blessed Virgin, we mean that they could not have thereby intended of set purpose to take no account of her in their Epistles, and to exclude her from their own consideration, and that of those to whom they wrote.

The one great central theme of all their teaching, whether oral or written, was our Lord Jesus Christ, the Word made flesh, the promised Messias and Saviour of the world. But His Virgin Mother is so intimately connected with Him; her ancestry, privileges, whole life and character are so closely interwoven with those of her Son; His claims to be believed in for what He professed to be, and was set forth to be by the Apostles, are so dependent on the truth of the recorded facts of Mary's history, that there could be no adequate teaching concerning Him without regard to her. Hence, the Apostles had necessarily to reckon, so to speak, with Mary in treating of Jesus Christ, and could not ignore her.

Moreover, everyone would, we think, admit that if we had had only the Apostolic Epistles to look to, our knowledge of our Lord Jesus Christ would be on many points very indefinite and imperfect. In order to complete this knowledge and to intelligently understand all that the Apostles write concerning Him in their Epistles, we must bring to them, as we read them, the knowledge we have of Him from whatever is elsewhere revealed in God's written word. But to this knowledge of Jesus Christ appertains all that is said in the sacred Scriptures, and especially in the Gospels, about Mary His Mother; as the Blessed one amongst women, foretold by God Himself in the primeval promise made to our first parents in paradise; the Virgin of virgins predicted by the prophets, saluted by Gabriel as full of grace; the true Mother of the Incarnate Word, whom on earth, above all others He honoured and obeyed as a most dutiful and loving Son; with whom He spent far the most part of His life, living and conversing with her alone; who was made at the Visitation the channel for communicating to others the first graces of His Incarnation; at whose prayer He anticipated the time for working miracles, whereby He first manifested His divine glory, and His disciples believed in Him; to whom He gave the chief share in His sufferings, and therefore of His graces, virtues, and merits, as also of His resurrection glory; to whom, when dying, He commended, as to their own Mother, all His brethren in the person of His beloved disciple, charging them at the same time that henceforth they should, as dutiful, loving children, regard her as their Mother; whom, in fine, the Holy Ghost had, by her own lips, foretold God's faithful in all generations should bless and praise.

Such a delineation of Mary's personal history, as well as of striking traits in her character, which at once appear from the incidents recorded of her, and remarks made about her by the Evangelists, is patent on the page of the Gospel to all who read what is there written with a believing and unprejudiced mind. And since, obviously, all that we know of Mary bears importantly on our knowledge of Jesus Christ, and serves to explain what is said of Him in Holy Scripture, it is evident that whoever would understand adequately what the Apostles wrote concerning Jesus Christ in their Epistles, must take with him in reading them what is elsewhere revealed of His Blessed Mother. And this all the more, because the authors of the Epistles, as Apostles, were in full possession of whatever had been revealed concerning Mary, and had, when writing, all this present to their minds, with an understanding and knowledge much more complete, clear, and profound than we can have. Besides, they lived in her own lifetime, had personally known her, and enjoyed intimate converse with her. This, too, was more or less incident to some, at least, of those whom the Apostles addressed, who, if they had not known or seen her personally, had, at any rate, seen and heard those who had known her, and from them learnt many circumstances of her life and character that are wanting to us, and which would go to fill in the sketch that is drawn in mere outline by the Evangelists, and to complete the marvellously beautiful idea of her, which even the little that they say brings up to our view.

Hence, from what we have said, it seems fair to conclude : that in whatever measure an explicit knowledge of the Blessed Virgin was needed for a full and adequate understanding of the Apostles' teaching concerning our Lord Jesus Christ in their Epistles, in the same measure they supposed that explicit knowledge of Mary to be in the possession of those to whom they wrote. In other words, so far was an implicit teaching on the Blessed Virgin, in this sense, contained in the Apostolic Epistles.

But, beside this argument, based to some extent, it may be thought, on *a priori* grounds—many passages of the Epistles bear positive evidence of such implicit teaching; since the principles and doctrines laid down in them point directly of themselves, and necessarily lead up to what was then known and believed about Our Lady, and to all that the Catholic Church has ever held concerning her. Many things, too, are said in the Epistles which seemingly would never have been written at all, were it not for the knowledge their authors had of Mary.

We shall bring many instances in proof of this assertion, from the words of the Apostles, when we go through their several Epistles in detail. It will suffice here summarily to observe that, whatever qualities of person, state, character, or office are spoken of in the Epistles, as grounds of dignity, claiming respectful attention, honour, praise, admiration, and love, on the part of Christians, meet with their perfect realisation, and, so to say, culminate in our Lady. Those virtues, too, which the Apostles most extol, and recommend to the faithful, are strikingly characteristic of, and exemplified in, Mary, as she is portrayed in the Gospels. Again, many of the metaphors, comparisons, and analogies that occur in the Epistles would seem to be directly borrowed from the idea of Mary, and to have been made use of by the Apostles, with the thought of her present to their mind, as they wrote; since, in her alone, they meet with their full and highest significance. And the same may be said, with due proportion, of illustrations, types, predictions, and promises taken from the Old Testament.

We will state our position and line of argument in another way, thus:—

The Blessed Virgin Mary is, in point of fact, through her ineffable union with Jesus Christ, the Word Incarnate, immeasurably above all the rest of creation in dignity, more well-pleasing and united to God than any other creature; and, consequently, was enriched with most noble graces of state, gifts, and privileges, and with a fulness of sanctifying grace and of the Holy Ghost beyond all others. By co-operating most faithfully with the graces she received, she surpassed all in acquired holiness and in the practice of every virtue, and through her perfect fidelity to grace, merited to be recompensed with a crown of glory greater than that of all others. Mary, as Mother of God, and through her exceeding grace and sanctity, is the most noble and excellent member of Christ's mystical Body, wherein she holds the highest place of state and office, after Jesus Christ, its Head. Mary is also the spiritual Mother of all Christians, who are the brethren of Christ; and in her they may find the Model of all virtues for their imitation. On all these grounds the Blessed Virgin should be an object of veneration, love, and hope to all Christians.

The foregoing points must, we think, be admitted as true by all who sincerely believe in Our Lord Jesus Christ as the Incarnate Son of God; and who seriously reflect on them, meditating, at the same time, on God's Attributes of Wisdom, Goodness, Faithfulness, and Justice.

But if this be so, we are in full accord with reason and truth, when we predicate of Mary, in its highest degree, whatever the Apostles say in their Epistles of dignity, honour, privileges, gifts, and graces that are bestowed on the rest of the faithful; whatever, too, they say in praise of Christian sanctity, virtues, and merits; and when we enhance, in her regard, the claims that they urge of any others on our veneration, hope, and love; and, when we contemplate her crown of eternal glory in heaven as surpassing far in splendour that with which they assure us all the elect are recompensed.

We say that to make such application to the Blessed Virgin of what is thus contained in the Epistles—even though this were beside the writers' intention—would entirely accord with reason and truth, because all these things are really applicable to Mary in the highest degree. But we say further, that implicitly it was the intention of the Apostles to make such application: since the professed theme of their Epistles was Jesus Christ, the Incarnate Word, with whom the thought of Mary, His Mother, is indissolubly united; and they were so well conscious of all that Mary was. We shall, moreover, point out several passages in the Epistles that bear trace of an explicit thought of the Blessed Virgin being present in the minds of the Apostles as they wrote.

What we now add may be deemed not strictly relevant to our particular inquiry. It is at any rate, one of those "undesigned coincidences" which will serve as a confirmation to our whole argument. And it is this, that the beautiful descriptions and praises of the various Christian virtues, which we read in the Epistles, exactly portray and vividly recall to mind that idea of Mary, as the type of all perfection, that is ever impressed on the minds and hearts of the faithful, as she has been depicted by the holy Fathers, Doctors, and Saints, and witnessed to by Catholic tradition in every age.

As, however, some consideration of this thought is necessary to better understand the full meaning and scope of our thesis, we shall devote the next chapter to its development.

CHAPTER VI.

THE CATHOLIC VIEW OF THE BLESSED VIRGIN AS AN IDEAL OF ALL CHRISTIAN PERFECTION.

As Mary's dignity, on account of her Divine Maternity, is revealed to us as transcendently sublime, reaching to a height and grandeur beyond all that created intelligence could of itself conceive, so in like manner has the Holy Church, which is ever animated and guided by the Spirit of Truth, uniformly contemplated Mary's grace and sanctity; the one only measure of these being the sublimity of her dignity as Mother of God.

In the same way, too, the spiritual instinct of the faithful ever prompts them to regard the Blessed Virgin, next after the Sacred Humanity of Jesus Christ, as the most perfect work of God's creation; the master-piece of His hands; the ideal type of all that is most excellent, pure, lovely, beautiful, gracious, virtuous, holy and well-pleasing to God; and as being through the fulness of grace bestowed upon her, and her own faithful co-operation, most like in thought, word, and work to Jesus Christ, her Son, the Divine Exemplar and Architype of all His elect.

Thus regarded, Mary is the norma and type, so to say, of all God's dealings with mankind in the supernatural order; the peculiar choice of all His elections and predestinations; pre-eminently the object of His most gracious Providence, and of the bestowal of His richest gifts and favours, so that she is, in a manner, the very impersonation of divine grace.

That she might be Mother of God with becoming worthiness, in her was perfectly fulfilled that Sovereign Canon of the Divine Spirit, which is expressed in the words of S. Bernardine of Sienna :

"For all singular graces communicated to any reasonable creature, the general rule is, that when ever the Divine favour has elected any one for some singular grace, or some sublime state, it bestows all those gifts of grace that are necessary for the person thus elected, and for his office, and which will plentifully adorn him." [1]

In the case of other Saints we must first know their lives and actions in order to form some judgment of their virtue and goodness, and we measure them according to a standard of which we seem to have a definitely formed idea already in our mind, whereas, in the case of Mary, we should rather first attain to some knowledge of what consummate virtue and perfection is, in order to know something of what she is; since we feel antecedently assured, that all we can conceive of sanctity, and of what is best and highest may be predicated of her, and still will fall short of the reality.

In other words, relatively to us, and so far as our thoughts can reach to the utmost bounds of excellence

---

[1] *Serm. de S. Joseph.* Tom. iv. p. 231. See S. Thomas, 3 *P.* qu. xxvii. art. 5, *ad* 1; art. 4, *concl.*; *art.* 5, *ad* 2.

in one who is but creature and finite, Mary is her own standard. For, just as the dignity to which God has been pleased to exalt her, by making her His own Mother, surpasses the limits of our comprehension, so does the perfection wherewith He has graced her, that she might be—adequately, that is, to her condition as a human creature—a Mother worthy of the Incarnate Word, exceed all our knowledge and conception.[1]

It was therefore unnecessary that much should be left on record regarding our Lady, and that we should have many and minute details of her life and conduct, or that all her virtues should be particularly described, and her praises of set purpose declared in Holy Writ. It was enough for us to know that she was the Virgin Mother, "of whom was born Jesus who is called Christ," to be well assured that God has endowed her with every grace and perfection proportioned to the sublime dignity to which He had chosen her.

"In fine," says S. Bernardine, "the greatness and

---

[1] "The Blessed Virgin is full of grace, not with the fulness of grace itself; for she had not grace in the highest degree of excellence in which it can be had, nor had she it as to all its effects; but she was said to be full of grace as to herself, because she had sufficient grace for that state to which she was chosen by God, that is, to be Mother of His Only-begotten Son." (S. Thom., *l.c. art.* 10, *ad* 1.)

"Hence it is we know that so great grace was conferred upon the Virgin; because she merited to conceive and give birth to God." (S. August., *De Nat. et Grat.* c. 36.)

"It was becoming that the Virgin should be entrusted with such gifts, that she might be full of grace, who gave to heaven glory, and God to earth." (S. Sophronius, *Serm. de Assump.*)

dignity of this Blessed Virgin are such that God alone does and can comprehend it." "In this reflection we have more than sufficient," remarks S. Thomas of Villanova, "to take away the surprise which might be caused on seeing that the Sacred Evangelists, who have so fully recorded the praises of a John the Baptist, and of a Magdalene, say so little of the precious gifts of Mary. It was sufficient to say of her: *Of whom was born Jesus.* What more could you wish the Evangelists to have said of the greatness of this Blessed Virgin?" continues the Saint. "Is it not enough that they declare that she was the Mother of God? In these few words they recorded the greatest, the whole, of her precious gifts: and since the whole was therein contained, it was unnecessary to enter into details.[1]

Hence it is that the Holy Church in her Liturgy applies to Mary so many passages from the Sapiential Books, which in their primary and highest sense are to be interpreted of the Divine uncreated Wisdom, because Mary above all other creatures is Its perfect mirror and type.

Hence, again, are bestowed on our Lady so many titles setting her before us as the created ideal of all virtue and sanctity, such as *Speculum justitiæ, Sedes sapientiæ, Vas honorablie, Vas insigne devotionis,* etc. Hence, too, the Church is so lavish of reiterated epithets, wherewith to praise her—styling her at once, *Sancta Dei Genitrix, Mater Christi, Mater Creatoris,* and *Mater Salvatoris;* and then again, *Sancta*

---

[1] See S. Alphonsus, *Glories of Mary,* p. 329.

Virgo virginum, Mater purissima, Mater castissima, Mater inviolata, Mater intemerata, and *Regina virginum*—as though each single title, however adequate in itself, were powerless to express, the full significance and meaning of Mary's Divine Maternity and Virginal purity, and as though the Holy Church would, by accumulated repetition, force human language to rise to something like a worthy utterance of her sublime dignity and perfection.

Harmonising with this view, it would seem that the holy Fathers and Saints in their praises of Mary, and when extolling the excellence of her virtues and sanctity, had not so much before their minds any particular recorded actions or incidents of her life and conduct, as virtue and sanctity in perfection, of which she was to them the ideal type, and to which everything that was most excellent might be with truth referred. In speaking of the Blessed Virgin, it is, as though they made application to her of the Apostle's words: "For the rest, brethren, whatsoever things are true, whatsoever modest, whatsoever just, whatsoever holy, whatsoever lovely, whatsoever of good fame, if there be any virtue, if there be any praise of discipline, think of these things:"[1] and think of them in Mary, for in her you will find them all.

Accordingly Catholic writers and the faithful generally are wont to predicate of Mary in surpassing measure and excellence whatever of virtue and perfection shines forth in the lives of all other

[1] *Philip.* iv. 8.

Saints, and whatever privileges or special gifts of grace and holiness any of these received, as belonging by right to her who is the Mother of our Lord, and the Queen of all Saints.[1] It is in this way, we incline to think, S. Ambrose has drawn his beautiful portrait of our Lady with a description of her virtues, which is contained in the Lections for so many of her Feasts.

It is worthy of notice, what at first sight might seem strange, that but little desire or curiosity is evinced generally by the faithful to know more details of Mary's history, and that comparatively few attempts have been made to write her life. It is as though Catholics are content with what is revealed concerning her in the Sacred Scriptures, and has been handed down in those few traditions upon which the Holy Church has set her seal; and as though there was felt a consciousness, that any more explicit record of her actions and virtues by human hand must needs be disappointing, and fall below that ideal standard, which is impressed on the minds and hearts of the faithful as belonging to the Mother of God.

If the Evangelists do not enter into many details about the Blessed Virgin, still in the little they do record of her, much is said. This is indeed, so much, and so pregnant, as to comprise all those sublime prerogatives and privileges which the Catholic Church ascribes to her, and to serve as the foundation of all

---

[1] See *infra* the quotation from Morales, S. J., in the *Comments* on *Coloss.* ii. 19.

that is believed of faith, or piously held concerning her by common consent of the faithful.

But even though in the divine revelation of the Word Incarnate, nothing had been explicitly told us regarding His Mother, still we may rest assured that she would, from the very nature of things, and from the necessary conviction we have of the essential harmony of truth, hold the place which she actually possesses in the minds and hearts of the faithful who believe fully and sincerely in the Gospel of Jesus Christ. The position of the Virgin Mother of the Incarnate Word is in all creation so unique, without parallel, beyond compare, her dignity so transcendent, her relations with the Divinity so intimate and personal, her office and functions so sublime, that, unless all our reason is at fault, or our faith irrational, and all our knowledge of God and man whether natural or supernatural to be ignored as of no account, we could not reasonably conceive that any who really believed, in all its fulness, the Incarnation of the Divine Word, should have other thoughts, than those of the Catholic Faith, concerning Mary, His own true Mother.

Hence, we say, if nothing had been known about Mary from the inspired Scriptures, or from tradition, and even her very name were left unrecorded, still the faithful would have found a name for the Mother of Jesus their Divine Redeemer, which would be enshrined with loving devotion in their hearts; and still would she be regarded as the first of all God's creatures, full of grace, the ideal type of whatever is most pure, holy and best in a creature; still would they hold her, because Mother of God, to be Queen of heaven, their Queen and Mother also, the Advocate of sinners with her Son, a channel of grace to all, and a worthy object of Christian hope, veneration, and love.

COMMENTS ON THE EPISTLES.

THE EPISTLE OF S. PAUL THE APOSTLE

TO THE

ROMANS.

CHAPTER I.

1 Paul, a servant of Jesus Christ, called to be an apostle, separated unto the Gospel of God,
2 Which he had promised before, by his prophets, in the holy scriptures,
3 Concerning his Son, who was made to him of the seed of David, according to the flesh,
4 Who was predestinated the Son of God in power, according to the spirit of santification, by the resurrection of our Lord Jesus Christ from the dead;
5 By whom we have received grace and apostleship for obedience to the faith, in all nations, for his name.

S. Paul in these verses, as at the commencement of other Epistles, gives the title of his authority from heaven, and the claim that he has on the respect and obedience of those whom he addresses. How much higher are Mary's claims. How would the terms of her commission run?

Mary, the handmaid of the Lord, chosen to be the Mother of Jesus Christ; that Virgin predicted by the prophets, separated for the Incarnation of the Divine Word, Who was made Flesh, conceived and born of me, by the overshadowing of the Holy Ghost, Our Lord Jesus Christ, my God, my Saviour, and my Son—through Whom I have found grace, and am full of grace and blessing, so that from henceforth all generations shall call me blessed; from Whom when dying on the Cross, I received the charge to be Mother of all His disciples and brethren, to the end that all the faithful in all nations should regard me with filial love and piety for His name.

S. Paul here dwells on his dignity in order to show with what authority he writes.

First, he delights in the title of being servant or slave (δοῦλος) of Jesus Christ, and considers it an honour. Next, he has been chosen by God to be one of His Apostles. He has been selected for a work of such mighty importance, that it has been foretold, or rather, that it has been the general burden of all the prophecies; this work being to make known the Gospel of God, that is, God's joyful news concerning His own Divine Son made Man.

Compare now Mary's dignity : she also delights in the title of handmaid (δούλη). Yet to what has God chosen her? Not to be an Apostle, or the first of them, but to be the Mother of His Son. She is that very *seed of David* which has been the object of so many prophecies. It was her office to *make Jesus Christ according to the flesh* for God His Father, and to give Him to the world. *Qui pro nobis natus, tulit esse tuus.*

S. Paul tells us that to fit him for his work, he was *separated unto the Gospel of God.* That is, he was removed from everything else, to be entirely consecrated to this. He was separated from his nation, his family, his home, his worldly pursuits and prospects; but above all from his former habits, prejudices, and sins. Since then Mary's office is so much higher, it is reasonable to suppose (as we know to be the fact), that *she was separated* for it by a much more perfect separation and consecration. Indeed, she was not one of the number of holy women, but blessed amongst them all. She was separated from the rest of men by her immaculate conception, by her presentation in the Temple, by her vow of virginity, by her fulness of grace. *Nec primam similem visa est, nec habere sequentem.*

"*But He was made of the seed of David according to the flesh*, as the Apostle says : That is, as though of the mould of earth, when there was no man to till the earth ; because no man wrought in the Virgin of whom Christ was born. 'But a spring rose out of the earth, watering all the face of the earth.' *The face of the earth, that is, the dignity of the earth, whereby is most rightly understood, the Mother of the Lord, the Virgin Mary, whom the Holy Spirit watered; for He is signified under the name of a Spring, and of Water in the Gospel: as though Christ, made of such mould, was to be the Man set in paradise to work and keep it, that is to say, in the will of His Father to fulfil and keep it.*[1]

9 For God is my witness, whom I serve in my spirit in the gospel of his Son, that without ceasing I make a commemoration of you;
10 Always in my prayers making request, if by any means now at length I may have a prosperous journey, by the will of God, to come unto you.
11 For I long to see you, that I may impart unto you some spiritual grace, to strengthen you:
12 That is to say, that I may be comforted together in you, by that which is common to us both, your faith and mine.

In almost every one of his Epistles the Apostle makes a protest, similar to this, of his fidelity in intercessory prayer, and ceaseless prayer, prayer "night and day," as he writes to S. Timothy.[2] So impressed is he with the importance of this duty, that he here even takes an oath that he fulfils it. Such intercessory prayer is not a mere external duty, which those perform who render to God only a perfunctory bodily service. No, S. Paul performed it otherwise, for, at the same time, *he served God in his spirit in the Gospel of His Son.*

But certainly the Blessed Mother of God *served God in her spirit in the Gospel of His Son.* This was nearer and dearer to her than to S. Paul. Certainly, then, she prayed day and night for the success of the Gospel when she was on earth; and certainly she does so still more fervently now that she is in heaven.

S. Paul longed to impart some spiritual grace. Had not Mary, has she not still, a more intense longing than the Apostle to *impart unto us some spiritual grace*, since she herself was "full of grace," having "found grace with God," and through her we have received the source of all grace? We

[1] S. Augustine, *De Genesi* L. ii. 36, on *Gen.* ii. 5-7.   [2] 2 *Tim.* i. 3.

see how Mary was appointed by God to be the channel of the first graces of the Incarnation; how eagerly she longed to impart grace, and how efficaciously she fulfilled her ministry, by what is told us by S. Luke. No sooner was the mystery of the Divine Maternity accomplished, than Mary arose with haste to visit with grace her cousin S. Elizabeth; and at the first sound of her salutation the yet unborn Baptist was sanctified, His Mother was filled with the Holy Ghost, and through the Blessed Virgin's coming, joy was brought to the whole household. And here, it may be remarked, that S. Paul does not hesitate, when speaking of himself, to use the word *impart*, though of course he could be only the channel, and not the source of grace. No one, however, could mistake his meaning. Can anyone, then, without perversity, mistake our meaning, when in prayers to Mary we do not simply ask her to pray for us, but to give us grace? By a similar form of speech S. Paul in another place speaks of *saving* men.[1] And may we not, regardless of the cavils of foolish men, ask Mary to save us?

14 To the Greeks and to the Barbarians, to the wise and to the unwise, I am a debtor.

S. Paul considered that he owed the Gospel to all men. Why? Because at the time of his marvellous conversion, he had asked our Lord what He would have him to do; and he had been told, as also had Ananias, that he was "a vessel of election to carry the Name of Jesus Christ before the Gentiles, and kings, and the children of Israel."[2]

Compare, now, Mary's vocation to her office with that of S. Paul. To him Jesus Christ appears and complains that he is His persecutor: Mary is saluted by the Angel as full of grace, blessed amongst women, and the Lord is said to be with her. Mary also asks what she is to do, or how the Divine pleasure shall be accomplished in her. She is told, not that she is to

---

[1] 1 *Tim.* iv. 16.

[2] *Acts* ix. 6, 7, 15, 16; xxii. 10, 14, 15; xxvi. 15-18. See *infra*, ch. ix. 22, the passage quoted from S. Basil of Seleucia.

be a vessel of election to carry the Name of Jesus to the world, but that she is to carry Jesus Himself, and give to Him His divine Name.[1] That Mary held that this dignity imposed an office upon her as regards men, and made her their debtor, is evident; for she at once makes herself the servant of Elizabeth and of John, carrying to them grace and joy with her Divine Son. Besides, S. John says: "He that saith he abideth in Jesus Christ, ought himself also to walk even as He walked."[2] What union more complete than that of Jesus and Mary, He in her, and she in Him. No wonder, then, that if He was "the servant of all,"[3] she esteemed herself a debtor to all.

"Mary," says S. Bernard, "has been made all things to all men: to the wise and to the unwise she hath made herself a debtor in her most abundant charity. To all she opens her bosom of mercy, that all may receive of her fulness: the captive redemption, the sick cure, the sad consolation, the sinner pardon, the just grace, the angels joy—in fine, the whole Trinity glory; the Person of the Son the substance of human flesh—so that none should be hid from the heat thereof."[4]

CHAPTER II.

6 Who will render to every man according to his works.
7 To them indeed, who according to patience in good work, seek glory, and honour, and incorruption, eternal life.

"What recompense will Christ render to the Blessed Virgin? Christ the Lord, the just judge, *gives rewards, says the Apostle, to every man according to his works.* As what Mary, His most holy Virgin Mother, has wrought is incomprehensible, and unspeakable the gift she received, so beyond all price and incomprehensible is the reward and the glory which she has merited. I say not amongst the rest of virgins, but also amongst all the Saints."[5]

---

[1] *Luke* i. .   [2] 2 *John* ii. 6.   [3] *Mark* x. 44, 45.   *Luke* xxii. 27.
[4] *Ps.* xviii. 7.   *Serm. De Verb. Apoc.*
[5] S. Ildephonsus, *Serm.* 2, *De Assump.*

"And who would there be, for whom the Lord would lay up greater merit and reserve greater reward than for His Mother?"[1]

10 But glory, and honour, and peace to every one that worketh good.

There is then an honour due to creatures, as well as to the Creator; though the honour due to the "only God"[2] cannot be shared by creatures. But, we may add, neither can the glory and honour due to creatures be given directly to God. Honour is due to excellence. Now, God's excellence is not only infinitely greater in degree than that of His creatures, but also essentially different in kind from theirs. Nay rather, they are not merely different, but contradictory. God's excellence is in His Infinite, Independent, Self-sufficing Nature. The honour due to this is *latria*, supreme adoration. The excellence of creatures is in their submission to God, their perfect dependence on Him, their absolute reference of themselves to Him. Mary, who of all creatures was the most humble, the most submissive, the most prostrate before God, is most deserving of honour as a creature. But this honour does not raise her up as a rival to God, but proclaims her the very humblest of His servants. If it places a crown on her brow, it is one which she casts at the feet of her Son.[3]

13 For not the hearers of the law are just before God; but the doers of the law shall be justified.

Mary is frequently praised in the Gospel as not a mere hearer but a doer. Indirectly she is thus commended by our Lord Himself in answer to the woman who exclaimed: "Blessed is the womb that bore thee," etc.; when He said, "Yea rather, blessed are they who hear the word of God and keep it."[4] And directly she is commended by the Evangelist, who records of Mary that she "performed all things according to the Law of the Lord,"[5] and carefully takes note of her

---

[1] S. Ambrose, *De Inst. Virg.* vi. 45.   [2] 1 *Tim.* i. 17.
[3] *Apoc.* iv. 10.   [4] *Luke* xi. 27, 28.   [5] *Ib.* ii. 39.

exact obedience.¹ Thus that blessedness of keeping God's word, which our Lord pronounced to be greater than that of the divine maternity, was pre-eminently Mary's: and hence pre-eminently was she *just before God.*

"Mary was more blessed," says S. Augustine, "in receiving the faith of Christ than in conceiving the flesh of Christ. For to one who said : 'Blessed is the womb that bore thee and the paps that gave thee suck,' He answered: 'Yea rather, blessed are they who hear the word of God and keep it.' What profited it His brethren, that is, His kindred according to the flesh, who did not believe in Him, their relationship? So, too, the near relationship of mother would have profited Mary nothing, had she not borne Christ in her heart, which was more blessed than bearing Him in her flesh. . . . Thus Mary, by doing the will of God corporally is only the Mother of Christ, but spiritually is both sister and mother."²

29 But he is a Jew, that is one inwardly; and the circumcision is that of the heart, in the spirit, not in the letter; whose praise is not of men, but of God.

Such was Nathanael, "an Israelite indeed, in whom was no guile;"³ thus praised by our Lord Himself. Such, still more, was Mary. It was not fitting that His earthly lips should directly praise her. But her interior piety is praised by the Angel and the Evangelist.⁴ "All the glory of the King's daughter is from within." ⁵

CHAPTER III.

23 For all men have sinned.

"Does this universal statement include the Blessed Virgin? By a special privilege granted to Mary an exception was made in her case to the general rule that all have sinned, as S. Augustine declares."⁶

---

[1] v.v. 21-27, 41, 43.   [2] *De Sanct. Virginit.* c.c. 3, 4.   [3] *John* i. 47.
[4] See *Luke* i. 28, 30, 41-45; ii. 19, 51.   [5] *Ps.* xliv. 15.
[6] S. Antoninus, P iv., Tit. 15, cap. 20, § 4.—See the passage from S. Augustine, *De Natura et gratia* c. xxxvi., *infra*, ad 1 *John* i. 8.

CHAPTER IV.

3 For what saith the scripture? Abraham believed God, and it was reputed to him unto justice.

16 Therefore it is of faith, that according to grace the promise might be firm to all the seed; not to that only which is of the law, but to that also which is of the faith of Abraham, who is the father of us all.

17 (As it is written: I have made thee a father of many nations) before God, whom he believed, who quickeneth the dead; and calleth those things that are not, as those that are.

18 Who against hope believed in hope; that he might be made the father of many nations, according to that which was said to him: So shall thy seed be.

19 And he was not weak in faith; neither did he consider his own body now dead, whereas he was almost an hundred years old, nor the dead womb of Sara.

20 In the promise also of God he staggered not by distrust; but was strengthened in faith, giving glory to God:

21 Most fully knowing, that whatsoever he has promised, he is able also to perform.

22 And therefore it was reputed to him unto justice.

23 Now it is not written only for him, that it was reputed to him unto justice,

24 But also for us, to whom it shall be reputed, if we believe in him, that raised up Jesus Christ, our Lord, from the dead,

25 Who was delivered up for our sins, and rose again for our justification.

How well and how truly might we not here substitute the name of Mary for Abraham. What saith the Gospel? "Blessed art thou that hast believed, because these things shall be accomplished that were spoken to thee by the Lord."[1] How much higher and more efficacious was Mary's *faith* than that of Abraham; and, consequently, how much greater and more perfect her *justice;* how much fuller and more extended the blessedness and *promised inheritance* resulting to her therefrom. Are these not proportioned to the immediate object of her faith, the Redeemer of the world, the Incarnate Lord of men and angels, who was so much greater than Isaac, the son of Sara, the immediate object of Abraham's faith?

Yes, Blessed, indeed, Mary, art thou amongst women, whom all generations, in time and eternity, shall pronounce Blessed.

---

[1] *Luke* i. 45.

Has not Mary, in a more true and far higher sense than Abraham is the father of the faithful, become through her faith *the Mother of us all?* She *who against hope believed in hope, that she might be the Mother* of her God, and of all generations of His faithful ones:[1] who *was not weak in faith,* considering not her virginal sterility; *in the promise also* that "the Holy Ghost should come upon her, and the power of the Most High overshadow her, and that there should be born of her the Holy, the Son of God," *staggered not by distrust; but strengthened in faith,* knowing that no word is impossible with God, said, "Behold the handmaid of the Lord, be it done to me according to Thy word;" and *giving to God all the glory,* exclaimed: "My soul doth magnify the Lord . . . because He that is Mighty hath done great things to me; and holy is His Name. *Now it is not written only for her, but also for us, if we believe;* as she herself declared: "His mercy is for them that fear Him throughout all generations."

"Blessed be the Babe," exclaims S. Ephrem, "whose Mother was Bride of the Holy One! . . . Sara had lulled Isaac as being a slave that bare the image of the King his Master on his shoulders, even the sign of His Cross, yea on his hands were bandages and sufferings, a type of the nails. Rachel cried to her husband, and said, Give me sons. Blessed be Mary, in whose womb, though she asked not, Thou didst dwell holily, O Gift, that poured itself upon them that received it. Anna with bitter tears asked a child, Sara and Rebecca with vows and words, Elizabeth also with her prayer: after having harassed themselves for a long time yet so obtained comfort. Blessed be Mary, who without vows and without prayers, in her virginity conceived and brought forth the Lord of all the sons of her companions, who have been or shall be chaste and righteous, priests and kings. Who ever lulled a son in her bosom as Mary did? Who ever dared to call her son, Son of the Maker, Son of the Creator, Son of the

---

[1] See *infra, Gal.* iii. 6-9, 16, 18, 22, 26-29; iv. 22-31. *Heb.* xi. 11, 12, 17-19. *James* ii. 21-23.

Most High? Who ever dared to speak to her son as in prayer? O Trust of Thy Mother as God, her Beloved and her Son as Mary, in fear and love it is meet for Thy Mother to stand before Thee."[1]

"Mary hid in us to-day leaven come from Abraham."[2]

The Blessed Virgin has alluded in her Magnificat to God's fidelity to His promises made to " Abraham and his seed for ever." The Jews in our Lord's time were fond of calling Abraham their father, but they were often degenerate children. The Pharisees were rebuked for this by S. John Baptist,[3] as well as by our Blessed Lord Himself,[4] Who told them to imitate or do the works of Abraham. Yet the great patriarch has some genuine children amongst his lineal descendants, and of these Mary was the chief. She was a true daughter of Abraham. But she was far more. She was the Mother of Him who was before Abraham,[5] and whose day Abraham rejoiced to see.[6] No doubt Abraham rejoiced also in the birth and life of his more favoured daughter. Abraham's faith and hope were great. Greater still were Mary's. He believed that his barren wife could be made fruitful, but Mary that a virgin could conceive. "Blessed art thou that didst believe." Abraham believed that though he should slay his child of promise, God's promises would still be fulfilled. Mary saw her Son die in shame, and even heard Him cry : " My God, My God, why hast Thou forsaken Me ? " Yet she believed in His resurrection and future reign. And so she *is the Mother of us all*, the Mother of many nations, the Mother whom all generations shall call Blessed.

"Was the faith of the Blessed Virgin greater than that of Abraham ? Abraham, indeed, believed in the hope of the promise made to him by the angel concerning a son who was to be born contrary to the hope that he had naturally that he

---

[1] *De Natal. Dom.* Hom. vi. *Opp. Syr.* ii. Morris, p. 36.
[2] *Ib.* Hom. i. p. 8.—S. Ephrem in his sermon on Abraham and Isaac draws out the analogy between the conception of Sara (*Gen.* xviii. 10-12, xxi. 7), and the Annuntiation to Mary, dwelling on the former only for the sake of the latter (*Opp. Græc.* iii. p. 376).
[3] *Matt.* iii. 9.   [4] *John* viii. 39.   [5] *John* viii. 58.   [6] *Ib.* v. 56.

should yet have a son, since he was very old and his wife barren. But the faith of the Blessed Virgin Mary was greater, for she believed the angel, that of herself a virgin should be born, not a man only, but the Son of the Most High. Magis enim est contra, vel potius supra naturam, virginem concipere, permanente virgine, et verum Deum et hominem, quam concipere vetulam ex vetulissimo, et purum hominem."[1]

CHAPTER V.

1 Being justified therefore by faith, let us have peace with God, through our Lord Jesus Christ:
2 By whom also we have access through faith into this grace, wherein we stand, and glory in the hope of the glory of the sons of God.
3 And not only so; but we glory also in tribulations, knowing that tribulation worketh patience;
4 And patience trial; and trial hope;
5 And hope confoundeth not; because the charity of God is poured forth in our hearts, by the Holy Ghost, who is given to us.

By faith we have access to our present grace. Faith is the beginning and root of our justification. The Church is the kingdom of faith. Without faith we cannot participate in its treasures. It is faith which gives us access to our sonship. "As many as received Him, He gave them power to be made the sons of God, to them that believe in His name."[2] Consequently it is faith which admits us to our hope of that eternal bliss, which God our Father will confer on His sons. "Dearly beloved, we are now the sons of God; and it hath not yet appeared what we shall be. We know that when He shall appear, we shall be like to Him, because we shall see Him as He is."[3] Now Mary was daughter, first-born daughter of God, and like us she obtained that grace by faith. But she was more than daughter: she was Mother. Mother of her Heavenly Father! And how had she access to this grace? By her faith. "Blessed art thou that hast believed, because those things shall be accomplished that were spoken to thee

---

[1] S. Antonin. P. iv. Tit. 15, cap. 19, § 3. [2] John i. 12.
[3] 1 John iii. 2.

by the Lord."[1] And note how Mary, *standing in this grace gloried in the hope of the glory of Mother of God.* No sooner had Elizabeth reminded her of the grace to which faith has given her access, than her spirit rejoiced in God her Saviour. "Because He hath regarded the humility of His handmaid: for behold from henceforth all generations shall call me blessed."[2] And now in heaven Mary possesses that for which she hoped. She who was hungry is filled with the good things of her Divine Son: she who was humble is exalted to His right hand. She "sees Him as He is," in the beatific vision—not, indeed, adequately, as He sees Himself; yet more perfectly than the saints or angels. And because she sees Him more perfectly, she is more "like to Him" than they. Oh! what vision! what likeness! It is part of the hope in which we glory that we shall one day see the Son reflected in the Mother, His spotless mirror.

If all Christians *have access, through their faith,* to the grace of reconciliation with God, and to the hope of future glory as His adopted children, what access to all graces must not Mary have obtained through her pre-eminent faith! *Beata, quæ credidisti.* She who was declared, even before her divine maternity, by God Himself to be perfectly united to Him, *Dominus tecum*; and to have already found grace and blessedness, and to be full of grace. What must be her glory, and what the hope wherewith she looked forward to it, as the Blessed amongst women, the elect daughter of the Father, the true Mother of the Incarnate Son, the immaculate Spouse of the Holy Ghost. Again: what *tribulations* like to hers, whose soul the sword of sorrow was to pierce through and through, as continually she contemplated, and herself was witness of, and sharer in, the Passion and Death of her beloved Jesus. What *glory in tribulations,* what perfect *trial,* what assuring *hope* was hers, in whose heart *the charity of God,* the love of Jesus her own Divine Son, was so superabundantly *poured forth, by the Holy Ghost,* who overshadowed her at the Incarnation, and again was given to her at Pentecost in all His fulness.

[1] *Luke* i. 45.   [2] *Luke* i. 46-48.

17 Much more they who receive abundance of grace, and of the gift, and of justice, shall reign in life through One, Jesus Christ.

According to the measure of the grace, gift, and justice, will be the reign in eternal life. What *abundance of grace* comparable with the fulness which Mary received? What *gift*, with that bestowed on her, to whom God was given to be her own true Son? What *justice* and sanctity with hers, to whom God from heaven declares Himself to be united, whom the holy Archangel salutes with his Ave as Queen? What, then, in eternal glory must be *the reign in life through Jesus Christ* of Mary, His own Mother, the holy Queen of angels and saints?

CHAPTER VI.

5 For if we have been planted together in the likeness of his death, we shall be also in the likeness of his resurrection.
8 Now if we be dead with Christ, we believe that we shall live also together with Christ.

The same sword which pierced the Heart of Jesus in death, pierced also the soul of Mary.[1] As she stood beside the Cross of Calvary, all the Passion and Death of her Divine Son Jesus was hers. Who then, as she, *was planted together in the likeness of His Death?* And who, as she, will be *in the likeness of His Resurrection glory?* United with Christ, as no other was, in His death, where must we believe is her place with Him in eternal life?

CHAPTER VIII.

10 And if Christ be in you, the body indeed is dead, because of sin; but the spirit liveth, because of justification.
11 And if the spirit of him that raised up Jesus from the dead, dwell in you; he that raised up Jesus Christ from the dead, shall quicken also your mortal bodies, because of his spirit that dwelleth in you.

It has ever been the teaching of the Holy Church, that, as S. Augustine expresses it, there is no question of sin with

---

[1] *Luke* ii. 35.

regard to the Mother of God. And it is now a defined dogma of the Faith, that Mary was conceived free from original sin. Consequently her holy body was not subject to the penal law of death, for *the body is dead,* i.e. subject to death, *because of sin* —" death is the wages of sin." The Blessed Virgin died, indeed, that in all things she might be conformed to the image of her Son, but not because of sin (in a strict penal sense) any more than He. It was fitting, then, and indeed due to her, that her body should not be left in the grave, nor her flesh should see corruption.[1] And, therefore, God raised her from the tomb—it being impossible that she should be holden by it; death and the grave having no right in her—and exalted her in her Assumption to the right hand of her Son. This has ever been the teaching of the Holy Church, and would seem to flow as a natural consequence from the Immaculate Conception of the Blessed Virgin Mary, and from the principle laid down by the Apostle, that the death of the body is an effect of sin.

"The Holy Ghost says that 'the glory of a man is from the honour of his father, and a father without honour is the disgrace of the son.'[2] 'Therefore it was,' says an ancient writer, 'that Jesus preserved the body of Mary from corruption after death; for it would have redounded to His dishonour, had that virginal flesh with which He had clothed Himself become the food of worms;' 'For,' he adds, 'corruption is a disgrace of human nature; and as Jesus was not subject to it, Mary was also exempted; for the flesh of Jesus is the flesh of Mary,'" etc.[3]

14 For whosoever are led by the spirit of God, they are the sons of God.

15 For you have not received the spirit of bondage again in fear; but you have received the spirit of adoption of sons, whereby we cry: Abba (Father).

16 For the Spirit himself giveth testimony to our spirit, that we are the sons of God.

---

[1] *Acts* ii. 31.   [2] *Ecclus.* iii. 13.
[3] *De Assump. B. M. V. int. op. S. Augustini.* S. Alphonsus, *Glories of Mary,* p. 251.

17 And if sons, heirs also; heirs indeed of God, and joint-heirs with Christ: yet so, if we suffer with him, that we may be also glorified with him.

How wonderfully here does each word of S. Paul reveal to us the grace and glory of Mary. It is the Spirit of God which makes us sons, "who are born not of blood, nor of the will of the flesh, but of God,"[1] Who having made us sons, gives testimony to our spirit that we are indeed sons. But who was ever visited, filled, *led by the Spirit of God*, like Mary? Who ever as she had the testimony of the Spirit that she was indeed the child of God? Mary, then, is God's first-born daughter by adoption, and pre-eminently, in a sense no other could be. She is heir of God, and joint-heir of the kingdom of glory with Christ His Only-begotten Son. Mary had, moreover, that other title, of the Divine Maternity. The same Holy Spirit Who gave to Mary the spirit of adoption as a child of God, made her also the Mother of God. Though the "Word was made flesh" of Mary, yet of her He was "born not of the will of the flesh, nor of the will of man, but of God." "The Holy Ghost shall come upon thee, and the power of the Most High shall overshadow thee, and therefore also the Holy which shall be born of thee shall be called the Son of God."[2] The same Holy Spirit gave ineffable testimony to Mary's spirit that she was indeed Mother. Hence not only could she by the spirit of adoption cry: Abba, Father; but also Magnificat, as she called God her Saviour, her Son[3]—not by adoption, but in a true and proper sense; for she is in truth the great Mother of God, and as such, has her place in His kingdom. Yet still more does she call herself His handmaid, *Ecce ancilla Domini*. We may here ask our Lord's question, putting the name of Mary for that of David: "If David, then, call Him Lord, how is He his Son?"[4] The Pharisees could not answer; but we can. Mary is at once the creature and the Mother of Jesus; and therefore the Holy Spirit teaches her to call Him both Lord and Son.

---

[1] *John* i. 13.   [2] *Luke* i. 35.   [3] *Luke* i. 46, 47; ii. 48.
[4] *Matt.* xxii. 43.

Joint-heirs with Christ, if we suffer with Him. Who fulfilled this condition as Mary? Her compassion with Christ, as His own Mother, was wholly different in kind, as well as degree, from that of all other saints, and so different in kind must be her glory in heaven. See that Mother standing at the foot of the Cross, while the sword pierces her soul: then lift your eyes to heaven, and see Jesus in His kingdom, on the throne of His father David, on His everlasting throne: "Thy throne, O God, is for ever and ever,"[1] etc. Who can doubt of Mary's place? "The Queen stood on thy right hand,"[2] etc.

18 For I reckon that the sufferings of this time are not worthy to be compared with the glory to come, that shall be revealed in us.
19 For the expectation of the creature waiteth for the revelation of the sons of God.

So also did Mary reckon. Great as were her dolours in her compassion she considered that all was not worthy to be compared with the glory to come, that should be revealed in her. Standing by the Cross, and throughout her life, she looked to and imitated the example of "Jesus the author and finisher of faith, Who having joy set before Him, endured the Cross, despising the shame, and sitteth on the right hand of the throne of God,"[3] and she too is sitting now on the right hand of her Son. And even as all creation looks forward to *the revelation of the glory of the children of God*, so in the Church are all the faithful waiting for the manifestation of the exceeding glory of His Mother.

26 Likewise the Spirit also helpeth our infirmity. For we know not what we should pray for as we ought; but the Spirit himself asketh for us with unspeakable groanings.
27 And he that searcheth the hearts, knoweth what the Spirit desireth; because he asketh for the saints according to God.

In our soul's distress the Holy Ghost not only thus helps and pleads for us Himself, but is often wont to inspire us to invoke the help and intercession of others, especially of some Saint in heaven. Thus S. Patrick records of himself: "On that same night, in my sleep, I was fiercely tempted by Satan

---

[1] *Heb.* i. 8, 9.   [2] *Ps.* xliv. 10.   [3] *Heb.* xii. 2.

(which I shall remember as long as body and soul hold together). There fell, as it were, a great stone upon me, and all my limbs were paralysed. Then it came in some way into my mind to call upon Elias, and at that moment I saw the sun rise in the heavens, and while I called with all my strength upon Elias, behold, the splendour of the sun fell upon me, and at once shook off the weight, and I believe that Christ my Lord cried out for me, and I hope that so it will be in the day of my distress."[1] Most especially does the Holy Ghost inspire us to invoke Mary, who knows so well what we should pray for, and who never fails to obtain from her Divine Son what she asks for us. For as King Solomon said to Bethsabee, so Jesus says to Mary, "My Mother, ask : for I must not turn away thy face."[2] Many Catholic writers have quoted these words of Solomon to Bethsabee with the same application. They have not, however, remarked, that, when Bethsabee did speak, she was so far from obtaining her request, that she drew death down on him who had prompted it. To use this illustration, it should be coupled with the conduct of our Blessed Lord at Cana. Bethsabee asks, and Solomon makes as if he would grant all, but rejects her petition. Mary asks, and Jesus seems to reject, yet in reality He grants her request.[3]

28 And we know that to them that love God, all things work together unto good, to such as, according to his purpose, are called to be saints.
29 For whom he foreknew, he also predestinated to be made conformable to the image of his Son ; that he might be the first-born amongst many brethren.
30 And whom he predestinated, them he also called. And whom he called, them he also justified   And whom he justified, them he also glorified.

Mary was called according to the divine purpose, not only to be a Saint, but to be the Mother of the Holy One, the King

---

[1] *Acta*, § 3 ; *Mart.* xvii., p. 535 ; Fr. Morris, *Life of S. Patrick*, p. 57.
[2] 3 Kings ii. 19.
[3] Protestants would fain prove from certain passages in the Gospel that Jesus Christ did not treat Mary as Mother of God ; and Socinians teach that Mary did not treat Jesus as God. Both are false, but the latter view is as easy to sustain from Scripture as the other.

of Saints. She loved God with a love surpassing that of all others. All things, then, of God's Providence worked together in a most special manner for her good. His " Wisdom which reacheth from end to end mightily, and ordereth all things sweetly,"[1] caused everything so to cooperate, that her end might correspond with the beginning; her glorification be equal and proportioned to her first vocation. God had fore-known her from everlasting as the Mother of His Only-begotten Son. He had predestined her in His eternal decrees to be prevented with extraordinary grace, so that she might be a worthy Mother most conformable to the image of His Son. He had elected her in time, and sanctified her fully. As no mind of angel or man could ever have imagined her predestined dignity, and God's accomplishment in time, so none can conceive her glory in eternity.

The life of Mary is written in these words. She was fore-known, and fore-told. She is the Woman between whom and the Serpent God promised to put enmity. She is the Virgin who should conceive Emmanuel. From her immaculate conception she was prepared to be like her Son. During the whole of her Son's life, she laid up in her heart every event which happened to Him, every word spoken of Him, every word spoken by Him, every look, every act, and so became more and more like Him. When Philip had been two or three years in the school of Jesus he was justly blamed for not having studied his Divine Master better. " Philip said: Lord shew us the Father, and it is enough for us. Jesus saith to him. So long a time have I been with you, and you have not known Me? Philip, he that seeth Me, seeth the Father also . . . Do you not believe that I am in the Father, and the Father in Me ?"[2] Mary was far longer in the school of Jesus, but she merited no such reproach. She knew and studied her Divine Son. On the same occasion our Lord said to His Apostles : " He that loveth Me shall be loved of My Father, and I will love him and will manifest Myself to him.

---

[1] *Wisdom*, viii. 1. [2] *John* xiv. 8-10.

Judas saith to Him (not Iscariot), Lord how is it that Thou wilt manifest Thyself to us, and not to the world? Jesus answered and said to him, If any man love Me, he will keep My word, and My Father will love him, and We will come, and will make our abode with him."[1] Did not Mary love her Divine Son? Did she not keep His word? Did He not manifest Himself to her? He came and took up His abode with her bodily, but only because He had already taken up His abode with her spiritually. "The Lord is with thee." *Prius in mente quam in ventre*, says S. Augustine.

32 He that spared not even his own Son, but delivered him up for us all, how hath he not also, with him, given us all things?

S. Paul's argument is, God has given for you His Son, in whom all good things are contained. All things are, therefore, yours, if you will. Now God gave His Son not only for Mary, but to Mary. She for His sake, was full of grace before she received Him actually as her Son. But He who gave her Jesus to be her Son, *how has He not also with Him given her all things?* Nothing is more excellent in itself, nothing more dear to God than His Only-begotten Son. His Father did not give other excellent gifts, such as angels and archangels, patriarchs, and prophets, and keep back or spare His Son. No, He gave Him, and Him especially and entirely. All His other gifts only led to and prepared for this one. It was complete. He gave Him not in part, but wholly. *He delivered Him up.* He did not lend Him, but gave Him for ever. If He has already done this, why do we hesitate or doubt about anything else? Is there anything greater, anything equal? Can anything be ever put in comparison with Him? Is not every other gift contained in Him, resulting from Him, and merited by Him? Is it more startling that I should be in heaven, than that the Only-begotten Son of God should be shivering in a crib? that I should enjoy eternal bliss, than that the Ever-Blessed should die accursed on a

[1] *John* xiv. 21-23.

Cross?[1] that I should gaze on the unveiled Majesty of God, than that God's glory should be veiled beneath the form of bread? If then the greater Gift has been given, the lesser one will not be refused. If the stranger work of mercy has already taken place, the less strange one may well take place also. How does this regard Mary? Thus:

> Monstra te esse matrem,
> Sumat per te preces,
> Qui pro nobis natus
> Tulit esse tuus.

Jesus became Mary's, yet for our sake, He became hers, that she might give Him for us, and to us. She did so at the Presentation. She did so on Calvary. She *spared not her own Son.* What then will she spare? her love, or her prayers that we may not lose that Son, and that He may not lose the fruit of His Incarnation and Death? Impossible.

35 Who then shall separate us from the love of Christ? Shall tribulation? or distress? or famine? or nakedness? or danger? or persecution? or the sword?
36 (As it is written: For thy sake we are put to death all the day long. We are accounted as sheep for the slaughter.)
37 But in all these things we overcome, because of him that hath loved us.
38 For I am sure that neither death, nor life, nor angels, nor principalities, nor powers, nor things present, nor things to come, nor might,
39 Nor height, nor depth, nor any other creature, shall be able to separate us from the love of God, which is in Christ Jesus our Lord.

If S. Paul was able thus with assured confidence to glory in his love of Jesus Christ, and challenge all sufferings and created powers to separate him therefrom, with much greater force could the Blessed Virgin Mary do so, whose love to God as far surpasses that of all other Saints, as does her Divine Maternity excel all other dignities. The trial, too, of Mary's love was correspondingly great: that is, her Dolours, which were exceeded only by the sufferings of Jesus Christ her Son, so that she has merited the title of *Mater dolorosissima,* and *Regina Martyrum.*

---

[1] See the passage from S. Chrysostom, *In Matt., Hom.* ii., n. 2, quoted above, p. 22, *note.*

CHAPTER IX.

1 I speak the truth in Christ, I lie not, my conscience bearing me witness in the Holy Ghost:
2 That I have great sadness, and continual sorrow in my heart.
3 For I wished myself to be an anathema from Christ, for my brethren, who are my kinsmen according to the flesh.

This most wonderful desire of the Apostle to sacrifice himself for the salvation of souls, even so far as to lose the fruition of Jesus Christ, provided he was not separated from His grace and charity, was actually realised in Mary. Of her own free consent she offered up her beloved Jesus, a thousand times dearer to her than her own self, for a life and death of shame and suffering, to be made even *an anathema* and a curse for us. In thus offering Him, she offered herself; for He to her was more than her own self; whilst the same sword of suffering and sorrow that pierced the Son, transfixed the Mother's heart also. Thus all her life long, she made an anathema of herself, and especially at the foot of the Cross, for the love of souls. "Her Son Jesus was hanging on the Cross," says S. Ambrose, "Mary, the while, was offering herself to the executioners."[1] For the salvation of sinners she bore in her own person, united to Him, the weight of God's anger against sin, whilst He hung there "as one struck by God," to turn away our curse. For love of her brethren, she consented during so many years after His Ascension to be separated from Him and from the glory into which He had entered, which was already her due. Oh how great was the *sadness and continual sorrow in her heart*, at seeing the mercy and love of God requited by so much ingratitude and hard-heartedness, and so many sins.

"The more ardent was Mary's charity, the more bitter was the compassion which she felt. How truly the words, *I wished . . . brethren*, apply to the Blessed Virgin. Mary was full of love from compassion for others, and still more so after the Ascension of her Son, on account of the blindness of her people.

[1] *De Inst. Virg.* 7.

Consequently, eager as she was for the salvation of all who were in blindness, she was able to say in the words of the Apostle, *I wished . . . brethren.* This indeed can be understood with greater truth and reason of the Blessed Virgin than of the Apostle Paul, since her charity was more ardent, and her compassion more bitter." [1]

> 4 Who are Israelites, to whom belongeth the adoption as of children, and the glory, and the testament, and the giving of the law, and the service of God, and the promises;
> 5 Whose are the fathers, and of whom is Christ, according to the flesh, who is over all things, God blessed for ever. Amen.

Consider well all these privileges, by the enumeration of which the Apostle enhances the claims of his kinsmen on his love and honour : and see how Mary possessed them all in a super-eminent degree, and in a far more true and spiritual sense ; especially the last and greatest, that one for the sake of which all the others were.

How would S. Paul have written of her, who was of the tribe of Juda, the Rod from the root of Jesse, the royal daughter of David, the Virgin Mother of Emmanuel, whom the Patriarchs had so ardently desired and the Prophets foretold—that Second Eve whom God had in the beginning set forth as destined to crush the head of the old Serpent? What would he have said of the claims on our love and honour of "Mary, of whom was born Jesus who is called Christ," [2] *Who is over all things, God blessed for ever. Amen?*

The Jewish people were Mary's people emphatically. She was the daughter of Juda and Jerusalem by excellence, the virgin daughter of Sion, the lily of Israel. In her God's chosen people, the holy city of Jerusalem and Mount Sion were personified by the Prophets. What love, then, must Mary have felt for her people. Among their special glories the greatest was this : *Of whom is Christ, according to the flesh,* her Christ, taken of her flesh. They, indeed, made void their glory by their incredulity ; but she not only accepted it by faith after it was accomplished, but by her faith brought about

---

[1] Ægidius Romanus, on the *Ave Maria.*   [2] *Matt.* i. 16.

its accomplishment: "Blessed art thou that didst believe, for those things shall be accomplished which were told thee by the Lord." The Incarnation and all its results were thus due to her faith. "It was through believing that the Blessed Mary conceived Christ; to whom also through believing she gave birth. . . . Mary, full of faith, and conceiving Christ in her mind before she did so in her womb, said: "Behold the handmaid of the Lord, be it done to me according to thy word."[1]———*Whose are the fathers.* The Jews were degenerate children of the patriarchs. But Our Lady was more than their child, she was their queen, *Regina Patriarcharum,* and the object of their sighs and hopes, *Aperiatur terra et germinet Salvatorem.*———*To whom belong the promises,* which on God's side were faithfully fulfilled: *Sicut locutus est ad patres nostros.* But what special promises were hers! All generations shall call her blessed. If Mary loved and prayed for her own people, faithless as they were for the most part, she loves and prays for the spiritual Israel, who have believed in, and welcomed her Divine Son. To call her Mother of God, and salute her by the Hail Mary is to awaken all her tenderness, could it ever for a moment slumber.

8 That is to say, not they that are the children of the flesh, are the children of God; but they that are the children of the promise are accounted for the seed.
9 For this is the word of promise: According to this time will I come; and Sara shall have a son.

What is the *word of promise* which was made to Abraham, compared to that made to Mary? The former was but a foreshadowing type of the latter, which was fulfilled in the fulness of time, when God sent forth His Son, made and born of Mary. The true children of the promise are, then, the children of Mary. *Suscepit Israel puerum suum recordatus misericordiæ suæ sicut locutus est ad patres nostros, Abraham et semini ejus in sæcula.*

23 That he might show the riches of his glory on the vessels of mercy, which he hath prepared unto glory.

[1] S. Augustine, *Serm.* 215, 4.

Is not Mary that *vessel made unto honour* (v. 21) above all others: *Vas honorabile*; and also *the vessel of mercy*, whereby we have received the Incarnate Word, the object of all our adoration and honour, the source of Mercy to us? *On her God showed the riches of His glory, and prepared her unto the glory,* which she now enjoys in body and soul at the right hand of Jesus Christ her Son. *Fecit mihi magna qui potens est. Misericordia ejus a progenie in progenies. Recordatus misericordiæ suæ.* "If Paul," says S. Basil of Seleucia, "was called a *vessel of election*. . . . what vessel will the Mother of God not be? Is she not the golden urn that received the manna, yea that received within her womb that heavenly Bread which is given for food and strength to the faithful?"[1]

32 Why so? Because they sought it not by faith, but as it were of works. For they stumbled at the stumbling-stone.

33 As it is written: Behold I lay in Sion a stumbling-stone and a rock of scandal; and whosoever believeth in him shall not be confounded.

Simeon in the Temple saw the accomplishment of this prophecy, *the laying of the Stone*; and bore witness, too, when he "said to Mary His Mother: Behold this child is set for the fall, and for the resurrection of many in Israel, and for a sign which shall be contradicted." With that Child, *the rock of scandal*, he united at the same time in suffering and contradiction the Mother, by immediately adding: "And thy own soul a sword shall pierce, that out of many hearts thoughts"—some of faith and love, some of unbelief and contradiction: of these for their fall of those for their resurrection—"may be revealed."[2] None can stumble at the Mother, without also stumbling at the Son.

CHAPTER X.

10 The same is Lord over all, rich unto all that call upon him.

"The liberality of Mary," says Richard of S. Laurence, "is like that of her Son, who always gives more than He is asked for, and is rich unto all that call upon Him."[3]

[1] *Orat.* x. *De Annunt. Deip.* [2] *Luke* ii. 34, 35.
[3] *De Laud. Virg.*, L. iv., c. 22.

15 And how shall they preach unless they be sent, as it is written: How beautiful are the feet of them that preach the gospel of peace, of them that bring glad tidings of good things!

If beautiful are the feet of those who preach the Gospel of Jesus Christ and bring glad tidings of His salvation ; how beautiful upon the mountains[1] of Judæa were the feet of Mary, as rising up with haste, she went forth, not, indeed, to preach the Gospel of Jesus Christ, or to bring glad tidings alone of good things ; but to bring with her the Source of all good, Jesus Christ Himself, and by the sweet voice of her salutation, to impart peace and joy of the Holy Ghost.[2] If those who preach the Gospel are worthy of honour and praise, how much more so is Mary! Thus indeed thought Elizabeth, when filled with the Holy Ghost, and conscious of the presence of her Incarnate God, she exclaimed, "Whence is this to me, that the Mother of my Lord should come to me ?"

"Imitate Mary, to whom admirably applies what was prophesied of the Church : ' Beautiful are seen thy steps in shoes, O daughter of Aminadab ' [or, O prince's daughter] ![3] Because with beauty did the Church go forth in the preaching of the Gospel. Beautifully, too, goes forth the soul, that uses the body as though a shoe ; so that whither it will, it may bear about its step without let or hindrance. In this shoe with beauty went forth Mary, who, with chastity inviolate, a Virgin most pure, gave birth to the Author of Salvation ; hence well says John : ' I am not worthy to loose the latchet of His shoes,' that is, I am not worthy to comprehend the mystery of the Incarnation within the straits of human intelligence, nor to compass it in the meanness of poor speech. Hence, too, Isaias saith : ' Who shall declare His generation ?' Beautiful, therefore, are the steps, whether of Mary or of the Church, since beautiful are the steps of the Evangelists. How beautiful also are all those things that were prophesied of Mary under the figure of the Church," etc.[4]

---

[1] *Isa.* lii. 7.   [2] *Luke* i. 39-45.   [3] *Cant.* vii. 1.
[4] S. Ambrose, *De Instit. Virg.*, Cap. xiv.

CHAPTER XI.

33 O the depth of the riches of the wisdom and of the knowledge of God. How incomprehensible are his judgments, and how unsearchable his ways!

34 For who hath known the mind of the Lord? Or who hath been his counsellor?

35 Or who hath first given to him, and recompense shall be made him?

36 For of him, and by him, and in him, are all things: to him be glory for ever. Amen.

What a great glory to our Lady, that, though she did not originate the plan of the Incarnation, yet in its execution she was taken into God's counsel, and her consent to it was asked. She could, indeed, only give to God what *He had first given to her.* Her faith was His gift, her humility, her purity, her soul and her body that had been prepared by Him. Yet *she did give to Him*, and proportionate *recompense was made to her.* The words: "God loveth a cheerful giver," have their highest application in Mary. We may well exclaim in thinking of all her graces and glories: *O altitudo divitiarum!*

CHAPTER XII.

1 I beseech you therefore, brethren, by the mercy of God, that you present your bodies a living sacrifice, holy, pleasing unto God, your reasonable service.

2 And be not conformed to this world; but be reformed in the newness of your mind, that you may prove what is the good, and the acceptable, and the perfect will of God.

Mary had practised these lessons in a more excellent manner than all others. She, according to the constant tradition of the Church, *presented herself, body and soul* from earliest years to God in the Temple to live in perpetual virginity. Moreover, she offered herself to Him throughout her life, together with her Son, *as a living sacrifice*, and especially when she presented Him to the Eternal Father in the Temple. She was indeed *holy* and *pleasing unto God*, so that she found grace before Him. *Invenisti gratiam apud Deum.* The world had no part in her, and so she was enabled to *prove and to do the good, acceptable, and perfect will of God. Ecce ancilla Domini, fiat mihi secundum verbum tuum.*

"To-day," writes S. Bernard, "earth's most excellent fruit is presented to the Creator. To-day an appeasing Sacrifice, *pleasing unto God,* by virgin hands is offered in the Temple, is borne by the parents, is expected by aged ones. Joseph and Mary offer the Sacrifice of praise, the morning sacrifice ; Simeon and Anna receive it."[1] "Offer thy Son, O Sacred Virgin, and present to the Lord the blessed fruit of thy womb. Offer for the reconciliation of us all *the Sacrifice holy, pleasing unto God.*"[2]

Beata Dei Genitrix Maria, exclaims Holy Church, Virgo perpetua, Templum Domini, Sacrarium Spiritus Sancti, sola sine exemplo placuisti Domino nostro Jesu Christo. Alleluia.[3]

4 For as in one body we have many members, but all the members have not the same office :
5 So we being many, are one body in Christ, and every one members one of another.
6 And having different gifts, according to the grace that is given us.

Mary as Mother of Christ, is Mother also of all the faithful who are the members of His mystical body, whereof He Himself is the Head. Mary is also the most excellent member of this body. She is sometimes compared to the neck, through which the energy and life of the head are derived to all the other members. As Mary's place and office in the Church are pre-eminent and unique, so also are the gifts, and the fulness of grace, bestowed upon her.[4]

9 Let love be without dissimulation. Hating that which is evil, cleaving to that which is good.
10 Loving one another with the charity of brotherhood, with honour preventing one another.
11 In carefulness not slothful. In spirit fervent. Serving the Lord.
12 Rejoicing in hope. Patient in tribulation. Instant in prayer.

---

[1] *De Purif. B. M. Serm.* ii.   [2] *Ib. Serm.* iii.
[3] *Ana ad Vesp. in Præsentat. B. M. V.*
[4] See *infra,* 1 Cor. xii. 26, 27 ; *Eph.* v. 29-32 ; *Col.* ii. 19.

13 Communicating to the necesisties of the saints. Pursuing hospitality.

We may gather what was the mind and spirit of Mary from her recorded words and acts. What an example does she give of humble *charity of brotherhood, with honour preventing one another* in her visit to Elizabeth when she was the first to salute her cousin.——*Serving the Lord:* " Ecce ancilla Domini." " Respexit humilitatem ancillæ suæ."——*In carefulness not slothful. In spirit fervent. Patient in tribulation.* Think of Mary's diligence in seeking her lost Jesus : " Dolentes quærebamus te ; "[1] and again on Calvary : " Stabant autem juxta crucem Jesu Mater ejus . . ."[2]——*Rejoicing in hope.* " Magnificat anima mea Dominum, et exultavit spiritus meus in Deo salutari meo."——*Instant in prayer;* as at Pentecost. " Hi omnes erant perseverantes unanimiter in oratione cum mulieribus, et Maria Matre Jesu ; "[3] and at Cana, where we see, too, her thoughtful care for others, in *communicating to the necessities of the saints, and pursuing hospitality.* " Deficiente vino, dicit mater Jesu ad eum : vinum non habent."[4]

14 Bless them that persecute you : bless, and curse not.
15 Rejoice with them that rejoice ; weep with them that weep.

Mary under inspiration of the Holy Ghost foretells that all generations of the true children of God shall bless her. God had Himself predicted the perpetual enmities that should exist between the seed of the evil one and the promised woman.[5] The wise man says, "There is a generation that doth not bless their mother."[6] What shall we think of those heretics who will not bless the Blessed Virgin Mary ; but almost curse her ? They are like Esau,[7] and worse than Balaam.[8] Catholics, animated with a different spirit, love to take part in the joys, sorrows, and glories of their Mother. This they do when they say the Rosary.

---

[1] *Luke*, ii. 44-48.   [2] *John*, xix. 25.   [3] *Acts* i. 14.   [4] *John* ii. 3 *sq.*
[5] *Luke* i. 48; *Gen.* iii. 15 ; 1 *Pet.* iii. 9.   [6] *Prov.* xxx. 11.
[7] *Gen.* xxvii. 41.   [8] *Numb.* xxii. 12, xxiii. 20.

"Though," says S. Chrysostom, "you cannot remove another's sorrow, yet give your tears, and you take away the greater part of it, and though you cannot increase his joy, yet rejoice with him, and you augment it much."

16 Being of one mind one towards another. Not minding high things, but consenting to the humble. Be not wise in your own conceits.

The Blessed Virgin loved humility, and was herself the most humble of all. "He hath regarded the humility of His handmaid. He hath scattered the proud in the conceit of their heart. He hath put down the mighty from their seat, and hath exalted the humble." "Mary kept all the words (that were told by the humble unlettered shepherds) pondering them in her heart."[1] Her place is recorded the last amongst the disciples and women in the Upper room awaiting the Descent of the Holy Ghost.[2]

CHAPTER XIII.

1 Let every soul be subject to the higher powers.

What a striking example Mary showed of submission, when according to the decree of Augustus, she went to be enrolled at Bethlehem.[3]

7 Render therefore to all men their dues. Tribute to whom tribute is due: custom, to whom custom: fear, to whom fear: honour, to whom honour.
8 Owe no man anything, but to love one another. For he that loveth his neighbour, hath fulfilled the law.

Is no honour then due to Mary? Is no love owed to Mary?

14 Put ye on the Lord Jesus Christ.

It was Mary who gave us the Lord Jesus Christ, wherewith to clothe ourselves.——"Because," says S. Ephrem, "He put His Mother's garment on, she clothed her body with His

---

[1] *Luke* ii. 16-19. [2] *Acts* i. 14. [3] *Luke* ii. 1-5.

glory."[1] And: "Thy Mother put on in her Virginity the garment of Glory that sufficeth for all."[2]

CHAPTER XIV.

1 Now him that is weak in faith, take unto you.

How beautifully is the Apostle's precept of condescension and bearing with the weakness of others illustrated by Mary; who, strong in faith, never doubting of our Lord's Resurrection as she watched His agony and death, associated herself with those who were weak in faith, viz., with Mary Magdalene and the other women, who by their coming to embalm his body, had evidently but little belief that He would rise again the third day, as He had promised. " Now there stood by the Cross of Jesus, His Mother, and His Mother's sister, Mary of Cleophas, and Mary Magdalene."[3]

8 For whether we live, we live unto the Lord; or whether we die, we die unto the Lord. Therefore, whether we live, or whether we die, we are the Lord's.

Who could say this in the same sense as Mary? Her whole life was for God, lost in God.[4] She was all for Jesus, from His first moment to His latest breath. What then was her death? As in the beginning, so was it then: Ecce ancilla Domini. Dominus tecum. *She was the Lord's.*

17 For the kingdom of God is not meat and drink; but justice, and peace, and joy in the Holy Ghost.
18 For he that in this serveth Christ, pleaseth God, and is approved of men.

"The kingdom of God is within you," said Jesus Christ.[5] In Mary's heart that divine kingdom was manifested in its fulness: and so that *Servant of Christ*, the Handmaid of the Lord, found grace with God, and all generations shall call her blessed. "Sola sine exemplo placuisti Domino."[6]

---

[1] S. Ephrem, *In Nat. Dom.* xi., Morris, p. 51. [2] *Ib.* p. 53.
[3] *John* xix. 25. [4] See *Col.* iii. 3. [5] *Luke* xvii. 21.
[6] See *supra*, ch. xii. 1.

CHAPTER XV.

2 Let every one of you please his neighbour unto good, to edification.

See *supra*, xiv. 1. Consider, too, Mary's visit to Elizabeth, and her compassionate conduct at the Marriage Feast of Cana.

12 And again Isaias saith: There shall be a root of Jesse; and he that shall rise up to rule the Gentiles, in him the Gentiles shall hope.

S. Paul quotes from *Isaias* xi. 10. The prophet had said just before (v. 1): "There shall come forth a rod out of the root of Jesse, and a flower shall rise up out of his root." That Rod is the Blessed Virgin Mary, and that Flower our Lord Jesus Christ. Mary then must have been present to the mind of the Apostle, in quoting this prophecy.

S. Jerome, quoting the above passage from *Isaias*, says: "The Mother of the Lord is the Rod, simple, pure, sincere, without any germ extrinsically cleaving to it, and, after the likeness of God, of itself alone fruitful. The Flower of the rod is Christ, who says: 'I am the flower of the field, and the lily of the valleys.'"[1] And S. Ambrose: "Mary was the Rod, graceful, delicate, and virgin, that blossomed forth Christ, as a flower, through the perfect purity of her body."[2] S. Cyril of Jerusalem shows that Mary was both the Rod of Aaron and of Jesse;[3] as do also many other Fathers.

13 Now the God of hope fill you with all joy and peace in believing; that you may abound in hope, and in the power of the Holy Ghost.

14 And I myself also, my brethren, am assured of you, that you also are full of love, replenished with all knowledge, so that you are able to admonish one another.

According to Mary's *joy and peace in believing*, wherewith her soul was filled ("Blessed art thou that hast believed;" "My spirit hath exulted in God,") so was the abundance of her hope and power of the Holy Ghost. We also ourselves are *assured of her, that she too is full of love*, love to her God, and maternal love to us; *replenished also with all knowledge*, from the lips of Jesus Christ Himself, whose intercourse she

---

[1] *Ep.* xxii. 19.   [2] *Inter opera, Serm.* 28.   [3] *Catec.* xii. 27.

alone enjoyed for well nigh thirty years, so that she was able, as no other could, to instruct, console and admonish the Apostles and first disciples—of whom our Lord had made her Mother—after His Ascension into heaven; even as the tradition of the Holy Church teaches us.

15 But I have written to you, brethren, more boldly in some sort, as it were putting you in mind; because of the grace which is given me from God.
16 That I should be the minister of Christ Jesus among the Gentiles; sanctifying the gospel of God, that the oblation of the Gentiles may be made acceptable and sanctified in the Holy Ghost.
17 I have therefore glory in Christ Jesus towards God.

If S. Paul, because of the commission laid upon him, and according to the grace given him from God as Minister of Christ Jesus, could offer up to God the oblation of the Gentiles, acceptable and sanctified in the Holy Ghost, and could therefrom have glory in Christ Jesus towards God—what glory must Mary have with God, to whom was given to be the Mother of Jesus Christ, and a fulness of grace proportioned to that dignity, that worthily she might fulfil its duties. To whom, too, was given to be the Mother of all His disciples, and corresponding grace. How efficaciously must she present her children, their prayers and good works, through her powerful intercession, before the throne of God, as the Mother of His Divine Son! And shall we not glorify and honour her, whom God has delighted so to honour?

29 And I know, that when I come to you, I shall come in the abundance of the blessing of the gospel of Christ.
30 I beseech you therefore, brethren, through our Lord Jesus Christ, and by the charity of the Holy Ghost, that you help me in your prayers for me to God,
31 That I may be delivered from the unbelievers that are in Judea, and that the oblation of my service may be acceptable in Jerusalem to the saints.
32 That I may come to you with joy, by the will of God, and may be refreshed with you.
33 Now the God of peace be with you all. Amen.

If S. Paul knew that by his coming he should be the means of imparting abundance of grace and blessing to the Romans, how much more may we be assured that the Mother of God, full of grace herself, is the great channel of grace to all. If such is an Apostle's visit, no wonder, then, that Elizabeth cried of the Mother of God's visit: "Whence is this to me, that the Mother of my Lord should come to me?"——And if S. Paul besought the Romans by all that was most sacred to pray for him, how much more should we beseech Mary to pray for us, through Jesus Christ her Son, by the grace and charity which she has received, that we may be delivered from our enemies, and that God may accept the service which we offer to Him.——S. Paul asks prayers; he recognises the power and importance of the intercession of God's servants, and he invokes them. He does this though he has just been instructing, and even rebuking them, and though he has just said that he will himself be to them a channel of grace, and even of abundance of grace. He thinks that the prayers of the Romans added to his own will ensure his deliverance from danger, and make his good works more fruitful. We ask the Saints to pray for us that we may be acceptable to God: *Orate pro nobis, ut digni efficiamur promissionibus Christi.* S. Paul asks the Saints to pray to God that he may be acceptable not only to God, but to God's Saints. How much greater reasons have we to ask the prayers of our Lady, for deliverance from bodily and spiritual dangers, for zeal in good works, and for their successful issue. And how much more forcible are the motives urged by S. Paul on the Romans, if addressed to our Lady, *through our Lord Jesus Christ, by the charity of the Holy Ghost.*—— What would S. Paul have thought of the modern objection, that it is derogatory to the Mediatorship of Jesus Christ to ask Mary's prayers? He considers that our Lord is not only Mediator between him and God, but between him and God's Saints. By our union in Him, by His love, by His claims, he calls on the Romans, *Help me, pray for me.* Surely all this action and reaction of God on His Saints, of the Saints on God, of the Saints on each other, of the Saints on sinners, and of sinners on Saints, is part of what S. Paul calls, *the abundance of the blessing of the Gospel of Christ*: the Communion of Saints in the Church of God.

CHAPTER XVI.

1 And I commend to you Phebe, our sister, who is in the ministry of the church, that is in Cenchre:
2 That you receive her in the Lord as becometh saints; and that you assist her in whatsoever business she shall have need of you. For she also hath assisted many, and myself also.
3 Salute Prisca and Aquila, my helpers in Christ Jesus,
4 (Who have for my life laid down their own necks: to whom not I only give thanks, but also all the churches of the Gentiles),
5 And the church which is in their house. Salute Epenetus, my beloved: who is the first fruits of Asia in Christ.
6 Salute Mary, who hath laboured much among you.
7 Salute Andronicus and Junias, my kinsmen and fellow-prisoners: who are of note among the apostles, who also were in Christ before me.
8 Salute Ampliatus, most beloved to me in the Lord.
9 Salute Urbanus, our helper in Christ Jesus, and Stachys, my beloved.
10 Salute Appelles, approved in Christ.
11 Salute them that are of Aristobulus's household. Salute Herodian, my kinsman. Salute them that are of Narcissus's household, who are in the Lord.
12 Salute Tryphena and Traphosa, who labour in the Lord. Salute Persis, the dearly beloved, who hath much labour in the Lord.
13 Salute Rufus, elect in the Lord, and his mother and mine.
14 Salute Asyncritus, Phlegon, Hermas, Patrobas, Hermes, and the brethren that are with them.
15 Salute Philologus and Julia, Nereus, and his sister, and Olympias; and all the saints that are with them.
16 Salute one another with an holy kiss. All the churches of Christ salute you.

Our Lord Jesus Christ made another commendation through the beloved disciple, to all His faithful, as He was on the point of expiring on the Cross: I commend to you Mary, My Mother, whom I give to be your Mother—"After that, He saith to the disciple: Behold thy Mother."[1]—that you receive her for My sake, look upon her, love, cherish, confide in her, honour her as your Mother, after My example, and precept, as becometh My disciples. For she also hath assisted many through her prayers, and is now assisting at My death. Should we not all imitate the example of that beloved disciple, who heard our Lord's commendation: "From that hour the disciple took her

[1] *John* xix. 27.

to his own"?[1]——In these words of the Apostle we may find by analogy great motives of devotion to our Lady, if we consider (1) the act which S. Paul enjoins, (2) by whom it is to be performed, (3) the reasons given. 1. *Salute.* An act of love, an act of reverence, an act of gratitude; a token of communion, as S. John says.[2] Salutation belongs by right to Mary; for it was the salutation she merited from heaven which was the beginning and cause of every loving Christian salutation. As Suarez says, there would have been no *Dominus vobiscum* in the Church, had not the word been spoken to Mary, *Dominus tecum.*——2. The Apostle writes to a whole Church, clergy and laity. The whole Church is to perform this public act of salutation. All were to salute each other with a holy kiss, but certain eminent members were to receive a more honourable and public salutation;——3. Why? They had eminently deserved it. (*a*) But what is it to have *helped* S. Paul, compared with having helped Jesus Christ as Mary did? If to have risked life for an Apostle merits the thanks of the whole Church, how much more to have offered up the life of an only son, and such a Son as Jesus, and to such a death. (*b*) If Epinetus was *the first-fruits in Asia*, what was Mary? Think of the thirty years she was *in Christ* before any one of the Apostles knew Him even by name. (*c*) If the Roman Mary *laboured* much, how had *the* Mary laboured and suffered? "All for us did she prefer the lily of virginity, and offer up her Son, the fruit of her fecundity, and pay for us the entire merit of her virtue."[3]

It was in the full realisation of the Communion of Saints that the Apostle saluted with such affectionate greetings so many of the faithful at Rome, naming each by name, and recounting the individual claims of each one on his memory. He and they were separated from bodily presence, but they were closely knit together in soul and spirit by the Communion of Saints. And is that communion lost, when the soul is set free, released from the prison of the flesh, and

---

[1] *John* xix. 27.   [2] 2 *John* i. 10, 11.   [3] B. Albert. Magn., *super Missus est.*

united to God in Paradise? Or, is not then the communion strengthened between the souls of those who are in God's grace on earth, and the souls of the Blessed in heaven? Hear our great Apostle: "You are come," he says, "to Mount Sion, and to the city of the living God, the heavenly Jerusalem, and to the company of many thousands of angels, and to the Church of the first-born, who are written in the heavens, and to God the Judge of all, and to the spirits of the just made perfect, and to Jesus the Mediator of the New Testament, and to the sprinkling of the Blood which speaketh better than that of Abel."[1] *We are come then to Mary* the glorious Mother of Jesus Christ, the Queen of Angels and of Saints; and we love to salute her, to give her thanks, to show her the devotion of our most tender love. If we recount the claims that she has on our heart's affections, we find them manifold more, and higher far than those of Prisca and Aquila and Epenetus and Apelles on the memory of S. Paul. How has Mary not *helped us in Jesus Christ* by her compassion and intercession with Him! Was she not ready *to lay down her own life*, and did she not in fact offer up a life ten thousand times more precious to her than her own, for our sakes? We salute her, then, and also all the Churches of the Catholic world salute and give her thanks: *Hail, Holy Queen, our Life, our Sweetness, and our Hope!* Shall we not greet her as, *Most beloved to us in the Lord;* the first-fruits of Redemption; that Mary who has laboured so much for us by her dolours, watchful care, and prayers; the Queen of Apostles, the *elect, and first, and most approved* of the disciples of Christ. As we salute Jesus our Redeemer, so do we *salute also His Mother and ours*—and Joseph her Spouse, together with our special patrons and protectors, *and all the Saints that are with them*. And do you, O blessed ones, *salute one another* for us in your bliss above, and obtain for us by your continual prayers that one day we may join you. We with *all the Churches of Christ on earth salute you.*

---

[1] *Heb.* xii. 22-24.

20 The God of peace crush Satan under your feet speedily. The grace of our Lord Jesus Christ be with you.

The Apostle prays that God may crush Satan under their feet shortly, and for this end supplicates for them the grace of our Lord Jesus Christ. He here refers to *Genesis* iii. 15. Where God promised that "the Woman," that is, Mary the Second Eve, should crush the serpent's head. From the first moment of her conception the grace of God was with Mary. *Dominus tecum*. She found grace, and was full of grace, so that she had not to wait *to crush Satan under her feet*, but did so effectually in the first moment of her existence, so that he never had any power against her, nor can have now against those whom she defends.

THE FIRST EPISTLE OF S. PAUL

TO THE

CORINTHIANS.

CHAPTER I.

4 I give thanks to my God always for you, for the grace of God that is given you in Christ Jesus.
5 That in all things you are made rich in him, in all utterance, and in all knowledge;
6 As the testimony of Christ was confirmed in you,
7 So that nothing is wanting to you in any grace, waiting for the manifestation of our Lord Jesus Christ.
8 Who also will confirm you unto the end without crime, in the day of the coming of our Lord Jesus Christ.
9 God is faithful: by whom you are called unto the fellowship of his Son Jesus Christ our Lord.

To encourage the Corinthian converts, the Apostle reminds them of God's faithfulness: that He who had been pleased to call them to the fellowship of His Son Jesus Christ, would assuredly not fail to confirm them by His grace, and enable them to persevere to the end in their Christian vocation. For whenever God calls anyone to a particular state or office, He gives at the same time graces proportioned thereto ; whereby he who is thus called may duly carry out his vocation and worthily fulfil its duties. So did God deal with Mary. *He was faithful to her.* In choosing Mary not alone for *fellowship with Jesus Christ,* but for the divine Maternity, He bestowed upon her the fulness of grace ; and in all things she was made rich in Him, so that nothing was wanting to her in any grace that might befit her to be the worthy Mother of His Son. He continued as He began. He confirmed her unto the end ; and the glory of her Assumption corresponded to the grace of her Immaculate Conception.

24 But unto them that are called, both Jews and Greeks, Christ the power of God, and the wisdom of God.
25 For the foolishness of God is wiser than men ; and the weakness of God is stronger than men.
26 For see your vocation, brethren, that there are not many wise according to the flesh, not many mighty, not many noble :
27 But the foolish things of the world hath God chosen, that he may confound the wise; and the weak things of the world hath God chosen, that he may confound the strong.
28 And the base things of the world, and the things that are contemptible hath God chosen, and things that are not, that he might bring to nought things that are :
29 That no flesh should glory in his sight.
30 But of him are you in Christ Jesus, who of God is made unto us wisdom, and justice, and sanctification, and redemption :
31 That, as it is written : He that glorieth, may glory in the Lord.

Mary is the ideal type of Divine vocation and election. In God's choice of the humble maiden of Nazareth to be the Mother of His Only-begotten Son, is perfectly exemplified all the Apostle here says, even according to her own words: " Ecce ancilla Domini. Respexit humilitatem ancillæ suæ. Fecit mihi magna qui potens est. Fecit potentiam in brachio suo. Dispersit superbos mente cordis sui. Deposuit potentes de sede, et exaltavit humiles."

"The more illustrious Mary and Joseph were by true and perfect nobility of birth, the more were they gentle, meek, mild, and humble. . . . The Apostle is here speaking especially of the preachers, by whom the world was to be converted to the Faith : and it was fitting that these should be plebeian and uneducated, lest to their own power and wisdom or dignity might be ascribed what God Himself wrought by His grace, and through their ministry, and thus 'the Cross of Christ should be made void.' But it was not fitting that in His domestic service the King of kings should be nurtured by the ignoble in mind or body: nor was it meet, that He, to whom myriads of angels minister, should select for His reputed father, one who was ignoble; nor that He who chose out a Virgin—whom the sun and moon, and all the citizens of the heavenly Jerusalem admire—for His Mother, should suffer her to be espoused to a man of mean origin. It, moreover, became Christ the Lord to exalt the Blessed Virgin as much as He was able, and she herself was capable, and to ennoble and magnify her, since it was unfitting that He should expose His own Mother to reproach of lack of nobility."[1]

"The sacerdotal line," says S. Austin, "differed from the royal line, which had its origin in one of David's sons, who, according to the custom, married a wife from the sacerdotal line. Hence Mary belonged to both tribes, and had her descent in the royal and sacerdotal lines."[2]——" Christ was born," says the Saint again, "of a Mother, who—although she conceived in perfect purity, and ever remained inviolate, a Virgin conceiving, a Virgin giving birth, a Virgin at death—yet was espoused to a carpenter, and thus extinguished in herself all pride of noble birth."[3]——If Jesus Christ has come to be, by so many titles, the glory of all Christians (see v.v. 24, 31), what has He not become to His own most blessed Mother?

CHAPTER II.

7 But we speak the wisdom of God in a mystery, a wisdom which is hidden, which God ordained before the world, unto our glory.
8 Which none of the princes of this world knew; for if they had known it, they would never have crucified the Lord of glory.

The Apostle seems to imply here what was said by S. Ignatius the Martyr in his Epistles to the Philippians and

---

[1] Morales, *L.* ii. *Tr.* 9.   [2] *De divers. Quæst.* 61, n. 2.
[3] *De catechizand. rudib.* n. 22.

Ephesians, viz., that the Virginity of Mary was concealed from the devil.[1]——If the demons (the princes of this world) had known Mary's virginity, they would have recognised the mystery of our Lord's Divinity, and then, far from exciting the Jews to the fury they exercised against Him, they would rather have dissuaded them from crucifying Him, in order thus to hinder the redemption of the world.

9 But, as it is written : That eye hath not seen, nor ear heard, neither hath it entered into the heart of man, what things God hath prepared for them that love him.
10 But to us God hath revealed them, by his Spirit. For the spirit searcheth all things, yea, the deep things of God.
11 For what man knoweth the things of a man, but the spirit of a man that is in him? So the things also that are of God no man knoweth, but the Spirit of God.
12 Now we have received not the spirit of this world, but the Spirit that is of God; that we may know the things that are given us from God.
16 For who hath known the mind of the Lord, that he may instruct him ? But we have the mind of Christ.

"What mind, then, can understand, what tongue, I do not say, tell forth and describe, but even barely mention, what things God hath prepared for this glorious Virgin ? Who of mortals can justly appraise the weight, number, and measure of good things wherewith that same God hath adorned *her* who gave Him birth, and her breasts to suck ; who nursed and nourished Him, and, holding more than the handmaid's place, ministered to all His needs, serving Him with so great affection and zeal ? She enjoys all that glory and beatitude which can possibly be imagined, or is worthy to be desired, after God. She is more holy than all the Saints, and more blessed than even the most blessed. It is not possible to find grace equal to her grace, nor glory equal to her glory."[2]

Of whom could it be said so truly, and in the same degree, as of Mary, that she had *received the Spirit that is of God?* She, whom the Holy Ghost overshadowed, in whom He wrought the mystery of the Incarnation of the Divine Word ; with whom the Angel proclaimed that God was united, *Do-*

---

[1] See *supra, Introd. Chap.* iii. p. 63.   [2] Alexius a Salo.

minus tecum; and on whom the Holy Spirit was poured at Pentecost. *Greater things were given from God* to Mary than even to the Apostles: she had, therefore, more of the Spirit of God to know them. Who as Mary had *the mind of Christ,* living as she did in close converse with Him alone for thirty years?[1]

CHAPTER III.

9 We are God's coadjutors: you are God's husbandry, you are God's building.

S. Paul could take to himself the title of *God's coadjutor,* on account of the work that he did in the vineyard of the Lord, and in edifying the faithful. With how much greater meaning may we give this title, or that of co-redemptress, to Mary, who co-operated in the divine work of our Redemption, by giving birth to the Lord of the vineyard, and in raising the true Temple of God, the Incarnate Word,[2] and also in forming the Mystical Body of Christ, as delegated Mother of the faithful, in a sense higher than S. Paul could be said to do. The part of the Apostles was to help in applying the Redemption, while that of Mary was to aid in accomplishing it.

16 Know you not, that you are the temple of God, and that the Spirit of God dwelleth in you?
17 But if any man violate the temple of God, him shall God destroy. For the temple of God is holy, which you are.

What then must be the sanctity of Mary, who is the Temple of God, not alone in a degree far surpassing that of all other Christians, but in a way in which no other could be? Not only was it said to Mary, *Ave gratia plena, Dominus tecum,* but also, *Spiritus Sanctus superveniet in te, et virtus Altissimi obumbrabit tibi. Ideoque et quod nascetur ex te Sanctum vocabitur Filius Dei.* If S. John could say: *Verbum caro factum est, et habitavit in nobis:* how much more might he say, *Habitavit in Maria.*

[1] All this chapter serves to explain the Magnificat. See S. Bernard, *De diligendo Deo,* Cap. 2.
[2] See *John* ii. 21. *Heb.* viii. 2; ix. 11; x. 20.

CHAPTER IV.

1 Let a man so account of us as of the ministers of Christ, and the dispensers of the mysteries of God.
2 Here now it is required among the dispensers, that a man be found faithful.

S. Paul claimed veneration for himself as an Apostle on account of his being a minister of Christ, and a dispenser of divine mysteries. Mary is the true Mother of Jesus Christ: by her we have received not divine mysteries, but God Incarnate Himself, and He has made her the dispenser of His graces. Hence, at once on her becoming the Mother of God, she dispensed His graces of justification and sanctification to S. John the Baptist and S. Elizabeth. Mary, the "Virgo fidelis," was *found faithful*. How then do our Lord and His Church will that we should account of her?

7 For who distinguisheth thee? Or what hast thou that thou hast not received? And if thou hast received, why dost thou glory, as if thou hadst not received it?

Mary in her Magnificat glories not in herself, but in Him *who distinguished her*, and from whom she *had received all*. If we glorify her as receiving, we give glory to God.

14 I write not these things to confound you; but I admonish you as my dearest children.
15 For if you have ten thousand instructors in Christ, yet not many fathers. For in Christ Jesus, by the gospel, I have begotten you.
16 Wherefore I beseech you, be ye followers of me, as I also am of Christ.

How much more is Mary our Mother than S. Paul our Father. And with how much more touching force might Mary say: "If you have ten thousand instructors in Christ, *yet no other Mother*: for at the foot of the Cross did I give you spiritual birth in Jesus Christ. Wherefore I admonish you as my dearest children, and beseech you, listen to the precept of our Saviour, who when dying said: 'Behold your Mother.' *Be ye, then, followers of Me, as I also am of Christ.*"

CHAPTER VI.

15 Know you not that your bodies are the members of Christ?
19 Or know you not, that your members are the temple of the Holy Ghost, who is in you, whom you have from God; and you are not your own?
20 For you are bought with a great price. Glorify and bear God in your body.

Great is the dignity of man in being created to the image of God, greater still in that God has by His Incarnation deigned to take the image of man, even the likeness of sinful flesh; but greatest of all when, by union with Christ through baptism and holy communion, he becomes almost identified with the God-Man. This union is so close that the very members of his body are looked upon as, in some sense, the members of Christ's virginal body. This identification is the work of the Holy Ghost, for He it is who forms Christ in us. Now these principles show us the incomparable dignity of Mary. The Holy Ghost overshadowed her, and she became His temple by a nobler consecration than ever was conferred on creature. He formed Christ in her, not metaphorically, not mystically, not by grace only, but literally, so that not only was her body a member of Christ, but the members of Christ were taken from her body.——*Mary was not her own.* She was created for, sanctified for, glorified for, her Son. She exists for Him. She was *bought at a great price.* What else could have been present in the Apostle's mind as the antitype of this, so to speak, mystical Incarnation, but the thought of Mary? Who will ever strive to separate Jesus and Mary. *Dominus tecum.*——" God does not dwell in any one," says S. Augustine, " whom the Holy Ghost has not first sanctified and purified. And even so to Mary, that Blessed Virgin, was it said, 'The Holy Ghost shall come upon thee,' no doubt to sanctify and purify her."

CHAPTER VII.

25 Now concerning virgins, I have no commandment of the Lord; but I give counsel, as having obtained mercy of the Lord, to be faithful.

¹ *Collat. cum Maxim.* 21.

34 And the unmarried woman and the virgin thinketh on the things of the Lord, that she may be holy both in body and in spirit. But she that is married thinketh on the things of the world, how she may please her husband.
35 And this I speak for your profit: not to cast a snare upon you; but for that which is decent, and which may give you power to attend upon the Lord, without impediment.
38 Therefore, both he that giveth his virgin in marriage, doth well; and he that giveth her not, doth better.
40 But more blessed shall she be, if she so remain, according to my counsel; and I think that I also have the spirit of God.

What Virgin was the antitype and ideal exemplar present here to the Apostle's mind, but Mary, the Virgin of virgins? She who was ever thinking on the things that concerned Jesus Christ, her Lord and Son, and pondering them in her heart. Here some words of Cardinal Newman, though on another matter, are of force: "I do not deny that under the image of the Woman the Church is signified, but what I would maintain is this, that the holy Apostle would not have spoken of the Church under this particular image, *unless* there had existed a Blessed Virgin, who was exalted on high, and the object of veneration to all the faithful."[1]

"Mary," says S. Austin, "alone of women is Mother and Virgin, not only in spirit, but also in body. And Mother she is, indeed, in spirit, not of our Head, who Himself is the Saviour, of whom rather she was herself spiritually born: since all who believe in Him, in whose number she is, are rightly called the children of the Bridegroom :[2] but she is clearly the spiritual Mother of His members, which we are; because she co-operated by her charity, that the faithful might be born into the Church; and these are the members of that same Head. For it was befitting that our Head should, according to the flesh, be born of a Virgin, for an admirable marvel, whereby He would signify that His members were to be born of a virgin Church, according to the Spirit. Consequently Mary alone is Mother and Virgin both in spirit and in body; both Mother of Christ and Virgin of Christ. But the Church, in the saints who will possess the Kingdom of God, is, if taken as a whole, in spirit

[1] *Letter to Dr. Pusey.*   [2] *Matt.* ix. 15.

indeed, Christ's Mother, and, as a whole, Christ's virgin; but not so, as a whole, in body; since in some she is Christ's virgin, in some a mother, but not of Christ."¹

"O prudent Virgin, O devout [devota, vowed] Virgin," exclaims S. Bernard, "who taught thee that virginity was pleasing to God? What law, what claim of justice, what page of the Old Testament, either commands, or counsels, or exhorts to live in the flesh not as in flesh, and to lead here on earth an angelic life? Where hadst thou read, Blessed Virgin, . . . of virgins that they sing a new canticle, which none other can sing, and 'follow the Lamb, whithersoever He goeth'?² Where hadst thou read: 'Though we walk in the flesh, we do not war according to the flesh,'³ and, *He that giveth his virgin in marriage doth well, and he that giveth her not doth better.* Where hadst thou heard, *I would that all men were even as myself?* and, *It is good for a man if he so remain according to my counsel?* and, *Concerning virgins I have no commandment of the Lord, but I give counsel?* But thou hadst—I will not say, neither commandment, nor counsel, nor example, but—nought save what the unction (of the Spirit) taught thee concerning all things, and that wherewith 'the Word of God, living and effectual,'⁴ Who first became thy teacher, ere He was made thy Son, previously instructed thy mind, before He put on thy flesh. *To Christ therefore thou vowest to present thyself a virgin,* and knowest not that to Him thou must be presented as His Mother also. Thou choosest to be contemptible in Israel, and, that 'thou mayest please Him to Whom thou hast engaged thyself,'⁵ to incur the curse of sterility: and, lo, the curse is exchanged for benediction, sterility is recompensed with fecundity."⁶

CHAPTER IX.

1 Am not I free? Am not I an apostle? Have not I seen Christ Jesus our Lord? Are not you my work in the Lord?

If these were so many claims on the respect and submission

---

¹ *De Sanct. Virginit.* Cap. vi.   ² *Apoc.* xiv. 4,   ³ 2 *Cor.* x. 3.
⁴ *Heb.* iv. 12.   ⁵ 2 *Tim.* ii. 4.   ⁶ *Super Missus est,* Hom. iii. 7.

of the Corinthian Christians, as being the grounds of S. Paul's dignity, how much greater are those of Mary. What is it to be an Apostle of Christ compared with being His own true Mother? If it was a great thing to have seen Jesus Christ for a few moments, what must it have been to have given Him birth, to have given Him her own breasts, to have brought Him up from childhood and lived with Him for thirty years? Deep was the debt which the Corinthians owed to S. Paul, chosen from the other Apostles to build up their spiritual edifice. But Mary's is a place that no other could supply. She alone is our Mother, who has given us our Saviour, and brought us forth to the life of grace.

5 Have we not power to carry about a woman a sister, as well as the rest of the apostles, and the brethren of the Lord, and Cephas?

Not without meaning does the Holy Ghost lead the Apostle to speak of, as a title of dignity, *the brethren of the Lord*.[1] S. Paul considers that this relationship with Jesus Christ was a claim to honour and authority. But it was all through Mary. In so far as they were nearly related to her, were they nearly related to her Divine Son Jesus Christ. She was the channel of whatever dignity they received from this relationship. S. Paul knew this well. How much greater veneration, then, in the Apostle's mind was due to her. How much more honour would he pay to her: for how much closer, and of what a different nature was her relationship to Jesus Christ, as His own true Mother. Because S. James, the brother (kinsman) of our Lord, was first bishop of Jerusalem, that Church was wont in ancient times to be styled with the dignity of *the Theadelphian See*: we might hence draw out from analogy the relationship of the Divine Mother with Christ's universal Church.

22 To the weak I became weak, that I might gain the weak. I became all things to all men, that I might save all.

"S. Paul made himself all to all by assimilation and condescension. The most blessed Virgin conformed herself, in

---

[1] See *Acts* i. 13, 14; *Gal.* i. 19; *Jude* 1.

truth and reality, to all in various times and states, even to such as were mutually most opposed. For she was a model at once to mothers, and virgins, and widows; to men, and angels."[1]

CHAPTER X.

31 Therefore, whether you eat or drink, or whatsoever else you do, do all to the glory of God.

"All human actions," says S. Antoninus, "may be referred to God. He, then, is the most perfect who refers all his actions to God. Since the Blessed Virgin was, of all mankind, alone exempt from every venial sin and imperfection, she alone was able actually to refer all she did to God, always throughout her life."[2]

33 As I also in all things please all men, not seeking that which is profitable to myself, but to many, that they may be saved.

If this was the zeal of the Apostle for the salvation of souls, how much more was it that of Mary at the foot of the Cross.

CHAPTER XI.

1 Be ye followers of me, as I also am of Christ.

If the Apostle can speak thus, how much more can Mary.[3]

3 But I would have you know, that the head of every man is Christ; and the head of the woman is the man; and the head of Christ is God.

7 The man indeed ought not to cover his head, because he is the image and glory of God; but the woman is the glory of the man.

8 For the man is not of the woman, but the woman of the man.

9 For the man was not created for the woman, but the woman for the man.

10 Therefore ought the woman to have a power over her head, because of the angels.

11 But yet neither is the man without the woman, nor the woman without the man, in the Lord.

12 For as the woman is of the man, so also is the man by the woman: but all things of God.

Most truly and forcibly may these words be applied in a

---

[1] B. Albert. Magn. *super Missus est*, c. 126. See *supra, Rom.* i. 14.
[2] *P. iv., Tit.* xv., c. 26, § 1. See also *infra,* 2 *Cor.* vi. 1.
[3] See *supra,* 1 *Cor.* iv. 16.

mystical sense to our Lord Jesus Christ and the Blessed Virgin Mary. Whether such mystical application was in the mind of S. Paul as he wrote or not, all that he here says is entirely in harmony with his teaching elsewhere, viz., that Jesus Christ is the ideal Man, "the second Man from heaven, heavenly;" "the Man Christ Jesus;"[1] "the brightness of God's glory and the figure of His substance;" "the image of the invisible God, the first-born of every creature."[2] As, then, Jesus Christ is the second Adam, so Mary is the second Eve, "the Woman," set forth in paradise to the hopes of our first parents, of whom in the fulness of time the Word became Man, our Redeemer Jesus Christ.[3] Mary is the glory of Jesus. All her grace and dignity is derived from Him. Yet neither is He, the Man, without her; but by her, and of her, since He derives His human existence from her: "Of whom was born Jesus who is called Christ."[4] Nor in the work of Redemption is He without her; since she co-operated with Him therein, even as the first Eve did with Adam in the Fall. If the entire passage be read in this mystical sense, it will be seen how beautifully everything contained in it, is applicable to Jesus and Mary.

Well does S. Ambrose say: "Go forth and see King Solomon in the crown, wherewith his mother crowned him in the day of his espousals, and in the day of the joy of his heart, because he made for himself, he says, charity from the daughters of Jerusalem. . . .'[5] Blessed Mother, Jerusalem, and blessed womb of Mary, which crowned so great a Lord. She crowned Him when she formed Him, she crowned Him when she brought Him forth . . . in that she conceived and bore Him for the salvation of all: she placed upon His head a crown of eternal piety, so that by the faith of them that believe, *Christ might become the head of every man.* . . . What there was of flesh He assumed from the Virgin, and in her formed the members of the last Adam, the Spotless Man."[6]

[1] See 1 Cor. xv. 45-47; 1 *Tim.* ii. 5. [2] *Heb.* i. 3; *Col.* i. 15.
[3] *Gal.* iv. 4. See *infra, Heb.* i. 1. [4] *Matt.* i. 16. [5] *Cant.* iii. 10, 11.
[6] *De Inst. Virg.*, Cap. xvi. 103.

"We must not pass over, Brethren," says S. Augustine, "and chiefly for the instruction of the women our sisters, the modesty, so holy of the Virgin Mary. She had given birth to Christ, the Angel had come to her, and had said to her, 'Behold, thou shalt conceive ... the Son of the Most High.'[1] She had merited to give birth to the Son of the Most High, and yet was she the most humble. She did not set herself above her husband; nor did she so in order of name, so as to say, 'I and Thy father;' but she says, 'Thy father and I.' Thus she did not pay attention to the dignity of her womb, but had regard to the conjugal order. It was not the humble Christ, who would have taught His Mother to be proud. She says, 'Thy father and I,' because *the head of the woman is the man*. How much less, then, ought the rest of women to be proud. Mary, too, is called a woman, not from loss of virginity, but according to the way of speaking proper to her country."

29 Not discerning the body of the Lord.

To discern rightly the Body of the Lord, we must discern rightly His Virgin Mother; for that Body was made of her. It is just those who have no discernment of Mary who fail to discern Christ's true Body and Blood in the Holy Eucharist.

Thus does S. Ephrem make Mary hold colloquy with her Babe:—"Thou art within me, and Thou art without me, O Thou that makest Thy Mother amazed; for I see that outward form of Thine before mine eyes, the hidden Form is shadowed forth in my mind, O Holy One. In Thy visible form I see Adam, and in Thy hidden Form I see Thy Father, who is blended with Thee. Hast Thou, then, shewn me alone Thy Beauty in two forms? Let Bread shadow forth Thee, and also the mind; dwell also in bread and in the eaters thereof. In secret and openly may Thy Church see Thee, as well as Thy Mother. He that hateth Thy Bread is like unto him that hateth Thy Body. He that is far off that desireth Thy Bread, and he that is near that loveth Thy Image, are alike. In the Bread and

[1] *Luke* i. 31, 32.   [2] *Serm.* 51, 11.

in the Body, the first and also the last have seen Thee. Yet Thy visible Bread is far more precious than Thy Body: for Thy Body even unbelievers have seen, but they have not seen Thy living Bread. They that were afar off rejoiced: their portion utterly scorneth that of those that were near. Lo! Thy Image is shadowed forth in the blood of the grapes on[1] the Bread; and it is shadowed forth on the heart with the finger of love, with the colours of faith. Blessed be He that by the Image of His Truth caused the graven images to pass away."

CHAPTER XII.

4 Now there are diversities of graces, but the same Spirit;
5 And there are diversities of ministries, but the same Lord;
6 And there are diversities of operations, but the same God, who worketh all in all.
7 And the manifestation of the Spirit is given to every man unto profit.
8 To one indeed, by the Spirit, is given the word of wisdom: and to another, the word of knowledge, according to the same Spirit;
9 To another, faith in the same Spirit; to another, the grace of healing in one Spirit;
10 To another, the working of miracles; to another, prophecy; to another, the discerning of spirits; to another, diverse kinds of tongues; to another, interpretation of speeches.
11 But all these things one and the same Spirit worketh, dividing to every one according as he will.

The Apostle teaches in this Chapter that, as in the natural body, so also in the mystical body of Christ, the members are of various degrees of dignity, according to the particular functions which they have to perform; and that they receive special gratuitous graces and gifts proportioned to their several dignity and office, for the profit of the other members, and the common good of the whole Church.—— Now the Blessed Virgin, as Mother of Jesus Christ, the Head of His mystical body, and as Mother of all the faithful,

---

[1] "This alludes to a rite in the Syrian Liturgy, in which the officiating Priest is instructed to dip one portion of the consecrated bread into the cup, and sprinkle the rest with it"—Ben. By the colours of faith, he means the outward words used to paint it, so to say, in the mind.

[2] S. Ephrem, *Opp. Syr.*, Tom. ii.; *Serm. In Nat. Dom.* xi., p. 429; Morris, p. 50.

holds the highest place of dignity amongst all the other members; and has consequently received in super-eminent degree such gifts and graces as are fitted for the worthy discharge of her sublime functions. Hence it is considered certain, according to S. Thomas and theologians generally, that Mary had all the gifts here enumerated in the highest degree, at least *inherently*, and also their actual *exercise*, so far as this was suitable to her sex and condition, and was expedient for the ministry to which she had been chosen by God.——Accordingly, she possessed the gift of *wisdom*, or an excellent intelligence, through contemplation,[1] of the most profound mysteries of revelation, such as the Trinity, the Incarnation, and Redemption; together with the faculty of explaining them to others. ——The gift of *knowledge* is said to refer especially to a deep understanding of, and the faculty of setting forth to others, all that is best and most perfect in practice. The marvellous prudence of the Blessed Virgin shows that she had this gift. But she had not the exercise either of this gift, nor of that of *wisdom* for public preaching or teaching, since this would have been out of order, and unbefitting her sex and condition.[2] She, however, exercised these gifts, in an unofficial and private capacity, so to say, and was, as tradition tells us, the instructress of the Apostles and Evangelists in many things, and especially in what related to the infancy, childhood, and hidden life of her Divine Son. And we may well believe that after the Ascension they often consulted her as the living commentary on all His words and acts, and the best interpreter of His mind and thoughts. Hence Eusebius of Emisa says: "Mary, being most wise, preserved in her heart all the words of Jesus Christ, and kept them for us, and caused them to be registered, in order that, according to her instruction, their recital and dictation should be published and preached throughout the world, and given to us to read." [3]——The *gift of faith*, as distinguished from the theological virtue of faith, is a firm trust and confidence in the power and help

[1] *Luke* ii. 19.   [2] 1 *Tim.* ii. 12.   [3] *Hom. in Evangel.*

of God, spite of all difficulties, obstacles, and even seeming impossibilities; such as, in the words of our Lord, can "remove mountains."[1] This gift was evidenced in the Blessed Virgin, when she believed the Angel's word that she should be Mother of the Son of God, and still remain a Virgin:[2] and again, when at the Marriage-feast she had firm confidence that our Lord would fulfil her desire, and work the miracle, though He seemed to refuse her petition. This gift of faith connotes also the power of easily convincing others of divine truths. It is thus bestowed on those especially whose ministry it is to preach God's Word. Mary, of course, had not such exercise of this gift: but that she possessed the gift of faith, understood in this sense, we may see clearly from the same miracle at Cana. For not only was her own faith and confidence so strong; but she had also the power of inspiring the domestics with faith, so that, when she bid them do whatever her Son commanded them, they at once acted on His word, believing that He would work the miracle, though all appearances were against it. This exercise of Mary's gift of faith was moreover, the root, so to say, of His disciples' faith, who, as the Evangelist records, then believed in our Lord.[3]——With regard to the *grace or gift of healing*, and of miracles generally, S. Thomas says that, "its exercise did not belong to the Blessed Virgin during her lifetime: because that was the time when Christ's doctrine had to be confirmed by miracles. And, therefore, for Christ alone, and His disciples who were the bearers of Christ's doctrine, was it fitting to work miracles. For the same reason, too, it is said of John the Baptist that 'he did no sign,'[4] in order, namely, that all might fix their attention on Christ."——The *working of miracles* (*operatio virtutum*) is considered to be greater than the last gift: comprising marvels and prodigies which have reference, not only to the body, but also to the soul, and all things else, such as to raise the dead to life, to cast out devils, and to work extraordinary miracles

---

[1] *Matt.* xvii. 19; xxi. 21.   *Mark* xi. 23.   1 *Cor.* xiii. 2.
[2] *Luke* i. 37, 38.   [3] *John* ii. 1-11.   [4] *John* x. 42.

in the order of grace. We may see Mary's exercise of this gift, as to the last effect, at the Visitation, when the yet unborn infant, John the Baptist, heard her salutation, and at the very sound of her voice leapt for joy, and was sanctified in his mother's womb; and at the same time Elizabeth was illuminated and filled with the Holy Ghost.——"That the Blessed Virgin had the exercise of *the gift of prophecy*," says S. Thomas, "is evident from the Canticle which she made: *Magnificat anima mea Dominum*," etc. S. Augustine referring to our Lord's words (*Matt.* xi. 13) enumerates those recorded in the New Testament as having prophesied before John, and adds: "We know, too, from the Gospel (*Luke* i. 46-55) that the Lord's Virgin Mother herself prophesied before John." [1]

S. Epiphanius writes: "'I went,' says Isaias, 'to the prophetess; and she conceived in her womb, and bore a son. And the Lord said to me: Call his name, hasten to take away the spoils: make haste to take away the prey,' etc.[2] By which words he shews the entrance of Gabriel to Mary; when he went forth to bring her the glad tidings that she was to give birth to the Son of God, the Saviour of the world, not from seed of man, but by the Holy Ghost."[3]

S. Jerome, commenting on the same text, says: "Some interpret the prophetess as the Blessed Virgin. That Mary was a prophetess there is no doubt, since she says herself in the Gospel: 'Behold from henceforth . . . great things.'[4] (*Luke* i. 48, 49.)

S. Nilus, too: "Thou hast asked us, why Mary the Mother of God is called by Isaias (vii. 14) a Prophetess. Remark in the Gospel her words, 'He hath regarded the humility of His handmaid: for behold from henceforth all generations shall call me blessed.' And if you do not find that the holy Mary is called blessed in all nations and in every tongue, because she bore in her womb God, made flesh of the Holy Ghost, and of her, and brought Him forth without corruption or any sort of stain, then give no credence to Isaias. But if through-

[1] *De Civit., Dei,* l. xvii. c. 22. [2] *Isa.* viii. 3. [3] *Hæres.* lxviii. 16.
[4] *Comment. in Isa.* l. iii.

out the world she is called blessed, and is extolled with praise, hymned forth, and eulogised—she, that land unsown and unwrought—together with her all-blessed and eternal Fruit, why dost thou further dispute whether Mary the Mother of God should be called a prophetess?"[1]

The gift of *the discerning of spirits*, that is to say, of thoughts and intentions, and consequently of words and actions—thereby to know whether they proceed from the natural spirit and instinct, or from the devil, or from God, or an angel, was possessed by the Blessed Virgin in the highest degree of perfection. She showed her exercise of this discernment especially at the Annuntiation. By this gift she knew for certain that he who then spoke to her the message, otherwise incomprehensible, was in truth the Angel of the Lord, and that his words were divine.——With regard to the gift of speaking *divers kinds of tongues*, the holy Virgin must have possessed it equally with the Apostles. It was fitting that she should not only understand foreign languages, but also speak them, because she would have been in want of this grace on many occasions, and God would not have deprived her of what was necessary for the accomplishment of the aims of His Divine Providence. For example, when the Magi came from the East to adore the Infant Jesus at Bethlehem, it was necessary that she should understand their language, as well as speak it. When she went into Egypt, and remained there several years, in order to save her Divine Infant from the persecution of Herod, it was necessary for her to understand and speak the language of those parts. Besides, it is reasonable to suppose and believe that after the Ascension of our Divine Lord, when the Christian faith began to be diffused and spread over the most distant countries, many came from afar to see the holy Mother of the Redeemer, and to honour her; she must then have understood them, and been able to speak their language. Again, we may well believe that they had the satisfaction of hearing in their own tongue the divine oracles from her

---

[1] *Epist.* l. ii. 212.

mouth.——By the gift of *interpretation of speeches*, is generally held to mean that of understanding and explaining especially the more obscure passages of Holy Scripture. Tradition tells us how versed Mary was in the Sacred Scriptures, and we might gather the same from several things said in the Gospels. We may see, too, her exercise of this gift in her Magnificat.[1]

26 And if one member suffer any thing, all the members suffer with it; or if one member glory, all the members rejoice with it.
27 Now you are the body of Christ, and members of member.

Hence in the Joyful, Sorrowful, and Glorious Mysteries of the Rosary the faithful not only take part in the Joys, Sufferings, and Glories of Jesus Christ the Head of the Body, but also in the Joys, Dolours, and Glories of Mary, who is the most excellent member of His Mystical Body.

"The Church," says S. Austin, "is a virgin." Thou wilt, perhaps, ask me: If she is a virgin, how does she give birth to children? And if she does not give birth to children, how is it we give in our names, that we might be born of her bowels? I answer: She is both virgin and brings forth children. She imitates Mary, who brought forth the Lord. Did not the holy Virgin Mary both bring forth and remain a virgin? So, too, the Church both brings forth and is a virgin. And if thou reflectest, she gives birth to Christ because those who are baptised are His members. *You*, says the Apostle, *are the body of Christ, and members.* If, therefore, she gives birth to Christ's members, she is most like to Mary."[2]——Again: "Mary is clearly the spiritual Mother of Christ's members, which we are, because she co-operated by charity, that the faithful who are members of the Head, should be born into the Church; and she is corporally Mother of that Head."[3]

---

[1] Quotations are made in the above comment from S. Thomas' *Summa* p. iii. qu. xxvii.; *Art* v. ad 3m.; *Cornel. a Lap. in loc.*; and *The Virgin Mary*, by Rev. R. Melia, D.D., P.S.M., pp. 152-156. For the Blessed Virgin's personal beauty, as a gratuitous grace, see the same work, pp. 157-161.

[2] *Serm*. 213, cap. 7. See also *supra*, vii. 34.

[3] *De Sanct. Virginit.* cap. vi.

CHAPTER XIII.

4 Charity is patient, is kind: charity envieth not, dealeth not perversely; is not puffed up;
5 Is not ambitious, seeketh not her own, is not provoked to anger, thinketh no evil;
6 Rejoiceth not in iniquity, but rejoiceth with the truth;
7 Beareth all things, believeth all things, hopeth all things, endureth all things.
8 Charity never falleth away.

"Charity is kind. God our Saviour showed Himself so kind to us, that He gave to us all that He had, and prayed for His crucifiers. His Mother imitated Him. The gold presented to her by the Magi, she soon generously bestowed upon the poor. The Apostle says, *Charity is kind*, and the greater the charity, the greater is the kindness. Hence, as Mary's charity exceeds that of all others, so too does her kindness." [2]

Think of Mary from what is said, and also from what is not said of her in the Gospels. Look then into your own thoughts about her: gather thence the necessary, inevitable idea of her impressed on the believing mind: compare with all this each clause of the Apostle's description of charity. Does not the idea perfectly harmonise with the description, and do not both tally the one with the other; bringing out distinctly to view that sweet character of the Blessed Virgin, which has been ever indelibly stamped on the mind of the Catholic Church, which has been uniformly expressed by the Saints, and been the consoling devotion of all the faithful in every age? O clemens, O pia, O dulcis Virgo Maria! Thou assuredly wert that living ideal whence the Apostle has drawn this picture of charity.

CHAPTER XV.

22 And as in Adam all die, so also in Christ all shall be made alive.

It is an unquestionable truth that the Blessed Virgin is the second Eve as our Lord Jesus Christ is the second Adam.

See *Tit.* iii. 4. [2] S. Antoninus, p. v., tit. xv., c. 26, § 4.

And since the certainty of this truth is established by other reasons, we may regard it as implicitly contained in these words of the Apostle although they do not formally express it. *As*, that is to say, in the same manner as the first man Adam wrought death, so did Christ the last Adam bring life (v. 45). But we know that the way by which the first Adam brought about our death was in direct co-operation with the first woman, Eve. So, in the same manner, with the co-operation of a woman, that is to say, Mary, the second Eve, did Christ the second Adam restore us to life. We may give the same extension to that other expression of S. Paul, viz., that the first Adam is the figure or form of the second: *Adam, qui est forma futuri*;[1] and conclude that Eve is the figure or form of Mary the second Eve; and that as the one woman co-operated in our fall, so the other co-operated in our redemption.[2]—— "Since by the female sex," says S. Augustine, "man fell, by the same sex is man restored. . . . By a woman death, by a woman life."[3] And S. Epiphanius: "Eve brought ruin on God's creatures by means of the transgression; allured as she was by the serpent's speech and promise, led astray from the commandment, and perverted in mind. For this cause the Lord and Saviour of all, wishing to heal the sore, build up what was fallen to ruin, and redress what was gone wrong, of a Virgin woman Himself was born, that He might banish death, supply what was wanting, and perfect what was impaired."[4]

23 But every one in his own order: the first-fruits Christ, then they that are of Christ, who have believed in his coming.

Who should be the next in order after Christ the first-fruits? What should be her place and order, who not only was *of Christ*, and was so signally blessed in *believing in His first coming*,[5] but "of whom was born Jesus" the *first-fruits of the Resurrection?*

---

[1] "After the similitude of the transgression of Adam, who is a figure of him who was to come"—*Rom.* v. 14.
[2] See *The Co-operation of the Blessed Virgin*, etc. Jeanjacquot, S. J.
[3] *Serm.* 232, 2.   [4] *Hæres.* 69, 9.   [5] *Luke* i. 45.

41 One is the glory of the sun, another the glory of the moon, and another the glory of the stars. For star differeth from star in glory.

Among the *bodies celestial* there is one that holds pre-eminence before all others, the Sun of Justice, our Lord Jesus Christ. Who is signified by that other orb, reflecting the sun, next in dignity and splendour, one and alone, differing utterly from, and excelling far, all stars in shining, *formosa ut luna?* Who but Mary? *Another is the glory of the moon, and another the glory of the stars* (the Saints of God), *for star differeth from star in glory.* The glory, then, of Mary not only surpasses far in degree, but is of a different kind from that of all the Saints. On this account the Church pays to the Blessed Virgin veneration and honour of a different order from what she gives to the other Saints.——" I keep silence," writes S. Jerome, " on Anna and Elisabeth, and the rest of the holy women, whose, so to say, tiny sparks of stars the bright, shining light of Mary eclipses."[1]——An ancient author writes : " Such was the splendour of Mary's life, as, in a manner, to obscure the lives of all others; for as in comparison with God no one is good, so in comparison with the Lord's Mother, no creature is found perfect, even though it be shewn to excel in virtues. One is our Father in heaven, one is our Mother on earth, one form of virtues Mary." [2]——" One is the glory of the sun, that is, the glory of Christ ; another the glory of the moon, that is, of the Virgin Mary ; and another the glory of the stars, that is, of the other Saints. Because according to their different merits, they will partake in various degrees of the light of glory, it is added, for star differeth from star in glory." [3]——" Of the Blessed Virgin, after Christ, is especially said : 'She is the brightness of eternal life, and an unspotted mirror,' on account of the exceeding beauty of her soul and body ; and again, 'She is more beautiful than the sun, and above all the order of the stars : being compared with the light, she is found more pure.' [4] S. Bonaventure, explaining this passage of the Blessed

---

[1] *Comment. in Sophon. Prol.*
[2] *Ep. ad Eustoch. et Paul. de Assump.* int. opera S. Hieron.
[3] Lyra, ap. Morales, lib. iii., tr. 2.   [4] *Sap.* vii. 26, 27.

Virgin, says as follows: 'Some read here *prior*, others *purior*; but both are applicable to our Star: for Mary is *before*, that is, more excellent or worthy: and Mary is also *more pure* than the sun, the stars, and light, because, as well in dignity and purity, she surpasses the sun, and stars, and all material light; nay, even all spiritual light, that is, all angelic creation.' Whence S. Anselm exclaims: 'O Blessed above women who excellest the Angels in purity, and the Saints in piety.'"[1]

"Christ," says Cardinal Hugo, "is the greater light to rule the day, that is, the just: Mary the lesser light to rule sinners."[2]

47 The first man was of the earth, earthly; the second man, from heaven, heavenly.

See *infra* (*Heb.* viii. 26) the passage from S. Ambrose alluding to these words, quoted by S. Alphonsus.——"Not," says Rupert, "that Jesus Christ who was born of Mary came with flesh from heaven, and passed through the Blessed Virgin—quasi per fistulam—as some heretics have asserted; but that the life of these two spouses, Joseph and Mary—or their union—was all heavenly, and the Holy Spirit was the conjugal love of both, since their conversation was entirely in heaven."[3]

THE SECOND EPISTLE OF S. PAUL

TO THE

CORINTHIANS.

CHAPTER I.

3 Blessed be the God and Father of our Lord Jesus Christ, the Father of mercies, and the God of all comfort.

4 Who comforteth us in all our tribulation; that we also may be able to comfort them who are in all distress, by the exhortation wherewith we also are exhorted by God.

---

[1] Morales ii. 10.   [2] In *Gen.* i.
[3] Rupert l. 1. *De gloria et honore Filii hominis.* Sup. *Matt.* i.

5 For as the sufferings of Christ abound in us: so also by Christ doth our comfort abound.

6 Now whether we be in tribulation, it is for your exhortation and salvation: or whether we be comforted, it is for your consolation: or whether we be exhorted, it is for your exhortation and salvation, which worketh the enduring of the same sufferings which we also suffer.

7 That our hope for you may be steadfast: knowing that as you are partakers of the sufferings, so shall you be also of the consolation.

If S. Paul could speak thus, much more could Mary. If we put his words into her lips, how much greater is their force and meaning. Try Mary by the canon laid down by the Apostle: *As the sufferings of Christ abound in us, so also by Christ doth our comfort abound.* Who can compare with Mary in abounding in the sufferings of Christ? Where then shall we look for such abounding comfort as in her? In the fulness of her joy on Easter-day, after the anguish of Good-Friday, well might she exclaim: "According to the multitude of my sorrows in my heart, Thy comforts have given joy to my soul."[1] And not only *in* Mary, but also *from* her may we look for most abundant comfort. For if S. Paul's own individual tribulations and comfort were all for our salvation and consolation, accomplishing *the enduring of the same sufferings* in measure in us, much more were Mary's dolours and joys for our salvation and consolation. Since Mary suffered and was consoled, not in general, as a disciple and servant of Jesus Christ, but she, as Mother of the Redeemer, took part in, or rather endured along with Him, all those particular sufferings which He Himself in person underwent for our redemption; and in like manner all His consolations and joys were her's also. If, then, S. Paul's sufferings and consolations were for the good of the faithful, how much more so were those of Mary the Mother of all the faithful. Should we not, therefore, bless the *Father of mercies* for giving us our Mother of Dolours to be such an example, hope, and consolation to us in our tribulations.

[1] *Ps.* xciii. 19.

10 Who hath delivered and doth deliver us out of so great dangers; in whom we trust that he will yet also deliver us.
11 You helping withal in prayer for us: that for this gift obtained for us, by the means of many persons, thanks may be given by many in our behalf.

If the Apostle could ascribe such signal mercies to the prayers of the Corinthians, trust so confidently in their intercession, and see therein only another great means of glorifying God, what must be the efficacy of the intercession of Mary the Mother of God. What should be our confidence and perseverance in asking it; and what immense glory will accrue to God therefrom. We see from this that hope in the prayers of Saints, especially of the Blessed Virgin, is not only consistent with, but also a great proof of, trust in God.

14 As also you have known us in part, that we are your glory, as you also are ours, in the day of our Lord Jesus Christ.

The Mother of Mercy is the glory of us poor sinners, and we poor sinners shall be her glory in eternity.

CHAPTER III.

6 Who also hath made us fit ministers of the New Testament, not in the letter, but in the spirit. For the letter killeth, but the spirit quickeneth.
7 Now if the ministration of death, engraven with letters upon stones, was glorious; so that the children of Israel could not steadfastly behold the face of Moses, for the glory of his countenance, which is made void:
8 How shall not the ministration of the Spirit be rather in glory?
9 For if the ministration of condemnation be glory, much more the ministration of justice aboundeth in glory.

If God rendered the Apostles every way fit for their office of delivering the message of the New Testament of Jesus Christ; He surely made her, by whom came Jesus Christ, in every way a worthy Mother of His Son.[1] How may we compare the ministration of the New Testament with the Divine Maternity? How, then, compare the gifts of the Apostles with those of the Divine Mother? Much more, then, must *she abound in glory.*

[1] See the citations from S. Bernardine of Sienna, S. Thomas, S. Augustine, and S. Sophronius, *supra*, p. 89.

18 But we all beholding the glory of the Lord with open face, are transformed into the same image from glory to glory, as by the Spirit of the Lord.

What astonishing words to be addressed to all Christians! What language may, then, be too great for her, who lived her life, as it were, for nothing else than to behold, as no other could, the glory of the Lord! "The Word was made flesh of me," might Mary say, "and dwelt in me, and with me, and I saw His glory, the glory, as it were, of the Only-begotten of the Father, full of grace and truth."[1] From what heights to what heights again of glory was Mary raised; and—as she lived, and lived beholding the glory of the Lord—how perfectly was she transformed into His image by the Spirit of the Lord, Who came upon her, overshadowed, and remained ever with her.——"With reason the Church ascribes to Mary things that literally are spoken of Divine Wisdom, for so wondrously had she part in the Divine Being, drank in so much of that divine fountain, was made so like to God, in such wise did He form Himself into her, that just as when we see a man endowed with very great wisdom we are wont to say that he seems to be wisdom itself: so divine titles are given to Mary, not that she is God, for she is but a creature, yet one so adorned with divine gifts, and abounding with heavenly riches, that we give her divine names. Every just man, for that matter, partakes of the divine likeness, and is, so to say, a sort of God, since in him is effected what the Apostle says: *We are transformed into the same image*; but in various manner, according to the different degree of the participation of God's grace; and since this in Mary was in all its plenitude, there was also in all its plenitude an assimilation of her to the Divine Wisdom and Goodness."[2]

CHAPTER IV.

6 For God, who commanded the light to shine out of darkness, hath shined in our hearts, to give the light of the knowledge of the glory of God, in the face of Christ Jesus.

[1] *John* i. 14.
[2] Osorius, *Conc.* 3 *De Concept. Mariæ*, ap. Morales, L. iii. Tr. 3.

What light of the knowledge of the glory of God shined in Mary's heart, as she lived in presence of, and gazed so unceasingly *in the Face of Christ Jesus*. The whole account of Him during the eighteen years of His hidden life is, that "He increased in wisdom and age and in grace with God and with men," that is, He continually manifested more and more His Divine Wisdom, grace, and perfections. But to whom ? Was it not to Mary, for the illumination and sanctification of her soul ?

10 Always bearing about in our body the mortification of Jesus, that the life also of Jesus may be made manifest in our bodies.
11 For we who live are always delivered unto death for Jesus' sake; that the life also of Jesus may be made manifest in our mortal flesh.

So did Mary also. She always *bore about in her body the mortification of Jesus*, suffering ever for, and with Him. She bore too about with her Jesus Himself, whom she had herself offered to death, and "whose sorrow was always before Him."[1] She bore, on Calvary, in her arms His body that had suffered, that body now dead. Hence *the life of Jesus was verily made manifest* in all resemblance, in its every feature, in her body, and visible in her life. Having given for us her Jesus to death, she lived as one *always delivered unto death for Jesus' sake*, and so *the resurrection life of Jesus was made manifest at once after death in her mortal flesh*.

15 For all things are for your sakes; that the grace abounding through many, may abound in thanksgiving unto the glory of God.

That fulness of grace, then, which Mary found and abounded in, is for our sakes too. On this account, therefore, it is for us to abound in thanksgiving, and so give glory to God.

17 For that which is at present momentary and light of our tribulation, worketh for us above measure exceedingly an eternal weight of glory.

What, then, must be the eternal weight of glory bestowed on Mary ?

[1] *Ps.* xxxvii. 18.

CHAPTER V.

6 Therefore having always confidence, knowing that, while we are in the body, we are absent from the Lord.
7 (For we walk by faith, and not by sight).
8 But we are confident, and have a good will to be absent rather from the body, and to be present with the Lord.
9 And therefore we labour, whether absent or present, to please him.

We have in these words an image of Mary's peaceful confidence, and at the same time of her continually longing desire to be again united to her Divine Son, during her life of earthly sojourn after His Ascension; whilst all the while her labour was, by complete conformity with His will, to please Him perfectly.——*Present with the Lord.*—"If Christ, the Life and the Truth, saith: 'Where I am, there also shall My minister be;' how much rather will not His Mother be with Him." [1]

16 Wherefore henceforth we know no man according to the flesh. And if we have known Christ according to the flesh; but now we know him so no longer.

Jesus too was estranged, so to say, in some sense from Mary: and Mary learned to give up and to be estranged from Jesus. But who can understand or express this mystery? [2]

CHAPTER VI.

1 And we helping do exhort you, that you receive not the grace of God in vain.

S. Paul calls himself and other sacred ministers God's co-adjutors. He attributes to them a share in man's reconciliation and redemption. Why then should we refuse to Mary, in a right sense, the title and office of co-redemptress?——"God gives grace," says S. Antoninus, "that man by co-operating with it may acquire for himself the merits of eternal life. He, then, who does not work when he can, *receives grace in vain* and to no purpose. Now though the Saints exercised themselves in grace in many things and by many good works, yet

---
[1] S. John Damasc., *Orat.* 2 *de Dormit. B. V. M.*
[2] See *Luke* ii. 48-50; *Matt.* xii. 47-50; *John* ii. 4.

there has been no one, who has always and in everything that he has wrought, followed the inspiration of grace, and has thus always merited by his works. But this was the privilege of singular grace in the Blessed Virgin Mary."[1]

3 Giving no offence to any man, that our ministry be not blamed:
4 But in all things let us exhibit ourselves as the ministers of God, in much patience, in tribulation, in necessities, in distresses,
5 In stripes, in prisons, in seditions, in labours, in watchings, in fastings,
6 In chastity, in knowledge, in long-suffering, in sweetness, in the Holy Ghost, in charity unfeigned,
7 In the word of truth, in the power of God; by the armour of justice on the right hand and on the left;
8 By honour and dishonour, by evil report and good report; as deceivers, and yet true; as unknown, and yet known;
9 As dying, and behold we live; as chastised, and not killed;
10 As sorrowful, yet always rejoicing; as needy, yet enriching many; as having nothing, and possessing all things.

If we were well to study the Blessed Virgin, even in the fragmentary sketch of her life and character given in the Gospels, we should see that each and all of those beautiful traits set forth by S. Paul, except such as belong peculiarly to the Apostolic life, are found in their perfection in Mary. And the proof of this is, that it is impossible for us to attempt any idea of Our Lady—unless the mind be distorted by perversity and prejudice—and not see in her the assemblage, and mirror, so to speak, of these and all other virtues.——"*Long-suffering* (v. 6), *i.e.* longanimity, is according to the Gloss, says S. Antoninus, not to give way, but to bear up in the expectation of good deferred. When anyone has to endure what is sad or grievous for a short time, or to wait for some great good which he will soon receive, he strives to bear up with equanimity, because the time is short. But when he sees, in such case, that he must endure long in toil or sorrow, or wait long for the attainment of some good, he is often led to grow tired and weary, and sometimes to give up altogether through the length of time. Now longanimity keeps a man from growing weary, helps him to persevere, though the toil last long, and

---

[1] P. iv., tit. 15, c. 20, § 6. See *supra*, 1 *Cor.* x. 3.

the good that is looked for tarry, and refreshes his mind with a sort of pledge and assurance of reward. Therefore, says the Apostle, *In all things let us exhibit ourselves . . . in longanimity.* The Blessed Virgin Mary was for many years in the tribulations of this world, and in expectation of glory deferred—about sixty years, according to the more common opinion—but, all the while, she continued ever more and more fervent and eager for every good work."—P. iv. tit. 15, c. 26, § 1.

11 Our mouth is open to you, O ye Corinthians, our heart is enlarged.
12 You are not straitened in us, but in your own bowels you are straitened.
13 But having the same recompense (I speak as to my children,) be you also enlarged.

The Apostle tenderly upbraids the Corinthians for their narrowed hearts and affections towards himself, and asks for their love, on account of, and in return for, his large love for them. He appeals to them as a father to his dear children. Much more might Mary speak thus to us. Is she not our Mother? Does she not love us with a Mother's heart? Why, then, should we not love her in return, and profess our love and devotion to her?

14 Bear not the yoke with unbelievers. For what participation hath justice with injustice? Or what fellowship hath light with darkness?
15 And what concord hath Christ with Belial? Or what part hath the faithful with the unbeliever?
16 And what agreement hath the temple of God with idols? For you are the temple of the living God; as God saith: I will dwell in them, and walk among them; and I will be their God, and they shall be my people.
17 Wherefore, Go out from among them, and be ye separate, saith the Lord, and touch not the unclean thing:
18 And I will receive you; and I will be a Father to you; and you shall be my sons and daughters, saith the Lord Almighty.

If the Apostle forbids to Christians, marriage and other intimate relations with unbelievers, on account of the utter opposition in the essential principles which constitute and actuate the faithful and unbelievers—how much more must Jesus Christ, the ideal Model of all perfection and sanctity, have separated Himself, as far as possible, from all that had relation to sin. "It was fitting that we should have such a High-priest, holy, innocent, undefiled, separate from sinners"[1] —and separated from them in every possible way, so far as such relation might touch upon His own sacred Person and Office. And such a holy High-priest "was He made, according to the power of an indissoluble life"—"not without an oath"—free from infirmity or imperfection of any sort; but "made higher than the heavens, the Son who is perfected for evermore."[2] Now as this Son, our great High-priest, was "made of a woman,"[3] it would, surely, be repugnant to the idea of absolute perfection, and separation from sinners, it would argue some sort of infirmity, some, at least indirect, remote *concord with Belial*—were she of whom "He was made," and from whom, in fact, He derived (by being her Son) the very essential constituent elements and principles of His priesthood, that is, flesh and humanity—for the Manhood of Jesus Christ enters as necessarily and essentially into the very constitution of our great High-priest, as does His Divinity[4]—were she, we say, Mary His Mother, any way, or at any time, under the dominion of sin and Satan; that is, if she were not conceived immaculate, and did not always remain entirely sinless, pure from all stain, as well of original, as of actual fault.——We are all, indeed, *temples of God*[5]: but Mary is so by excellence, and in quite another way from other Christians. She must therefore be pure and undefiled in another and more excellent way than the rest.——"As the story goes," writes S. Jerome, "a man who was unknown to the world, and not able to think of any good deed whereby to bring himself into notice, set the temple of Diana on fire; and when nobody could say whose the sacrilege was, he came before the public himself and owned that he had done it to gain notoriety. But you, Helvidius, have set on fire the Temple of the

---

[1] *Heb.* vii. 26.   [2] *Ib.* vv. 16, 17, 20, 21, 26, 28. . . .   [3] *Gal.* iv. 4.
[4] See *Heb.* ii, 9, 14-16, 17, 18; iv. 15; v. 1, 2, 7-10; 1 *Tim.* ii. 5, 6.
[5] 2 *Cor.* vi. 16.

Lord's Body, and defiled the Sanctuary of the Holy Ghost, by denying Mary's perpetual virginity."[1]——All Christians are *sons and daughters*. But Mary, the blessed amongst women, with whom, before the Incarnation, God declared Himself to be united (*Dominus tecum*), was His beloved Daughter by excellence, the one chosen alone above all others. She was *received* into His love from the first moment of her creation, nay from all eternity : "*Dominus possedit me in initio viarum suarum*."[2] Never had she *to go out from them, i.e.* His enemies, for never was she amongst them ; nor did she ever come in contact with *the unclean thing*. No need had she of *cleansing herself from defilement of the flesh and of the spirit*, for she was ever most pure, and was constantly from the very first *perfecting sanctification in the fear of God*: "*Sanctificavit tabernaculum suum Altissimus*."[3] "*Misericordia ejus . . . timentibus eum*."[4]

CHAPTER VIII.

9 For you know the grace of our Lord Jesus Christ, that being rich he became poor, for your sakes; that through his poverty you might be rich.

"Who," S. Ephrem makes Mary ask her Divine Infant, "hath given Thee to me? O Son of the Rich One, that hated the bosom of the rich women : who led Thee to the poor? For Joseph was needy and I also in want, yet Thy merchants have come, and brought gold to the house of the poor."[5]—— "The High One became as a little child, and in Him was hidden a treasure sufficing for all. Though Most High, yet He sucked the milk of Mary, and of His goodness all creatures suck ! . . . When He sucked the milk of Mary, He was suckling all with life. While He was lying on His Mother's bosom, in His bosom were all creatures lying. . . . Whilst he was increasing in stature among the poor, from an abundant treasury He was nourishing all. . . . It was by power from Him that Mary was able to bear in her bosom Him that beareth up all

---

[1] *Contr. Helvid.* See *infra*, Heb. ix. 2-4.   [2] *Prov.* viii. 22.   [3] *Ps.* xlv. 5.
[4] *Luke* i. 50.   [5] *In Nat. Dom.* x. *Opp. Syr.*, Morris, p. 48.

things. It was from the great store-house of all creatures Mary gave Him all that she did give Him. She gave Him milk from Himself that prepared it, she gave Him food from Himself that made it. He gave milk unto Mary as God; again He sucked it from her as the Son of Man. . . . She wove for Him, and clothed Him because He had put off His glory. She measured Him and wove for Him, since He had made Himself little."[1]——"Who shall open his mouth to speak of Him that feedeth all, who was yet brought up at the poor table of Joseph and of Mary! Coming from the Bosom great and rich, which maketh all rich, in the poor bosom of Mary wert Thou brought up."[2]

23 The apostles of the churches, the glory of Christ.

Is not Mary the Mother of Jesus also, and much more than were the Apostles, His glory?

CHAPTER IX.

6 Now this I say: He who soweth sparingly, shall also reap sparingly: and he who soweth in blessings, shall also reap blessings.

Mary sowed in blessings the blessed fruit of her womb, therefore she reaps the blessings of all generations. "No one sowed so liberally as that Blessed one amongst women, who poured forth the Blessed Seed from her womb. Of her own blessings Mary consequently will reap: even she who is in a singular manner to receive the blessing of all nations. 'All generations,' she says, 'shall call me blessed.' But this is too little; all the orders of the blessed spirits shall call thee blessed."[3]

CHAPTER X.

4 For the weapons of our warfare are not carnal, but mighty through God unto the pulling down of fortifications, destroying counsels,
5 And every height that exalteth itself against the knowledge of God, and bringing into captivity every understanding unto the obedience of Christ.

---

[1] *In Nat. Dom.* x. *Opp. Syr.*, iii. pp. 22-24.
[2] *Ib.* [3] Guerric. *Serm.* 4 *De Assump.*

This is according to what Mary herself says: "Fecit mihi magna qui potens est. Fecit potentiam in brachio suo. Dispersit superbos mente cordis sui. Deposuit potentes de sede, et exaltavit humiles."

17 But he that glorieth, let him glory in the Lord.
18 For not he who commendeth himself is approved, but he whom God commendeth.

God commended Mary, and she gloried only in the Lord: Magnificat, etc.[1]

CHAPTER XI.

2 For I am jealous of you with the jealousy of God. For I have espoused you to one husband, that I may present you as a chaste virgin to Christ.
3 But I fear lest, as the serpent seduced Eve by his subtilty, so your minds should be corrupted, and fall from the simplicity that is in Christ.

What ideal chaste virgin could have been in the mind of the Apostle here but the Blessed Virgin Mary, the Virgin of virgins, predicted as such by the Prophets, testified as such in the Gospel? What other was espoused to One, even to the Divine Spouse and faithful, as was Mary? *Virgo fidelis. Virum non cognosco. Dominus tecum.*——" This is He, beautiful above the sons of men," writes S. Augustine, "the Son of holy Mary, the Bridegroom of the holy Church, whom He has rendered like to His Mother: for He hath made her for us a mother, and hath kept her for Himself a virgin. To her it is, S. Paul speaks, *I have joined you as a chaste virgin to Christ.* Of her again, he says, that our mother is not a bondwoman, but free, and that the children of her who before was desolate, are more in number than hers who hath a husband.[2] Thus also in the case of the Church, as in that of Mary, it is perpetual virginity and incorrupt fecundity. For what Mary merited in flesh the Church hath preserved in spirit . . . with this difference, that Mary gave birth to One, whilst the Church gives birth to many, to be gathered

---

[1] See *supra*, 1 Cor. i. 24-31.   [2] *Gal.* iv. 26, 27.

together into One, by One (that is, Christ). . . . He came forth from His bride-chamber, and rejoiced as a giant to run His way.[1] . . . Abiding in the bosom of His Father, He filled the womb of His Mother. And in this bride-chamber, that is, in Mary's womb, the Divine Nature united itself to the human nature; and there the word was made flesh for us, that going forth from His Mother, He might dwell in us, and going before to His Father, He might prepare a place for us wherein to dwell." [2]——"May Christ assist us," says the same holy Doctor, "the Son of a Virgin, and the Spouse of virgins, corporally born from a virginal womb, spiritually married in virginal wedlock. Since, then, the whole universal Church herself *is espoused to one Man,* Christ, as saith the Apostle, of how great honour are His members worthy, who keep this (virginity) in their very flesh, which she, as a whole, keeps in the faith; thus imitating the Mother of their Bridegroom and their Lord! For the Church also is both a Mother and a Virgin. And of whose purity, in sooth, do we take account, if she be not a virgin? or of whom do we predicate offspring, if she be not a mother. Mary corporally gave birth to the Head of this body, the Church spiritually gives birth to the members of that Head. Both in one and the other virginity is no hindrance to fecundity. In both one and the other fecundity takes not away virginity. Hence, since the Church universal is holy both in body and spirit, and yet the universal Church is not virgin in body, but in spirit. How much holier is it in those members, wherein it is virgin both in body and in spirit." [3]

And again: "It was in this virginal womb that the Onlybegotten Son of God deigned to assume human nature, that He might unite to Himself, the spotless Head, the spotless Church; which the Apostle calls a virgin, not only taking account of the virgins in body within her, but from the desire he had to see the souls of all incorrupt. *For,* says he, *I have espoused you to one husband, that I may present you as a*

---

[1] *Psalm* xviii. 6. [2] *Serm.* 195 (alias *de Tempore* 12).
[3] *De Sanct. Virginit.* cap. ii.

chaste virgin to Christ. The Church, then, *in imitating the Mother of her Lord,* since she could not do so in body, is yet both mother and virgin in spirit. Think not, then, that Christ by His birth in any way detracted from the virginity of His Mother—He who made the Church virgin by redeeming her from the fornication of demons (*i.e.*, idolatry). It is from this incorrupt virginity that you have been brought forth, O holy virgins, who spurning earthly nuptials, have elected to be virgins in flesh also. Celebrate, then, with solemnity and joy this day of the virginal Child-birth . . . He who has conferred on you this privilege so dear to you, has not taken it away from His Mother. He who heals in you what you inherited from Eve—far be it from you to think that He should not keep intact what you have so much loved in Mary. You follow the footsteps of the Virgin . . . imitate her as much as you are able ; not indeed by fecundity ; for this you cannot do whilst preserving virginity. . . . She alone had this double prerogative, she who gave birth to the Omnipotent. . . . But think not, therefore, that Christ is nothing to you, because He is Son of one only Virgin. Him, whom you cannot give birth to in flesh, you may have in heart for your Spouse. . . . Nor think that you are sterile by remaining virgins. For holy virginity of body brings with it fruitfulness of soul. Do what the Apostle says,—since you think not of things of the world, nor how you may please husbands—think of the things of God, that you may please Him in all things,[1] and be fruitful, not in body but in soul, by the practice of virtues. . . . What you admire in the flesh of Mary, reproduce in the hiding-places of your soul. Whoso believes in the heart unto justice, conceives Christ ; whoso confesses unto salvation, brings forth Christ.[2] Thus may

---

[1] *1 Cor.* vii. 32-34.
[2] " 'Tis to believers Christ is pleased to come.
The heart of fickle faith that doubts, he spurns
Unhonoured, and withholds His proffered grace.
Virginity and ready faith drink in
Christ to the inmost soul, from whence there formed,
In hiding-places pure, they bring Him forth. "
—Prudentius, *Apotheosis* v. v. 580-4.

fruitfulness united to persevering virginity abound in your souls."[1]

"The Blessed Virgin," writes Morales, "was the figure of the Church, which is both a virgin and the spouse of Christ. It was meet therefore that the Mother of God should be both a Virgin and a Spouse. Hence S. Ambrose speaks thus on this likeness and figure: 'As the Blessed Virgin was married to one (Joseph), yet filled by Another, that is to say, by the Holy Ghost; so is the Church outwardly married to the visible priest, yet filled by the Holy Ghost, in order to form children of adoption, according to the Apostle's words, 'I have planted, Apollo watered, but God gave the increase. But neither he who watereth, nor he who planteth is anything, but God who gives the increase.'[2] And S. Isidore: 'Joseph typically represents Christ, Whose office is to guard the holy Church which hath not spot nor wrinkle. But Mary signifies the Church, which being espoused to Christ, as a virgin hath conceived us of the Holy Ghost, and as a virgin hath also given us birth.'[3] From hence the greatest glory and incomparable praise result to our Blessed Joseph, since—from his having been protector and guardian of Christ our Lord, the Spouse of the Church, and of the Blessed Mother of God, who is a type of the Church, as we have just said—this same S. Joseph was and is the protector and guardian of the Church, and kept the living Bread from heaven, not for himself, but for the whole world, as S. Bernard has said (*Hom. 2 super Missus est*)."[4]

The immediate mention that S. Paul here makes of Eve and her seduction to sin almost forces upon us the conviction that he had Mary distinctly—though it might be only implicitly—in view, in setting forth a Virgin, pure and chaste, espoused to One alone, and faithful to Him, as the exemplar to the Corinthians of their spiritual union with Christ, in opposition to Eve's infidelity. For this antithesis of Eve and

---

[1] *Serm.* 171, 2, 3.   [2] 1 *Cor.* iii. 6, 7.   S. Ambrose *L.* 2, *in Luc.*
[3] *Allegoriæ ex N. Test.*   [4] *Lib.* ii., *Tr.* 6.

Mary forms the very earliest tradition of the Fathers, and is so prominent in their writings of the century next to that of the Apostles, as, we might almost say, to be the one only doctrine with regard to the Blessed Virgin of that age now on record. It is the special theme of S. Justin, S. Irenaeus, and Tertullian. These Fathers insist on the point that Eve and Mary were alike virgins, when each took her part, the one in the Fall, the other in the Redemption of mankind : also, that both virgins were each alike espoused to one alone. They then contrast the infidelity of Eve with the faithfulness of Mary, and the opposite effects of life and death which thence resulted. From this we conclude that the doctrine of Mary the Second Eve forms an integral part of S. Paul's implicit teaching, as that of Jesus Christ the Second Adam does of his explicit exposition. We here remark that the description of Mary by the Evangelists as *an espoused Virgin*[1] forms, as though, a title peculiarly attaching to our Blessed Lady, of which no other instance is to be found in Holy Writ to suggest such thought to S. Paul's mind. Moreover, the figure that he gives of a chaste virgin espoused to a virginal husband well illustrates the marriage of the Blessed Virgin and S. Joseph. " Does it not seem," writes Père D'Argentan, "that the admirable words of the great Apostle S. Paul, *Despondi vos uni viro virginem castam exhibere Christo*, were expressly written to show the excellence of the marriage with S. Joseph ? See here a marriage indeed extraordinary, which is made only to consecrate virginity. You are married to a man, but it is not for the man who espouses you, but it is for God in Whose name he is espoused to you."[2]

[1] *Matt.* i. 18. *Luke* i. 27, ii. 5.
[2] *Conferences sur la S. V. Marie.* ix. p. 280.

THE EPISTLE OF S. PAUL

TO THE

GALATIANS.

CHAPTER I.

15 But when it pleased him, who separated me from my mother's womb, and called me by his grace,
16 To reveal his Son in me, that I might preach him among the Gentiles, immediately I condescended not to flesh and blood.

What was S. Paul's predestination and call by grace compared with Mary's, who, conceived immaculate, was full of grace from her Mother's womb? How far more excellently was the Eternal Son of God revealed in Mary! Not that she might preach Him, but that, as the fruit of her womb, He might be made of her, be suckled, nourished, guarded, educated, offered up in sacrifice by her. Mary *condescended not to flesh and blood.* From tenderest years she gave herself entirely to God, forgetting her kindred, and her parents' home. She condescended not to natural affection, even for her Jesus, foregoing much of His dear companionship during the three years of His public ministry: and at last on Calvary she sacrificed Him to death, as she allowed the sword of sorrow to pierce her Mother's heart for the salvation of sinners.

19 Saving James the brother of the Lord.

See what is said *supra*, 1 *Cor.* ix. 5.

24 And they glorified God in me.

Much more in our praises of Mary, may we glorify God in her.

CHAPTER II.

19 For I, through the law, am dead to the law, that I may live to God: with Christ I am nailed to the Cross.
20 And I live, now not I; but Christ liveth in me. And that I live now in the flesh: I live in the faith of the Son of God, who loved me, and delivered himself for me.

In a far higher sense than S. Paul, could Mary say: *With Christ I am nailed to the Cross*—that Mother who stood those three hours by the Cross whereon her own Son was hanging nailed, whilst their two hearts one sword was piercing. What else was her heart's language on Calvary, but, *With Christ I am nailed to the Cross?*——" By the King of Martyrs stood the Martyrs' Queen, wounded with her Son's wounds, crucified together with the Crucified, transfixed with the same sword of sorrow, so that better could she say than S. Paul *With Christ am I nailed to the Cross.*"[1]——What else her language during those long lingering years that followed, but, *I live, now not I*, etc.?——*Who loved me, and delivered Himself for me.* If the Apostle could thus, so to say, individualise to himself his Saviour's redeeming love, in a far higher sense could Mary do this, as being redeemed and loved in a more excellent way than the Apostle. Hence she exclaims: " *Exultavit spiritus meus in Deo salutari meo.*"

CHAPTER III.

1 Before whose eyes Jesus Christ hath been set forth, crucified among you.

If to have Jesus crucified vividly represented before their eyes were a great grace for the Galatians, and a motive and means of their loving obedience: had not Mary this and much more? *Stabant juxta crucem.*——" You," says S. Ambrose, "behold indeed a painful funeral. But holy Mary, too, stood close to the Cross of her Son, and the Virgin gazed at the passion of her only Child. I read of her standing, I read not of her weeping. Hence her Son said to her: 'Woman, behold thy son;' and to the disciple He said: 'Behold thy Mother,'[2] bequeathing to them the inheritance of His charity and grace."[3]

6 Abraham believed God, and it was reputed to him unto justice.
7 Know ye therefore, that they who are of faith, the same are the children of Abraham.

---

[1] *Summa Aurea, De Laud. B.M.V.* Tom. 4, p. 1337.
[2] *John* xix. 26, 27.   [3] *De obitu Valent. Consolatio*, 30.

8 And the Scripture foreseeing, that God justifieth the Gentiles by faith, told unto Abraham before: In thee shall all nations be blessed.
9 Therefore they that are of faith, shall be blessed with faithful Abraham.

See *supra*, *Rom.* iv. 3, 18. How much more in Mary, than in Abraham, are all these promises fulfilled. How much more blessed are we as children of Mary, than as children of Abraham. All the blessing that attaches to the seed and children of Abraham culminates in Mary [1]: and she appropriates it peculiarly to herself.[2] From her it is derived to her children.[3] The type has given place to the antitype. Now it is Mary's, rather than Abraham's, blessed seed. If we keep part in Mary's living faith, we shall be blessed with *faithful Mary*.

14 That the blessing of Abraham might come on the Gentiles through Jesus Christ: that we may receive the promise of the Spirit by faith.
16 To Abraham were the promises made, and to his seed. He saith not, And to his seeds, as of many: but as of one, And to thy seed, which is Christ.
18 For if the inheritance be of the law, it is no more of promise. But God gave it to Abraham by promise.
22 But the Scripture hath concluded all under sin, that the promise, by the faith of Jesus Christ, might be given to them that believe.
26 For you are all the children of God by faith, in Christ Jesus.
27 For as many of you as have been baptised in Christ, have put on Christ.
29 But if you be Christ's, then are you the seed of Abraham, heirs according to the promise.

To Mary, may we say, the promises were fulfilled, and to her own Son Jesus Christ, *that the blessing of Mary might come upon all generations through Jesus Christ: that we might receive the promise of the Spirit by faith*, being baptised into Christ, and putting on Christ. Made thus one in Christ Jesus, and being Christ's, we are all the children of Mary, His Mother and ours, and *heirs according to the promise:* "He that believeth, and is baptised, shall be saved."[4]

---

[1] *Luke* i. 28, 42; xi. 27, 28. *Ps.* lxxxiv. 1.   [2] *Luke* i. 48.
[3] *Ib.* v. 50, 54, 55.   [4] *Mark* xvi. 16.

CHAPTER IV.

1 Now I say: as long as the heir is a child, he differeth nothing from a servant, though he be lord of all:
2 But is under tutors and governors until the time appointed by the father.

"Not only was Joseph the nurturer of Christ," writes Morales, "but also His most apt tutor, governor, and protector: since His tender age required many services, which a mother by herself cannot conveniently render. Hence well said Augustine (*in Luc.* i.): 'The Virgin was espoused, that Joseph might himself take care of the Infant, whether in going to Egypt, or returning thence.' Joseph, therefore, was in truth Christ's tutor, according to the words of S. Paul: *As long as the heir . . . by the father.*" [1]

On the same text S. Thomas says: "Christ was even as a servant, because, though Lord of all,[2] He seemed to differ nothing in outward things from a servant, and, so far as man, He debased Himself, taking the form of a servant, and was in habit found as a man.[3] Hence, indeed, it is no wonder that He should render humble obedience to Joseph, since He came to serve."[4] At this thought Gerson exclaims: "Oh, utterly marvellous sublimity is thine, O Joseph! O incomparable dignity, that the Mother of God, the Queen of heaven, and Mistress of the world should think to call thee a no unworthy lord! I know not, in truth, which here is the more wonderful, Mary's humility, or Joseph's sublimity: although incomparably surpasses both, their Child Jesus, Blessed for ever, of whom is written: *Et erat subditus illis.* Subject to a creature is He who made the morning light and the sun.[5] Subject to a weaving woman is He to whom bows every knee of those that are in heaven, on earth, and under the earth."[6]

---

[1] L. ii. tr. 1. [2] *Ps.* cix. 1. [3] *Philip.* ii. 7.
[4] *Is.* xliii. 10. *Mark* x. 45. [5] *Ps.* lxxiii. 16.
[6] *Philip.* ii. 10. *Serm. de Nativ. Virg. Consid.* 3. ap. Morales l. tr. 6.

"According to *the form of a servant*,[1] the Child Jesus was even less than His parents."[2]

4 But when the fulness of the time was come, God sent his Son, made of a woman, made under the law:
5 That he might redeem them who were under the law: that we might receive the adoption of sons.
6 And because you are sons, God hath sent the Spirit of his Son into your hearts, crying: Abba, Father.
7 Therefore now he is not a servant, but a son. And if a son, an heir also through God.

This is the one only passage in all the Epistles wherein the person of the Blessed Virgin Mary is explicitly mentioned: *Made of a woman.* God, says the Apostle, sent His Only-begotten co-equal Son, made of the substance of the Blessed Virgin man, one of ourselves, under the Law, to redeem us from servitude to true liberty, that we might become sons of God by adoption; and that, through the Spirit of His Son in our hearts, being now the brethren of Jesus Christ, we might be able to call God our Father. Being sons, we are heirs, joint-heirs with Jesus Christ our elder Brother, of God's kingdom of glory. All that is Christ's, is now ours. Not only is His Father ours, but also His Mother. Consequently that same Spirit of His Son, which enables us *to cry, Abba, Father,* prompts us to call Mary His Mother, our Mother. And as God the Father of our Lord Jesus Christ, has through Him adopted us, and treats us as His children; so the Blessed Virgin Mary the Mother of our Lord Jesus Christ, through Him, by that same Divine Spirit Who came upon her and overshadowed her, and on account of the dying bequest of Jesus Christ her Son, is our true and most loving Mother, would have us cherish her as our Mother, and treats us as her own most dear children.

"Mary," says S. Augustine, "is called a woman, not from any detriment to virginity, but according to the manner of speaking proper to her country. Hence, the Apostle, in saying that our Lord Jesus Christ was *made of a woman,* does not break in upon the order and texture of our faith,

---

[1] *Phil.* II. 7.   [2] S. August. *Contr. Maximin.* c. 18.

whereby we confess Him to be born of the Holy Ghost and the Virgin Mary. For virgin she conceived, virgin brought forth, and virgin remained. But they called all females women, according to the Hebrew idiom. Of this we have an evident example in Eve, whom God made by taking her from the side of Adam, who was called woman whilst still a virgin, and before, with her husband, she went forth from paradise."[1]

"We read of Eve, that she was made from man," remarks Estius, "because she was made and formed from his substance. So the Son of God was made from a woman, because He received flesh of a woman's substance. And as Eve was from man alone, so Christ was from woman alone. Adam was not, however, father of Eve, as Mary is Mother of Christ, for Eve was not made from man by way of generation and birth, as Christ from woman. Still, even so, the Apostle preferred to say *made of a woman*, rather than born of a woman, as some have supposed should be read."[2]

The Angelic Doctor further explains this distinction between *made* and *born*, showing how certain ancient heresies against the Incarnation are confuted, and the truth of the mystery is clearly established by the language of the Apostle. We give the words of S. Thomas, and also some of Cardinal Cajetan, as follows: Per hoc quod dicitur *ex muliere* factus, destruuntur duo errores, scilicet Valentini dicentis Christum non sumpsisse corpus de Virgine, sed attulisse illud de cœlo, et per Beatam Virginem, sicut per fistulam, seu canale transivisse. Sed hoc est falsum, quia si verum esset quod dicit; non fuisset factus *ex muliere*, ut Apostolus dicit; hæc enim præpositio *ex*, causam materialem designat. Item error Nestorii dicentis Beatam Virginem non esse Matrem Filii Dei, sed filii hominis; quod falsum esse ostenditur, per hoc quod dicit Apostolus hic, quod *misit Deus Filium suum factum ex muliere*; qui enim fit ex muliere, est filius ejus.

---

[1] *Gen.* ii. 22, 23; iii. 12, 13, 15, 16, 24; iv. 1—*Serm.* li. c. 11.
[2] *In loc.*

Si ergo Filius Dei est factus *ex muliere*, scilicet ex Beata Virgine, manifestum est, quod Beata Virgo est Mater Filii Dei. Licet autem posset dici natus ex muliere, signanter autem dicit *factum* et non natum. Nasci enim aliquid, est ipsum produci solum ex principio conjuncto ; sed fieri est produci ex principio separato ; area enim fit ab artifice, sed fructus nascitur ex arbore. Principium autem humanae generationis est duplex, scilicet materiale, et quantum ad hoc Christus processit ex principio conjuncto, quia materiam sui corporis sumpsit ex Virgine, unde secundum hoc dicitur, nasci de ea (*Matt.* i. 16) : *De qua natus est Jesus.* Aliud est principium activum, quod quidem in Christo quantum ad id quod principium habuit, id est quantum ad formationem corporis, non fuit conjunctum, sed separatum ; quia virtus Spiritus Sancti formavit illud, et quantum ad hoc, non dicitur, *natus ex muliere*, sed *factus*, quasi ex principio exteriori ; ex quo patet, quod hoc, quod dicit : *Ex muliere*, non dicit corruptionem, quia dixisset natum, et non factum."[1]——And Cardinal Cajetan : " Plus explicavit dicendo, *Factum ex muliere*, quam factum in carne : quoniam non solum carneam naturam ex muliere sumptam, sed etiam sine virili semine significat dicendo : *Factum ex muliere.* Quod enim ex muliere, virili semine formatur, non proprie *factum*, sed natum dicitur, ad significandum, quod ex muliere virgine, ex muliere sola factus est, et ad significandum, quod non est factus in carne quemadmodum Adam, sed ex muliere."[2]

19 My little children, of whom I am in labour again, until Christ be formed in you.
20 And I would willingly be present with you now.

Who was that ideal mother present to the mind of the Apostle ; that mother in, and of whom, Christ was really formed, and who first brought Him forth ; that mother to whom S. Paul would here liken himself ? What mother,

---
[1] S. Thomas, *Comment. in loc.*
[2] Ap. *Sum. Aur. De Laud. B.M.V.* tom. ii. p. 1254.

too, would recur to the thoughts of the Galatian converts as the antitype whence this figurative language of the Apostle was borrowed? Was it only some mother in general, or was there no mother in particular, who had a great part in Christ and His religion? We should here remember that the Galatians were recent converts, and the chief lessons they had been taught would be the historical facts of the Gospel, but above all that of the Incarnation. Who then could be that mother but Mary, "of whom was born Jesus"? Mary, whom that same Jesus when dying had given from His Cross to be our spiritual Mother, Mary who at the foot of the Cross, travailed in pangs of sorrow for us, as she gave her Jesus up to death, that thus He might be the Life of our souls; Mary, who still wearies not *until Christ be formed in us*. O how much more truly might she use the language of the Apostle, *My little children* . . . in her loving desire for our conversion and sanctification. Still in heaven is she mindful of us, *and willingly would she be present with us now*, and is indeed present with us by her ever-anxious care, and powerful intercession with her Son, whilst we are exiles mourning and weeping in this vale of tears. Does not S. Paul speak as though Mary was in his thoughts? As though he would fain put on the tender love of that Mother for his children? As though, too, he was setting her forth for their imitation, as their model, and wishing them to strive that Jesus Christ might be formed in their hearts, through that same Holy Spirit, Who formed Him in her, really and corporally as her Son, as well as spiritually in her soul by grace?

22 For it is written that Abraham had two sons: the one by a bond-woman, and the other by a free-woman.

23 But he who was of the bond-woman, was born according to the flesh: but he of the free-woman, was by promise.

24 Which things are said by an allegory. For these are the two testaments. The one from mount Sina, engendering unto bondage; which is Agar:

25 For Sina is a mountain in Arabia, which hath affinity to that Jerusalem which now is, and is in bondage with her children.

26 But that Jerusalem, which is above, is free: which is our mother.

27 For it is written: Rejoice, thou barren, that bearest not: break forth and cry, thou that travailest not: for many are the children of the desolate, more than of her that hath a husband.

28 Now we, brethren, as Isaac was, are the children of promise.

29 But as then he, that was born according to the flesh, persecuted him that was after the spirit: so also it is now.

30 But what saith the scripture? Cast out the bond-woman and her son; for the son of the bond-woman shall not be heir with the son of the free-woman.

31 So then, brethren, we are not the children of the bond-woman, but of the free: by the freedom wherewith Christ has made us free.

Which things are said by an allegory. May they not be well applied, in a really true mystical sense, to the Blessed Virgin Mary? Is she not the true, the heavenly Jerusalem?[1] Is she not free? Was she ever a bondswoman to Satan? Is she not that Jerusalem which is our Mother? Is she not indeed our Mother? Are we not her children? Was it not of this Virgin Mother that the Prophet sang: *Rejoice thou barren* etc.?[2] Was it Sara, was it Isaac, in whom the Promise was fulfilled? Which, then, was the real promise, "Sara shall have a son,"[3] or Mary shall have a Son? Was not the former but the type of the latter? This thought caused S. Ambrose to exclaim: "Come then, O Lord, and seek Thy sheep, not now by servants, not by mercenaries, but by Thine own self. Do thou in flesh which in Adam fell, receive me. Receive me not from Sara, but from Mary: that it may be a Virgin incorrupt, a Virgin by grace intact, and free from all stain of sin."[4]

Was the persecution here alluded to of Isaac by Ishmael anything but a figure of the enmities between the Serpent and the Woman, and between the Serpent's seed and that of Mary? Is not this the distinguishing note, that is being fulfilled every day, of the generations of the faithful, and of the seed of error, devotion to, or aversion from, the Blessed Virgin Mary? She herself foretold it: *Ecce enim* . . . Mark it well—Henceforth all the generations of God's faithful

---

[1] *Ps.* lxxxvi., cxxi.   [2] *Isa.* liv. 1.   [3] *Rom.* ix. 8.

[4] *In Ps.* cxviii. n. 30 v. 176.

children, the children of the free-woman, my children, shall bless and praise me. *So then, brethren, we are not the children of the bond-woman, but of the free: by the freedom wherewith Christ hath made us free. Which things are said by an allegory.*

"With rival words," writes S. Ephrem, "did Mary wax hot, yea she lulled Him, saying, Who hath given *me, the barren,* that I should conceive and bring forth this One, that is manifold, a little One, that is great; for that He is wholly with me, and wholly everywhere? The day that Gabriel came in unto my low estate, *he made me free instead of a handmaid,* of a sudden: for I was the handmaid of Thy Divine Nature, and am also the Mother of Thy human nature, O Lord and Son! Of a sudden the handmaid became the King's daughter in Thee, Thou Son of the King. Lo, the meanest in the house of David by reason of Thee, Thou Son of David, lo, a daughter of earth hath attained unto heaven by the Heavenly One!"[1]

"The free-woman, my Son, is Thy handmaid."[2]

CHAPTER V.

13 By charity of the Spirit serve one another.

What an example of humble charity did the Mother of God show forth, when filled with the charity of the Spirit, she hasted to visit Elizabeth, and abode serving and ministering to her for three months.

22 But the fruit of the Spirit is, charity, joy, peace, patience, benignity, goodness, longanimity,
23 Mildness, faith, modesty, continency, chastity. Against such there is no law.
24 And they that are Christ's, have crucified their flesh, with the vices and concupiscences.
25 If we live in the Spirit, let us also walk in the Spirit.

Here we have Mary's portrait drawn with her beautiful characteristic features. What was said above at 2 *Cor.* iv. 6, 10, is applicable here also.

---

[1] *Rhythm* iv. *on the Nativity. Opp. Syr.*, Morris, p. 28.   [2] *Id. R.* xii. p. 54.

CHAPTER VI.

2 Bear ye one another's burdens: and so you shall fulfil the law of Christ.

Christ bore our burdens, as He carried His Cross: and Mary helped Him by her sympathy and dolours.

8 For what things a man shall sow, those also shall he reap. . . . He that soweth in the spirit of the Spirit shall reap life everlasting.

Mary sowed blessings to the world, what wonder then that she has reaped the blessing of the world? "The soul that blesseth shall be made fat: and he that inebriateth, shall be inebriated also himself."[1] Mary's whole life from beginning to end was all *in the Spirit:* what then must be the harvest of glory she has gathered in life everlasting?

14 God forbid that I should glory, save on the Cross of our Lord Jesus Christ, by whom the world is crucified to me, and I to the world.
17 I bear the marks of the Lord Jesus in my body.

Who could use this language in any way comparably with Mary, the Mother of the Crucified?

THE EPISTLE OF S. PAUL
TO THE
EPHESIANS.

CHAPTER I.

3 Blessed be the God and Father of our Lord Jesus Christ, who hath blessed us with spiritual blessings in heavenly places, in Christ:
4 As he chose us in him before the foundation of the world, that we should be holy and unspotted in his sight in charity.
5 Who hath predestinated us unto the adoption of children through Jesus Christ unto himself: according to the purpose of his will.

---

[1] *Prov.* xi. 25. See 2 *Cor.* ix. 6, *supra.*

6 Unto the praise of the glory of his grace, in which he hath graced us in his beloved Son.
7 In whom we have redemption through his blood, the remission of sins according to the riches of his grace,
8 Which hath superabounded in us in all wisdom and prudence,
9 That he might make known unto us the mystery of his will, according to his good pleasure, which he hath purposed in him,
10 In the dispensation of the fulness of times, to re-establish all things in Christ, that are in heaven and on earth, in him.
11 In whom we also are called by lot, being predestinated according to the purpose of him who worketh all things according to the counsel of his will.
12 That we may be unto the praise of his glory, we who before hoped in Christ.

How sublime is the Apostle's description of the grace and purpose of God in his regard ! But were Mary to tell forth the great things which He Who is Mighty had done for her, what words would be adequate ? He blessed her with all spiritual blessings above all the heavenly choirs. He chose her before the foundation of the world to be holy and immaculate, from the first moment of her existence, in His sight, in charity ; predestined, as she was, to be His most beloved daughter, through Jesus Christ, according to His blessed Will, that in her His grace, wherewith He graced and made her full, might be praised and glorified through Jesus Christ His Only-begotten Son, of whom she was to be Mother, and by whom she received redemption through His Blood, in the most excellent manner, even the preservation from all stain of sin, original and actual, by an excess of richest grace, which superabounded in her in sublimest wisdom and prudence. So that He accomplished by her the greatest mystery of His Will, the Incarnation of the Divine Word, as He had in the good pleasure of His eternal decrees purposed to do, when the fulness of time should come : viz., to send His Son, made of a woman, that He might by His Incarnate Word redeem mankind, and thus re-establish all things on earth, and in heaven also ; by filling up with the redeemed of men, those thrones which the rebel angels had forfeited. Through whose infinite merits Mary was chosen too to such an excellent dignity, and to take in this mystery so sublime a part ; being graciously elected thereto from eternity, according to the Divine Will which knows how to accomplish in all things its counsel, and to bring all to shew forth His own praise and glory.

17 That the God of our Lord Jesus Christ, the Father of glory, may give unto you the spirit of wisdom and of revelation, in the knowledge of him :
18 The eyes of your heart enlightened, that you may know what the hope is of his calling, and what are the riches of the glory of his inheritance in the saints.

S. Paul not only preached in order to enlighten, as he says in this same epistle ;[1] but he prayed God to enlighten. It requires to have *the eyes of the heart* opened and enlightened, in order to understand what is the present work of grace, and future hope of glory, even in the least of the saints. Who then even among the saints can know what grace and glory have done for Mary ? If the saintly Doctors tell us marvellous things of her, we must remember that the eyes of their hearts were enlightened, while ours are very dim.——But what *spirit of wisdom* must the Father of glory have given to her in the knowledge of Himself and His Divine Son. S. Paul tells the Ephesians that from the few words he had written they might judge of *his knowledge in the mystery of Christ.*[2] So from the Magnificat we can form some little conception of Mary's gift of wisdom. Yet those words were uttered before her Son's birth. Now we are told with what attention she pondered over every circumstance regarding Him ;[3] with what attention, then, must she have listened to all His words, and studied all His acts while He lived with her. It pleases God to reveal His mysteries to little ones.[4] Who so little as Mary in the true sense ? "No man knoweth the Son, but the Father, neither doth anyone know the Father, but the Son, and he to whom the Son will reveal Him."[5] Did it not please Jesus to reveal His Father to His Mother ? And did not the Father reveal the Son to the Mother ? If He revealed Him to S. Peter, how much more to Mary.

[1] iii. 8, 9.   [2] iii. 3, 4.   [3] *Luke* ii. 19, 51.   [4] *Matt.* xi. 25, 26.
[5] *Ib.* 27.

19 And what is the exceeding greatness of his power to us, who believe according to the operation of the might of his power.

20 Which he wrought in Christ, raising him up from the dead, and setting him on his right hand in the heavenly places.

21 Above all principality, and power, and virtue, and dominion, and every name that is named, not only in this world, but also in that which is to come.

22 And he hath subjected all things under his feet, and hath made him head over all the church,

23 Which is his body, and the fulness of him who is filled all in all.

In enumerating the magnificent titles of the Angelic Choirs, and thus glorifying them, S. Paul enhances, and sets off the super-eminent dignity and glory of the Man, Christ Jesus, over all of which He is placed. Surely, in thus glorifying the pre-eminent dignity and excellence of Mary's Son, the Apostle indirectly and implicitly enhances the dignity and glory of the Mother, from whom He derives that nature so exalted, and through whom He is in fact what He is, viz., Jesus Christ, the God-man, constituted King of Angels and Saints. Is it conceivable that she, His Mother, should be set lower than His servants and ministering spirits—she, to whom "the Father of the world to come" made Himself on earth subject? No.—*Sedes tua Deus, in sæculum sæculi. Dixit Dominus Domino meo, sede a dextris meis.* Such is Thy glorious throne, O Word Incarnate: and where shall that of Thy royal Mother be? David again shall speak. *Astitit Regina a dextris tuis.* The more, therefore, the Apostle glorifies the Angelic Choirs, the more does he enhance the glory of the Mother of God, which is above theirs.

CHAPTER II.

18 For by him we have access both in one Spirit to the Father.

19 Now therefore you are no more strangers and foreigners: but you are fellow-citizens with the saints, and the domestics of God.

20 Built upon the foundation of the apostles and prophets, Jesus Christ himself being the chief corner-stone:

21 In whom all the building being framed together, groweth up into an holy temple in the Lord.

22 In whom you also are built together into an habitation of God in the Spirit.

The Apostle says that if we are in communion with God, the ever-Blessed Trinity—*by* the Son, *in* the Spirit, *to* the Father—we have then full communion with God's Saints; we belong to the same city, the same household; we form with the Saints one temple built of living stones in which God Himself dwells. How wondrously did He dwell in Mary, first in her soul, then in her body; and by her He became the chief corner-stone, uniting all nations. No wonder, all nations and all generations call her blessed. For is it not to her co-operation in the Incarnation, and to her prayers on earth and in heaven, we owe it, that we are no longer strangers and foreigners to the Divine Family?

Built upon the foundation of the Apostles and Prophets. Mary is called by the Church Queen of Apostles, and Queen of Prophets. She was not one of the Apostles, who are represented by S. John as the twelve foundations of the heavenly Jerusalem.[1] But she was far more. She was the subject of Apostolic teaching. She was the Woman revealed to prophets, and she herself was the great prophetess, who sketched the outlines of her Son's Kingdom, and her own glory in it. She is also one of the principal agents of the Holy Ghost in building up the living walls of the temple of God. Oh! happy we to have part in such mysteries. "One same end, one same beatitude, one same joy, one same glory, one same kingdom with God Himself."[2] This is what we share with the Saints, and with Mary their Queen.

CHAPTER III.

1 For this cause, I Paul the prisoner of Jesus Christ, for you gentiles:
2 If yet you have heard of the dispensation of the grace of God, which is given me towards you:
3 How that according to revelation, the mystery has been made known to me, as I have written above in few words:
4 As you reading may understand my knowledge in the mystery of Christ.

---

[1] *Apoc.* xxi. 14.   [2] Tauler.

5 Which in other generations was not known to the sons of men, as it is now revealed to his holy apostles, and prophets in the Spirit.
12 In whom we have boldness and access with confidence by the faith of him.
13 Wherefore I pray you not to faint at my tribulations for you which is your glory.
14 For this cause I bow my knees to the Father of our Lord Jesus Christ,
15 Of whom all paternity in heaven and earth is named.
16 That he would grant you, according to the riches of his glory, to be strengthened by his Spirit with might unto the inward man.
17 That Christ may dwell by faith in your hearts : that being rooted and founded in charity,
18 You may be able to comprehend, with all the saints, what is the breadth, and length, and height, and depth.
19 To know also the charity of Christ, which surpasseth all knowledge, that you may be filled unto all the fulness of God.
20 Now to him who is able to do all things more abundantly than we desire or understand, according to the power that worketh in us :
21 To him be glory in the church, and in Christ Jesus, unto all generations world without end. Amen.

The more S. Paul magnifies the grace and excellence of his own apostleship, the more does he give grounds for magnifying far more exceedingly the grace and dignity of the Mother of God. For what part does an Apostle hold in the great Mystery of Christ comparable with that of Mary? She, the little humble handmaid of the Lord, was made His Mother by the fulness *of the grace of God which was given to her*, according to the power of the Highest Who came upon her, and the Mighty One who did great things unto her, so that she gave to the whole world God manifested in the flesh, and showed Him first to simple Jewish shepherds, and then to royal sages of the Gentiles with all His unsearchable riches, as an earnest that He should be manifested to all mankind, "the light of the Gentiles, and the glory of Israel". It was through Mary that for all eternity the manifold wisdom of God in this mystery of the Incarnation, should be made known to all the principalities and powers in heaven ; since she, the human Mother, is there the ever-living witness and testimony of its truth, the gage and the pledge that God her Son is ever and very Man—that "great mystery of godliness, which was manifested in the flesh, was justified in the Spirit, appeared unto Angels, hath been preached unto the Gentiles, is believed in the world, is taken up to glory."[1]

What was Mary's *knowledge in the Mystery of Christ? Illi solum datum est nosse,* says S. Bernard, *cui datum est experiri.* In the Annuntiation she had a full revelation of the Mystery. In the Virginal Conception an experimental knowledge. How was she *strengthened by the Spirit with might unto the inward man,* when that Spirit ineffably overshadowed her, *that Christ might dwell,* not merely *by faith in her heart* (though for that she was praised by the Holy Ghost Himself), but by the wondrous union of maternity. *The charity, in which she was rooted and founded,* was not merely that of a creature to its Creator, but that of a mother to a son. Yet it was a most supernatural charity, having God for its object, and the Holy Ghost for its author. God, *Who is able to do all things more abundantly than we can desire or understand,* Himself wrought these works of sanctification in Mary. Well, then, does she say, Fecit mihi magna *qui potens est,* et sanctum nomen ejus. More abundant are they than *we* could desire : but Mary had in its fulness the beatitude of the hungry : and *esurientes implevit bonis.* What creature, then, save the Blessed Virgin Mary, the Mother of Christ, the Incarnate Word, could be the ideal present to the Apostle's mind, as he wrote his burning words ?—Strengthened inwardly in all perfection, so far as a pure creature is capable thereof, by the Divine Spirit ; her heart united to Jesus Christ, and rooted in charity above all others ; comprehending beyond the other saints the intensity and extension of the exceeding love of Christ ; approaching, as far as the finite may, to the infinite fulness of God. "Our Lord and Saviour, Himself ever-Virgin, had a Virgin for His Mother. He offered in His own person an example of virginity to men, and in His Mother to women. Whereby is clearly shown, how in both sexes blessed purity merited to have *the fulness of the*

---

[1] 1 Tim. iii. 16.

Divinity, since all that there is in the Son was found in the Mother."[1]

In whom we have boldness. The Apostle, in order to encourage the Ephesian converts, reminds them of the freedom and confidence wherewith Christians might have access to Jesus Christ, through faith in Him; and entreats them by this consideration, not to lose heart on account of his own present tribulations. These sufferings, he tells them, he is enduring for their sakes, and that they are their glory. That is, the persecution of S. Paul ought to be a ground for their rejoicing and thanksgiving to God, that he, the Apostle of the Gentiles, was accounted worthy thus to suffer in their behalf for the Name of Jesus, and thereby to glorify God, and their holy faith. It was the Apostle's glory to suffer for Christ, and this his glory redounded on them.[2] His sufferings were their glory, too, as being an efficacious means of grace and glory to them, for whom he suffered. For his own part, the persecutions he endured for Christ so greatly strengthened his confidence, as to constrain him, with most earnest devotion and humble reverence, to beseech the Father of our Lord Jesus Christ, in Whose cause he suffered, to pour in abundance upon the Ephesian Christians the richest blessings of grace.

To make application of the foregoing to Mary, it is enough to suggest one or other thought which meditation will unfold. 1. What confident access[3] must His most holy Mother have to Jesus Christ her Son. 2. How great is our ground for hope, consolation, thanksgiving, and joy, in the thought of all Mary's dolours which she underwent on our account. How powerful and meritorious must these dolours render her intercession. How efficacious in obtaining mercy and grace for us. 3. What great glory must these dolours have given to God; suffered, as they were, in union with the Passion of Jesus Christ her Son to satisfy the Divine Majesty outraged by sin.

[1] *Int. opp.* Sulpic. Sever. *Ep.* 2.   [2] 1 *Pet.* ii. 19-21.
[3] *Rom.* v. 2.

What grateful compensation did Mary's perfect compassion render to our Saviour for all the indifference and ingratitude shewn to Him by men in His Sacred Passion. 4. How glorious are Mary's dolours for the Church of Jesus Christ and for His holy Name. 5. How fruitful in virtue, merit, and glory for herself. For since Jesus, " whereas, indeed, He was the Son of God, learned obedience by the things that He suffered;[1] so too Mary, His Mother, had to acquire virtue and perfection worthy of her sublime dignity and office, by means of suffering: and as it was by His sufferings He became for us before God a merciful High-priest and Saviour, so also through her dolours has Mary become for us our Mother of Mercy, and a Consoler of the afflicted, who can have compassion on our miseries, and is able to succour us in our temptations—a Mother to whom we may go at all times with confidence, beseeching her to obtain mercy, and grace to help us in seasonable aid.[2] In fine, as it behoved Christ to suffer and thus to enter into His glory,[3] so also did it behove Mary His Mother to earn by suffering her glorious crown.

Of whom all paternity, etc. God the Father has willed that all in heaven and earth should be brought into relationship with Himself, through our Lord Jesus Christ, His Only-begotten Son made man: and through Him the Eternal Father is the Father of all His adopted children. Equally true is it—though not in the same, but in another sense—that all these are brought also into relationship with Mary, the Mother of Jesus Christ, as her children. Through Him she has become the Mother of all in heaven and earth; that is, of all those who can claim the paternity of the Father of our Lord Jesus Christ. Hence in such secondary sense of Mary it may be said, *Of whom all maternity in heaven and earth is named.*[4]

---

[1] *Heb.* v. 8.   [2] *Ib.* ii. 17, 18; iv. 15, 16.   [3] *Luke* xxiv. 26.
[4] *Rom.* vii. 15, 16.   *Gal.* iv. 5, 6.   See *infra*, Note A, pp. 275-9.

CHAPTER IV.

7 But to every one of us is given grace, according to the measure of the giving of Christ.

8 Wherefore he saith : *Ascending on high he led captivity captive; he gave gifts to men.*

9 Now that he ascended, what is it but because he also descended first into the lower parts of the earth?

10 He that descended is the same also that ascended above all the heavens, that he might fill all things.

11 And he gave some apostles and some prophets, and other some evangelists, and other some pastors and doctors.

12 For the perfecting of the saints, for the work of the ministry, for the edifying of the body of Christ :

13 Until we all meet into the unity of faith, and of the knowledge of the Son of God, unto a perfect man, unto the measure of the age of the fulness of Christ.

As Christ *gave* to Mary, far, far above all others, viz., Himself to be her own true Son, so is *the measure of her grace* in proportion to the gift. And she is *full of grace.*——*He gave some apostles*, etc., but He gave Himself one only Mother. To His Church, too, He gave but one Mother, *for the perfecting of the saints, for the edifying of His body.* That as she nurtured His human body of flesh, watched over and brought Him up from infancy to childhood, and on to maturity ; so also might she care for His mystical body, and each individual member of the same, *until we all meet unto a perfect man, unto the measure of the age of the fulness of Christ.*

" *Now that He ascended,* etc., (v.v. 9, 10). That is, He who thus most profoundly humbled Himself was exalted to a height of dignity most sublime. This is also applicable, after our Lord Jesus Christ, to the Blessed Virgin Mary, who, above the nine choirs of Angels, herself alone fills with her majesty a tenth choir, which is as much more glorious than the others, as she is nearer to God, and receives a more perfect participation of the divinity."

CHAPTER V.

1 Be ye therefore followers of God, as most dear children :

2 And walk in love, as Christ also hath loved us, and hath delivered himself for us, an oblation and a sacrifice to God for an odour of sweetness.

---

[1] *Summ. Aur. de Laud. B.M.V.* tom. iv. p. 848

The perfection of a creature is to copy its Creator in things imitable. "Be ye perfect as your heavenly Father is perfect," said our Lord, and in so saying, He referred especially to His perfection in bounty and mercy, even to His enemies. The perfection of a Christian is to imitate Christ in the spirit of generosity and self-sacrifice. Most strikingly was this two-fold imitation exemplified in Mary. How perfect was our Blessed Queen, both as the *most dear Child* of the Eternal Father, and most dear Mother of the Son. What a dolorous *walk of love* was that of Mary from the Crib to the Cross—every step *a sacrifice*, every breath *an odour of sweetness* in union with the Sweetness of Jesus.

"The name of Mary," says S. Ambrose, "is as ointment poured forth. May that same ointment descend into the inmost depths and recesses of our souls, whereby holy Mary was redolent not of odours of (earthly) delights, but of the breathings of divine grace." [1]

8 For you were heretofore darkness, but now light in the Lord. Walk then as children of the light.

Our Blessed Lord contrasts the children of light and the children of the world; the former are the seed of the woman, the latter of the serpent. The children of Mary are the children of light.

18 Be ye filled with the Holy Spirit:
19 Speaking to yourselves in psalms, and hymns, and spiritual canticles, singing and making melody in your hearts to the Lord:
20 Giving thanks always for all things, in the name of our Lord Jesus Christ, to God and the Father.

Mary was the first to set an example in the New Testament of what the Apostle here recommends, by her Magnificat. She first gave thanks to God the Father through our Lord Jesus Christ.

When the Church wants to make sweet melody and to pour out thanksgiving to God, evening by evening she borrows the words of Mary: *Magnificat anima mea Dominum.*

---

[1] *De Inst. Virg.* c. 13.

"I will sing to Thee on a harp of ten strings," says the Psalmist: *In psalterio decachordo*.[1]

There are exactly ten chords touched by the hand of Mary in the Magnificat.
1. She magnifies the Lord—chord of adoration.
2. She rejoices in God—chord of joyful thanksgiving.
3. Thrill of humility—He hath regarded my lowliness.
4. Exultation in His greatness and holiness, as exhibited to herself.
5. Exultation in His mercy, as exhibited to others.
6. Exultation in His power, and justice.
7. Exultation in His grandeur, and condescension.
8. Exultation in His bounty, and severity.
9. Exultation in His special love.
10. Exultation in His everlasting fidelity to His promises.

22 Let women be subject to their husbands, as to the Lord:
23 Because the husband is the head of the wife, as Christ is head of the Church. He is the saviour of his body.
24 Therefore as the Church is subject to Christ, so also let the wives be to their husbands in all things.

What a beautiful example of conjugal obedience did the Blessed Virgin shew in her conduct towards S. Joseph, following in all things his guidance.[2] She had at the same time wonderful motives for this submission in the enlightenment and foreknowledge which she possessed with regard to the mysteries of the Church and of her Divine Son.

29 For no man ever hated his own flesh; but nourisheth it and cherisheth it, as also Christ doth the church:
30 Because we are members of his body, of his flesh, and of his bones.
31 *For this cause shall a man leave his father and mother, and shall cleave to his wife, and they shall be two in one flesh.*
32 This is a great sacrament; but I speak in Christ and in the church.

---
[1] *Ps*. cxliii. 10.
[2] See *Luke* ii. 5, 16, 39, 41-44, 51—*Matt*. ii. 14, 21, 23. Also S. Augustine's words quoted *supra*, 1 *Cor*. xi. 3.

No man hates his own flesh. Even if he denies, and chastises it, it is from enlightened love. "He that loseth his life for My sake shall find it."[1] But Mary must have loved her own flesh in Him who was "made of a woman," far better than in herself: since in Him that flesh was deified, in her it could only be glorified, though with unutterable glory. Mary consented to see this Flesh scourged, pierced with nails, and quivering with pain, because she believed "in the operation of the might of His power, which He (would work) in Christ, raising Him up from the dead, and setting Him at His right hand in the heavenly places above all principality and power and virtue and dominion, and every named that is named."[2] So Christ loves His Church, nourishes and cherishes it, even as our Lady fed the Divine Child at her breast, yet giving over its most precious members to every kind of martyrdom; but numbering each hair of their head for eternal glory. And though He cherished most of all His blessed Mother, He made her the Queen of Martyrs.

We are members of His body, of His flesh, and of His bones. How much more she! He was of her body, of her flesh, and of her bones. *We are members of His body.* How then must Mary cherish us for His sake in Him. *We are members of His body.* How ought we then to cherish her, His Mother and ours. Is she not indeed our Mother, if we are His members?

This great sacrament in Christ and in the Church: the mystery of the Incarnation, or the hypostatic union of the Word with human nature, is the model of the Sacrament of Matrimony, or the Christian union of man and wife. This mystery was accomplished in the womb of the Blessed Virgin Mary. It was shadowed forth in the virginal marriage of Joseph and Mary, wherein were found the greatest goods of marriage, *proles, fides, sacramentum,* as says S. Augustine. This mystery is the model, after which, was formed the union between Christ and His Church.

"From Mary," writes S. Epiphanius, "is taken that Scrip-

---

[1] *Matt.* x. 39. [2] *Ephes.* i. 19-21.

ture, which is applicable also to the Church: *For this cause . . . one flesh:* whereon the holy Apostle says: *This is a great sacrament: but I speak as to Christ and the Church.* And observe, the accuracy of the Scriptures. For of Adam it is said that God formed him; but of Eve it is not said she was formed, but was 'built.' Since we read that God took one of Adam's ribs, and built it for him into a woman; thus to show, that when the Lord had formed again a body for Himself from Mary, it was from the rib from her the Church was built, in the piercing of His side, and that the mysteries of the Blood and Water were made baths for us."[1]

"Let us now bring forward that celebrated passage of the Apostle," says S. Ambrose, "where is written: *For this cause . . . in Christ and in the Church.* We remark, then, that by a woman has this heavenly mystery of the Church been fulfilled, in her grace been figured forth, for whose sake Christ came down, and completed that eternal work of human redemption. Hence, too, Adam called the name of his wife *Life*,[2] for it is by means of woman that the series and propagation of the human race is diffused through the world, and by means of the Church that eternal life is bestowed."[3]

CHAPTER VI.

1 Children, obey your parents in the Lord, for this is just.

In the Lord, that is, conformably to the precept and also to the example of Jesus Christ, Who obeyed His parents.[4] *This is just*: Mary then received as her due, as a matter of justice, the obedience and honour of her Son.[4]

"The Lord Jesus was subject to His parents," says S. Jerome, "He honoured His Mother, whose Father He Himself was. He reverenced His nursing father, whom He had nourished, and remembered that He had been Himself carried in the womb of another, and borne in another's arms. For this cause also when hanging on the Cross, He commends to the

---

[1] *Hæres.* 78. n. 20.   [2] *Gen.* ii. 23.   [3] *De Instit. Virg.* iii. 24.
[4] *Luke* ii. 51.

disciples that parent, whom before the time of His Cross, He had never given up."[1]

17 And take unto you the helmet of salvation, and the sword of the Spirit (which is the word of God).

18 By all prayer and supplication praying at all times in the spirit; and in the same watching with all instance and supplication for all the saints:

19 And for me . . .

"It is of this *sword of the Spirit*," says S. Antoninus, "that S. Ambrose seems to explain the words: 'And thy own soul a sword shall pierce.'[2] 'Simeon,' says the holy Doctor, 'shows here that Mary's prudence was not ignorant of the mystery.' The sword of the word of God therefore pierced through the intellectual soul of Mary, since she understood the word spoken by Simeon, viz., that her Son was set for the ruin of the Jewish people, and for the resurrection of the Gentiles who should be converted to the Faith: and for a sign which should be contradicted by many in regard to the truth of the mystery of the Incarnation—to wit, by Pagans, Jews, and heretics, and through the evil lives of many bad Christians. All the mysteries of Christ, of His birth, life, passion, and resurrection were, in fact, foretold and figured forth by the prophets; so that when the Blessed Virgin Mary read and heard the Scriptures, and saw the several mysteries successively accomplished, *the sword of the word of God* pierced through her intellectual soul by reason of the acute and perfect understanding which she had of them."[3]

—— If the prayers of Christians are of so much avail, what efficacy must the prayers of the Divine Mother possess: and if the duty of continual mutual intercession is incumbent on all, how must Mary have practised it when she was on earth, and still maintain its exercise in heaven.

24 Grace be with all them that love our Lord Jesus Christ in incorruption. Amen.

In incorruption, that is, with a pure and perfect love. Who thus *loved our Lord Jesus Christ* as Mary, and who so *full of grace*?

[1] *Ep.* 117, n. 2.   [2] *Luke* ii. 35.   [3] *P.* iv. *T.* 15 c. 36 § 2.

THE EPISTLE OF S. PAUL

TO THE

PHILIPPIANS.

CHAPTER I.

3 I give thanks to my God in every remembrance of you,
4 Always in all my prayers making supplication for you all, with joy.
5 For your communication in the gospel of Christ from the first day until now.
6 Being confident of this very thing, that he, who hath begun a good work in you, will perfect it unto the day of Christ Jesus.
7 As it is meet for me to think this for you all, for that I have you in my heart; and that in my bands, and in the defence and confirmation of the gospel, you all are partakers of my joy.
8 For God is my witness, how I long after you all in the bowels of Jesus Christ.
9 And this I pray, that your charity may more and more abound in knowledge, and in all understanding :
10 That you may approve the better things, that you may be sincere and without offence unto the day of Christ,
11 Filled with the fruit of justice, through Jesus Christ, unto the glory and praise of God.

1. Note how we should thank God, whenever we remember our Blessed Lady, for her communication of the Gospel of Christ from the first day of her Immaculate Conception until now.—2. Note S. Paul's confidence that, as far as God was concerned, the end would correspond with the beginning. Such is exactly the Church's confidence that He who began a good work in Mary by her Immaculate Conception, perfected it until the day of her Assumption and Coronation. " For His wisdom reacheth from end to end mightily, and ordereth all things sweetly."[1] As was the greatness of Mary's commencement, so must be her progress, and the greatness of the glory perfected in her end.—3. Note why S. Paul prays for the Philippians. Not because he doubts of God's love for them, but because he is confident of it; not to communicate to God, as it were, the love which he feels for

[1] *Wisd.* viii. 1.

his fellow-men, but on the contrary, because God has communicated to him some of the love which burns in His Sacred Heart for the men He has created and redeemed. S. Paul *has them in his heart,* because he longs after them in the Heart of Jesus Christ. Christ lives in him, therefore Christ loves in him, and Christ teaches him to pray for those whom he loves, and Christ hears his prayers, and so perfects the work He has begun. If therefore the Philippians, knowing all this, had asked S. Paul's prayers, it would not have been from any distrust of God, but rather from their very confidence and love. How much more than S. Paul must Mary love us in the bowels, that is, in the Heart of Jesus Christ. Could she have fire in her bosom—*Beata riscera,* etc.—and not burn?

"To whom," writes a devout author, "will the children of misery have recourse, if the Mother of Mercy rejects them? For this Mother desires for us all good things, as a mother for her children. And hence she too seems to say to all Christians: *God is my witness, how I long after you all in the bowels of Jesus Christ my Son.* For this Mother does not disdain sinners, any more than a good mother does her child that is covered with sores; because for the sake of sinners it is, that she sees herself made the Mother of Mercy: for where there is no misery, mercy has no place." [1]

And this I pray, etc. (v.v. 9-11). If in Mary was actually realised all that the Apostle here supplicates for the Philippians—as with grateful joy we love to acknowledge—surely then, our praise of her redounds *unto the glory and praise of God.*

19 For I know that this shall fall out to me unto salvation, through your prayer, and the supply of the Spirit of Jesus Christ,
20 According to my expectation and hope; that in nothing I shall be confounded, but with all confidence, as always, so now also shall Christ be magnified in my body, whether it be by life or by death.
21 For to me, to live is Christ: and to die is gain.
22 And if to live in the flesh, this is to me the fruit of labour, and what I shall choose I know not.

[1] Daniel Agricola. *Corona duodecim Stellarum.*

23 But I am straitened between two: having a desire to be dissolved and to be with Christ, a thing by far the better.
24 But to abide still in the flesh, is needful for you.

vv. 19, 20. What assured confidence, then, should we not have in Mary's prayer. If *Christ was magnified in S. Paul's body*, much more was He magnified in Mary's body—from which He took His own—during her life on earth; and will be magnified therein for all eternity, now that she is assumed into heaven.——v. 21. Who could say these words like Mary?——vv. 22-24. Such would have been the language of Mary, but in a far deeper sense than the Apostle could use it, during those years after the Ascension that her life on earth was prolonged.

"In the Virgin's heart two loves and two sorrows were in conflict. The two loves were the love of her Son, and the love of mankind. The love of her Son was unwilling that Christ should suffer. The love of mankind willed that He should suffer. And this love of mankind overcame the love of her Son. In like manner two sorrows were in conflict, viz., the sorrow which Mary would have for our perdition, and the sorrow she would have on account of the death of her Son, and the former sorrow overcame the latter. Hence she was able to say with the Apostle: *To me to live is Christ, and to die is gain.* As though she said: The life of my Son is the life of my heart, but His death is the gain of mankind."[1]

29 For unto you it is given for Christ, not only to believe in him, but also to suffer for him.

If these be choice graces, who received them as Mary?

CHAPTER II.

1 If there be therefore any consolation in Christ, if any comfort of charity, if any society of the spirit, if any bowels of commiseration.

S. Paul is touching the hearts of his disciples by recalling the consolations of the faith. Catholic experience will tell how much these are bound up with devotion to Mary, and all that relates to her.

---

[1] B. Jacobus de Voragine. *Serm. 2. Sabbat. Sanct.*

5 For let this mind be in you, which was also in Christ Jesus:
6 Who being in the form of God, thought it not robbery to be equal with God:
7 But emptied himself, taking the form of a servant, being made in the likeness of men, and in habit found as a man.
8 He humbled himself, becoming obedient unto death, even to the death of the cross.
9 For which cause God also hath exalted him, and hath given him a name that is above every name:
10 That in the name of Jesus every knee should bow, of those that are in heaven, on earth, and in hell;
11 And that every tongue should confess that the Lord Jesus Christ is in the glory of God the Father.

The Incarnation was the school of humility, who then profited in it like Mary who kept that school, so to say? But the Incarnation itself, that is, the taking the form of a servant by Him who was in the form of God, only took place, when she who was saluted as Mother of God, took the title of handmaid. None ever had *this mind which was in Christ Jesus* as Mary. No one, as she, was made to be so like to Him in His humility and in His glory. We might say that Mary, though the true Mother of God, also emptied herself, taking the title and form of a servant, appearing as though she were but one amongst other ordinary women, humbling herself, and humbled by her Son:[1] associating herself with all the humiliations and shame of Jesus Christ her Son, unto His death, even His death of the ignominious Cross. So, indeed, was she humbled: but as much in turn exalted by God and by His Church:[2] and her name, next to that of her Divine Son, is held in honour above every other Name, revered in the mouth of men and Angels.[3] And after the Lord Jesus Christ, the Blessed Virgin Mary, the Mother of God, is confessed by all to *be in the glory of God the Father.*

"Jesus Christ," says S. Antoninus, "began this humiliation in the womb of His Mother, since in the first instant of His formation, He was found less than all infants. Let man, says S. Augustine, blush to become proud, when his Lord has

---

[1] *Luke* i. 31, 32, 35, 43; 38, 48, 56; ii. 22; 49; xii. 46-50; *John* ii. 4.
[2] *Luke* i. 48. *Apoc.* xii. 1.   [3] *Luke* i. 30.

become humiliated.—A like Mother, too, did He choose in the Blessed Virgin, whom He knew to be of all creatures the most humble, and whose humility drew Him down from heaven."[1]

"Because Mary humbly acknowledged herself to be what she was, a servant, therefore she merited to be raised to what she was not. For she debased herself after the example of her Son, taking the form of a servant, for which cause God exalted her also, and hath given her a name that is above every name after that of her Son, that in her name every knee should bow, of those that are in heaven, on earth, and under the earth, that at her name the demons should tremble."[2]

"The same Spirit granted to thee, O Mary," says S. Ildephonsus, "that in thy name, every knee should bow of those in heaven, on earth, in hell, and that every tongue should confess that thou art the Mother of our Lord Jesus Christ, seated in the glory of God the Father at the right hand of thy most loving Spouse and only Son, crowned conspicuously with an unfading crown of seven stars of brilliant splendour, accompanied by bands of virgins, exalted marvellously above all other Saints, amidst the hymns of alternate choirs of angels, in the everlasting verdure of paradise."

29 Receive him therefore with all joy in the Lord; and treat with honour such as he is.

30 Because for the work of Christ he came to the point of death; delivering his life, that he might fulfil that which on your part was wanting towards my service.

Epaphroditus suffered and risked his life for an Apostle of Christ; Mary's heart was pierced for Christ, and for us. How much more is she worthy of honour.

CHAPTER III.

10 That I may know him, and the power of his resurrection, and the fellowship of his sufferings, being made conformable to his death,

11 If by any means I may attain to the resurrection which is from the dead.

Who as Mary had so great fellowship in the sufferings of Jesus Christ, and was made so conformable to His death?

[1] *P. iv. T.* 15, *C.* 21.   [2] Dan. Agric.

Who, then, as she knew the power of His resurrection? The Blessed Virgin, according to the Gospel narrative, and the united voice of Tradition, had fellowship of these mysteries in a way more real and perfect than the Apostle here even desired for himself.

17 Be followers of me, brethren, and observe them who walk so as you have our model.

Why should we not study Mary, and the virgins who walked according to her model? How great the honour to be allowed to have the name of children, servants, followers of Mary.

20 But our conversation is in heaven; from whence also we look for the Saviour, our Lord Jesus Christ,
21 Who will reform the body of our lowness, made like to the body of his glory, according to the operation whereby also he is able to subdue all things unto himself.

This was Mary's life after the Resurrection of her Son. At length He came Himself to receive her blessed soul, and *reformed the body of her lowness, which was made like to the body of His glory*, in her Assumption to heaven.

CHAPTER IV.

1 Therefore, my dearly beloved brethren, and most desired, my joy and my crown; so stand fast in the Lord, my dearly beloved.

S. Paul calls the Philippians *his joy and his crown*: why may we not call Mary "our life, our sweetness and our hope"?

So stand fast . . . "That is," as S. Antoninus remarks, "by conformity to the will of God. The Blessed Virgin stood by the Cross, conforming herself to the divine will. She knew that it was God's will that her Son should suffer, and that for this He came into the world. The Scriptures, too, which were well known to her, foretold this; and they must be accomplished. And since in all things she sought for rest, as is written of her [1]—and this can be found in no other way than

---

[1] *Ecclus.* xxiv. 11.

by conformity to the divine will according to reason—for this cause she stood, and did not murmur because her most innocent Son had to suffer: she did not speak evil of the Jews, because He was so cruelly treated by them, though He had done them so much good: she did not seek for vengeance from Him, that they should be swallowed up by the earth alive, as they deserved: she did not tear her hair and face, because she was being left a desolate widow, and without son to console her: but she *stood*, reverend, modest, full of tears, overwhelmed by sorrows." [1]

4 Rejoice in the Lord always; again, I say, rejoice.
5 Let your modesty be known to all men. The Lord is nigh.
6 Be nothing solicitous; but in everything, by prayer and supplication, with thanksgiving, let your petitions be made known to God.
7 And the peace of God, which surpasseth all understanding, keep your hearts and minds in Christ Jesus.
8 For the rest, brethren, whatsoever things are true, whatsoever modest, whatsoever just, whatsoever holy, whatsoever lovely, whatsoever of good fame, if there be any virtue, if any praise of discipline, think on these things.
9 The things which you have both learned, and received, and heard, and seen in me, these do ye, and the God of peace shall be with you.

Where shall we see all these precepts fulfilled, and these virtues shown forth, as in the Blessed Virgin Mary? What a theme is she for our meditation, what a model for us to imitate!

21 Salute ye every saint in Christ Jesus.

If we are to salute Saints on earth, why not Saints in heaven? Why not the Queen of Saints? Are not they, is not she, *in Christ Jesus?* Is not such salutation *in Christ Jesus?* Ave, Maria, gratia plena, Dominus tecum.

[1] *P.* iv. tit. 15, c. 41, § 1.

THE EPISTLE OF S. PAUL
TO THE
COLOSSIANS.

CHAPTER I.

15 Who is the image of the invisible God, the first-born of every creature:
16 For in him were all things created in heaven and on earth, visible and invisible, whether thrones, or dominations, or principalities, or powers: all things were created by him and in him.
17 And he is before all, and by him all things consist.
18 And he is the head of the body, the church, who is the beginning, the first-born from the dead; that in all things he may hold the primacy:
19 Because in him it hath well-pleased the Father, that all fulness should dwell.

And He dwelt in the bosom of Mary!

21 And you, whereas you were some time alienated and enemies in mind in evil works;
22 Yet now he hath reconciled in the body of his flesh through death, to present you holy and unspotted, and blameless before him.

What marvel, if she from whom He took that body of His flesh which reconciles sinners with God, was never alienated and enemy in mind, but was always holy and unspotted and blameless before Him?

24 Who now rejoice in my sufferings for you, and fill up those things that are wanting of the sufferings of Christ, in my flesh, for his body, which is the church;
25 Whereof I am made a minister according to the dispensation of God, which is given me towards you, that I may fulfil the word of God:
26 The mystery which hath been hidden from ages and generations, but now is manifested to his saints,
27 To whom God would make known the riches of the glory of this mystery among the Gentiles, which is Christ, in you the hope of glory.

If S. Paul could suffer meritoriously for others, and could speak of his sufferings as supplying what was *wanting of the sufferings of Christ for the Church*, and thus bear, in a sense, the office of co-redeemer with Jesus Christ our Redeemer, how much more did Mary fulfil such an office. Why may we not give to her, and in a far more eminent sense than to S. Paul, that title? S. Paul as minister of the Church, Mary as Mother of Jesus Christ, the Head of the Church was made *to fulfil the Word of God*—Fiat mihi secundum verbum tuum.

That mystery, hidden from ages, was first, and by express embassy from heaven, made manifest to Mary only, viz., Christ in, and of her, "the Word made flesh." Through her was He given and made manifest to all others, Angels as well as men,[1] and became *in them the hope of glory.*

28 That we may present every man perfect in Christ Jesus.

And shall not Mary perfect us, and present us before Jesus Christ?

CHAPTER II.

1 For I would have you know, what manner of care I have for you and for them that are at Laodicea, and whosoever have not seen my face in the flesh:
5 For though I be absent in body, yet in spirit I am with you; rejoicing, and beholding your order, and the steadfastness of your faith which is in Christ.

Then Mary, too, may in heaven have a care for her children still on earth, and may wish us to know that loving care: for we are all as much Mary's children as S. John, whom Jesus Christ from the Cross gave to her for a son, and who saw her face in the flesh. And though now absent in body, she may yet be present with us in spirit, rejoicing and beholding our order and the steadfastness of our faith which is in Christ.

3 In whom are hid all the treasures of wisdom and knowledge.
9 For in him dwelleth all the fulness of the Godhead corporally;
10 And you are filled in him, who is the head of all principality and power.

These words might literally, though in another sense, have been written of Mary in whom the Divine Word with all His infinite treasures of wisdom and knowledge dwelt corporally

[1] 1 *Tim.* iii. 16.

for nine months. As says S. Anselm, "Christ is in Mary. Therefore *in Mary are all the treasures of God's wisdom and knowledge.*"[1] And Isidore, Archbishop of Thessalonica: "To Mary may be applied the words of the great Apostle, concerning her Son, that in her were hid all treasures of wisdom and knowledge."[2]

19 And not holding the head, from which the whole body, by joints and bands, being supplied with nourishment and compacted, groweth unto the increase of God.

"In the mystical body of Christ," writes Morales, "He Himself holds the place of head, as the Apostle said above,[3] and all the faithful are its members.[4] But between the head and the members comes the neck. . . . Now the Blessed Virgin is most fitly represented by the neck: for as on the neck are hung costly chains, jewels, necklaces, and precious stones, so has Christ conferred all gifts of graces, all virtues, all beauties, in a word all perfections upon His Mother Mary, His Spouse, of whom is well understood what is written in the Canticles: 'Thy neck is as the tower of David, which is built with bulwarks; a thousand bucklers hang upon it, all the armour of valiant men.'[5] For in the Virgin are, and from her neck hang, all the beauties of Esther, of Judith, of Rachel, and Rebecca, the reverend modesty of Sara, the amiability of Rebecca, the fruitfulness of Leah, the prudence of Abigail, the courage and fortitude of Judith, the graciousness of Esther, the chastity of Susanna, the thoughtful diligence of the Sunamitess, the hospitality of the widow of Sarepta, the purity of Angels, the dignity of Apostles, the constancy of Martyrs, the wisdom of Doctors, the abstinence of Confessors, the modesty of Virgins, the humility and obedience of Religious; in a word, whatever else there is of beauty, nobility, riches, learning, strength, prudence, chastity, and any other virtue or excellence: since the Blessed Virgin

---

[1] In *Luc.* c. x.
[2] Ap. *Summ. Aur. B. M. V.* tom. iv., p. 610.
[3] i. 18, and ii. 10.
[4] See *Rom.* xii. 4, 5, and 1 *Cor.* xii. 27, *supra.*   [5] *Cant.* iv. 4.

contains them all in most surpassing measure: and they are bulwarks most strong for warding off all the darts of the enemy, the world, and the flesh. With good reason, therefore, have we said of the Blessed Virgin: 'Thy neck is as the tower of David,' etc.: since whatever belongs to Christ, or the Eternal Word, and is attributed in Holy Writ to the Church, His mystical body, by participation, is all to be ascribed to the Blessed Virgin pre-eminently and by excellence. Hence she is called Mother of Mercy, our Life, Sweetness and Hope; our Advocate, Queen and Lady; the Spouse, Sister, Friend, and Daughter."[1] "Again, under this same similitude is understood Mary's patronage—her favour and intercession with God,—since her intercession is, so to say, the neck through which all divine graces and helps pass from Christ the Head to men."[2]

"An ancient author, probably S. Sophronius, in a sermon on the Assumption, published with the works of S. Jerome, says that 'the plenitude of grace, which is in Jesus Christ, came into Mary, though in a different way,' meaning, that it is in our Lord, as in the head, from which the vital spirits (that is, Divine help to obtain eternal salvation) flow into us, who are the members of His mystical body, and that the same plenitude is in Mary, as in the neck, through which these vital spirits pass to the members."[3]

CHAPTER III.

1 Therefore, if you be risen with Christ, seek the things that are above; where Christ is sitting at the right hand of God:
2 Mind the things that are above, not the things that are upon the earth.
3 For you are dead; and your life is hid with Christ in God.
4 When Christ shall appear, who is your life, then you also shall appear with him in glory.

[1] In cap. i. *Matt.*, etc. L. ii., tr. x. See a striking passage from S. Antoninus (P. iv., tit. 15, cap. 14, § 7) where, applying to the B. V. M. the words of S. Paul, *Heb.* iv. 16, he teaches that in Mary are found, in eminent degree, the perfections of God, and the virtues of all the Saints of the Old and New Testament, whose examples are recorded for our instruction.
[2] See *Ib.* l. iii. tr. x.
[3] S. Alph. Lig. *Glories of Mary*, p. 127. See S. Bernardine of Sienna *infra*, James i. 17.

All that S. Paul here says is applicable in a most excellent manner to Mary, as descriptive of her life after the Resurrection and Ascension of her Son, and of her future glorious manifestation at the last day.

15 And let the peace of Christ rejoice in your hearts, wherein also you are called in one body: and be ye thankful.
16 Let the word of Christ dwell in you abundantly, in all wisdom: teaching and admonishing one another in psalms, hymns, and spiritual canticles, singing in grace in your hearts to God.
17 All whatsoever you do in word or in work, do all in the name of the Lord Jesus Christ, giving thanks to God and the Father by him.

It was Mary who gave in the New Testament the first example of *singing in grace in the heart to the Lord*, and the great model of *spiritual canticles* by her sublime Magnificat.[1] As she uttered it, not alone *the word to Christ and His peace* were dwelling and rejoicing in her heart, but Christ Himself the Incarnate Word and Wisdom of God was dwelling in her and rejoicing with her.

"Since thou art once for all dead to the world, touch not, I beg thee, taste not, handle not any more the things of the world;[2] but ever in psalms, and hymns, and spiritual canticles, withdraw thyself from the world's converse, singing not to man but to God. And, as was used to do the holy Mary, ponder in thy heart.[3] As a good little lamb, ruminate in thy mouth the divine commandments, that thou too mayest say: 'I shall be exercised in thy wondrous works.'"[4]

18 Wives, be subject to your husbands, as it behoveth in the Lord.
20 Children, obey your parents in all things: for this is well pleasing to the Lord.

See *supra*, *Eph.* v. 22-24, vi. 1.

24 Serve ye the Lord Christ.

Ecce ancilla Domini. See *supra*, *Rom.* xii. 11, xiv. 18.

---

[1] See *supra*, *Eph.* v. 18-20.　　[2] *Col.* ii. 20-21.　　[3] *Luke* ii. 19.
[4] *Ps.* cxviii. 27. S. Ambrose, *De Inst. Virg.* xvi. 103.

CHAPTER IV.

12 Epaphras saluteth you, who is one of you, a servant of Christ Jesus, who is always solicitous for you in prayers, that you may stand perfect, and full in all the will of God.

Is not Mary the Mother of Christ Jesus always solicitous for us in prayers, and for the same end, viz., that we may stand perfect, fulfilling in all things the will of God.

18 Be mindful of my bonds.

Much more may Mary appeal to us her children, and say: *Be mindful of my Dolours.*

THE FIRST EPISTLE OF S. PAUL
TO THE
THESSALONIANS.

CHAPTER II.

7 Whereas we might have been burdensome to you, as the apostles of Christ: but we became little ones in the midst of you, as if a nurse should cherish her children:

8 So desirous of you, we would gladly impart unto you not only the gospel of God, but also our own souls: because you were become most dear unto us.

11 As you know in what manner, entreating and comforting you (as a father doth his children).

Might not Mary say: Though the great Mother of God, I have become amongst you the little servant of the Lord, not claiming any burdensome honour, but as your own dear Mother cherishing you as my children: not only giving you my own Son, who is the Son of God, to be your Saviour, but willing gladly to give you my own soul and life a thousand times with Him, because you were become most dear unto me: entreating and comforting you as a mother doth her children, that so I may secure your soul's salvation, and win for myself your filial devotion, and tender love. See *supra*, 2 *Cor.* vi. 11-13.

17 But we, brethren, being taken away from you for a short time, in sight, not in heart, have hastened the more abundantly to see your face with great desire.
18 For we would have come unto you, I Paul indeed, once and again: but satan hath hindered us.
19 For what is our hope, or joy, or crown of glory? Are not you, in the presence of our Lord Jesus Christ at his coming?
20 For you are our glory and joy.

How well might these burning words of the Apostle be applied to Mary. Thus, and far more ardently than S. Paul on earth did over his dear converts, does Mary in heaven yearn over, and long to see, us, her own beloved children, who are her crown, and glory, and joy. And shall not Mary be also to us one day our crown, and glory, and joy, who is now our life, our sweetness, and our hope?

CHAPTER V.

23 And may the God of peace himself sanctify you in all things; that your whole spirit, and soul, and body, may be preserved blameless in the coming of our Lord Jesus Christ.

Mary attained this spotlessness and sanctification in perfection from the beginning to prepare her for the first coming of our Lord Jesus Christ.

" In Mary were three things, spirit, soul, and body, and these three she gave to her Son: for she gave her *body* and her womb for Him to dwell in; she united her *soul* to the soul of Christ by love, and in a manner made both one; and she indissolubly conjoined her *spirit* with the divinity of Christ."——" In the Blessed Virgin were three places-of-repose (*reclinatoria*), her spirit, soul, and body, whereof is said: *May your whole spirit, and soul, and body be preserved blameless.* In these three Christ rested: in her spirit, inasmuch as she gave herself to continual contemplation; in her soul, in that her reason was never withdrawn from Christ; in her body since sensuality never opposed her reason."——" Mary had the perfect integrity of purity, in her body, because she ever preserved it inviolate; in her soul, since she cut off every evil movement and sense; in her spirit, for never was she separated from God by any sin."[1]

[1] B. Jacob. de Voragine *Serm.* 2. *Sabbat.* v., *hebdomadæ Quadrag.*, also *Serm.* 2 et 5, *De Nativ. B. V. M.*

THE SECOND EPISTLE OF S. PAUL
TO THE
THESSALONIANS.

CHAPTER I.

4 So that we ourselves also glory in you in the churches of God, for your patience and faith, and in all your persecutions and tribulations, which you endure.

With much more reason should the faithful throughout the Church glory in the graces and virtues of Mary, and take part in all her dolours.

10 When he shall come to be glorified in his saints, and to be made wonderful in all them who have believed.

How glorious will Jesus Christ be then seen in His holy Mother, the Queen of Saints. How wonderful will He then be made in her, whose faith surpassed far that of all other believers.—O gloriosa Virginum, Regina sanctorum omnium, Mater admirabilis, Virgo fidelis, Beata quæ credidisti.

11 Wherefore also we pray always for you; that our God would make you worthy of his vocation, and fulfil all the good pleasure of his goodness and the work of faith in power;
12 That the name of our Lord Jesus may be glorified in you, and you in him, according to the grace of our God, and of the Lord Jesus Christ.

Mary was, as far as a creature could be, every way worthy of God's sublime vocation regarding her; and in her was fulfilled *all the good pleasure of His goodness*, through her perfect correspondence to His will: Ecce ancilla Domini, fiat mihi secundum verbum tuum.——In her, too, was accomplished *the work of faith in power:* Beata quæ credidisti, quoniam perficientur ea quæ dicta sunt tibi a Domino. Fecit mihi magna qui potens est.——How greatly, then, was *the name of our Lord Jesus glorified in Mary, and she in Him.* The more she is magnified, the more is God magnified in her: Magnificat anima mea Dominum. Consequently the more we glorify

Mary, the more do we glorify God, and *that* in proportionate *accordance to the fulness of grace*, which God bestowed upon her: Ave gratia plena, Dominus tecum!

CHAPTER II.

3 Unless . . . the man of sin be revealed, the son of perdition,
4 Who opposeth, and is lifted up above all that is called God, or that is worshipped, so that he sitteth in the temple of God, shewing himself as if he were God.

Mary, the Virgin Mother of God, the blessed amongst women, has been revealed to us; and how different is her character and spirit from that of the man of sin, the son of perdition. She, indeed, as the true Mother of God is lifted up and worshipped in the Church above all other creatures, above all that is *not* called God. But she takes herself the handmaid's place, and is in all things humble and entirely submissive to the Divine Will: Ecce ancilla Domini, fiat mihi . . . Respexit humilitatem ancillæ suæ. And for this very reason shall she be praised and exalted the more in the Church through every age: Ecce enim ex hoc beatam me dicent omnes generationes. Hence the distinctive mark of the true faithful of Christ in all generations is devotion to His Mother, whilst that of the children of perdition is aversion to her: Inimicitias ponam inter te et mulierem, et semen tuum et semen illius.[1]

12 But we ought to give thanks to God always for you, brethren, beloved of God, for that God hath chosen you first-fruits unto salvation, in sanctification of the spirit, and faith of the truth:
13 Whereunto also he hath called you by our gospel, unto the purchasing of the glory of our Lord Jesus Christ.

Should we not then give unceasing thanks to God on account of Mary, and especially on her Feasts, for the graces which God has bestowed upon her? Was she not *chosen the first-fruits unto salvation, in sanctification of the Spirit, and faith of the truth, unto predestined glory?*

---

[1] *Gen.* iii. 15.

CHAPTER III.

1 Brethren, pray for us.

Sancta Maria Mater Dei, Ora pro nobis.[1]

9 That we might give ourselves a pattern unto you to imitate us.

Mary is given to us for a pattern, *Speculum justitiæ*, expressly that we may strive to imitate her.

THE FIRST EPISTLE OF S. PAUL
TO
TIMOTHY.

CHAPTER I.

5 Now the end of the commandment is charity, from a pure heart, and a good conscience, and an unfeigned faith.

To attain this end, let us frequently meditate on what is said of Mary in the Gospels; for the qualities of charity here mentioned are specially characteristic of her. See *supra*, 2 *Thess.* iii. 9.

CHAPTER II.

1 I desire therefore, first of all, that supplications, prayers, intercessions, and thanksgivings be made for all men:
2 For kings, and for all that are in high station: that we may lead a quiet and a peaceable life in all piety and chastity.
3 For this is good and acceptable in the sight of God our Saviour,
4 Who will have all men to be saved, and to come to the knowledge of the truth.
5 For there is one God, and one mediator of God and men, the man Jesus Christ:
6 Who gave himself a redemption for all, a testimony in due times.

The words in v. 5 are equivalent to: As there is one only God, so there is one only Mediator between God and men, the

---

[1] See *Job* xlii. 8; *Ezech.* xx. 29, 30; *Rom.* xv. 30; *Eph.* vi. 18; 1 *Thess.* v. 25; *Acts* x. 4; xii. 5; *Zach.* i. 12; *Dan.* viii. 16; ix. 21; x. 19; xii. 1; *Job* xii. 12, 13; 4 *Kings* xix. 34; 2 *Mac.* xv. 22; *Luke* xv. 7, 10; *Heb.* i. 14; *Apoc.* v. 8; viii. 3, 4.

Man Christ Jesus. This however, according to S. Paul, does not exclude other mediators in another and most true sense. For all those who pray, and by their prayers obtain graces in behalf of others, are really mediators between God and men: and S. Paul had just before said that Christians should thus be mediators by interceding for all men: this being well-pleasing to God and conducive to man's salvation (v.v. 1, 3, 4); and just for this very reason, because there is one only Mediator (that is, of justice, and *per se*), the Man Christ Jesus, in and through Whom all others must mediate. "*For* there is one God," etc. (v.v. 5, 6). The fact is, the more exclusively, in a right sense, we look to Jesus Christ as our one only Mediator with God, the more efficacious may we consider the mediation of others, and pre-eminently that of His holy Mother. And the more we exalt, in a right sense, Mary as our mediatress (by grace), and trust in the power of her intercession, the more do we exalt and attribute efficacy to the one only mediation (of justice) of our Lord Jesus Christ, through and from which all other mediation with God derives its efficacy. In the same way Our Lord says that there is none good but God alone; and yet He says too, "Be ye perfect as your heavenly Father is perfect." And the Church says, *Tu solus Sanctus*; and yet God says, "Sancti eritis quoniam Ego sanctus sum." So too Jesus Christ says: "Call none your father upon earth: for one is your Father who is in heaven;" yet S. Paul speaks of himself as a father to his converts.

9 In like manner, women also in decent apparel: adorning themselves with modesty and sobriety, not with plaited hair, or gold, or pearls, or costly attire,
10 But as it becometh women professing godliness, with good works.
11 Let the woman learn in silence, with all subjection.
12 But I suffer not a woman to teach, nor to use authority over the man: but to be in silence.

How completely are these Apostolic injunctions (incidentally, as it were) conformable to the Catholic traditional idea of the Blessed Virgin Mary, as expressed by S. Ambrose and other Fathers, and as shown forth by all those Catholic women, who have in every age endeavoured to take Mary as their model, and professed to walk in her footsteps. It was doubtless, because Mary was to be the ideal of a perfect Christian woman, whose character was entirely conformed to that of her Divine Son, and because such a view of her was from the beginning deeply impressed in the mind of the Catholic Church, that so little is explicitly said of her in Holy Scripture.——We may note the prudent silence of our Lady from the words: "Mary kept all these things in her heart;"[1] and from her silence with regard to the doubt of S. Joseph.

15 Yet she shall be saved through child-bearing ; if she continue in faith, and love, and sanctification, with sobriety.

Mary, through her glorious child-bearing, was made to us the instrument of our salvation, and was thereby herself the more sanctified, magnified, and glorified. Through her blessed child-bearing comes, as it were, the reversal to Christian mothers of the primeval sentence pronounced on the daughters of Eve : " In sorrow shalt thou bring forth children : "[2] and now amongst the faithful, since women are children of Mary, the Second Eve and true Mother of the living, child-bearing and the rearing up of Christian children have become to them a source of glory and merit, and a means of salvation. And Christian mothers are themselves also, in a certain sense, after Mary mothers of the living, that is, of Christian children, who shall live to God here on earth by faith, and for ever in heavenly glory.

"Theophylact says that some understand *through child-bearing* (διὰ τῆς τεκνογονίας) to mean the child-birth of the Blessed Virgin Mary, which effected women's salvation: for she gave birth to Christ, and in Him to many Christian sons and daughters. . . . The preposition, *through* (per), here denotes the cause and merit—that is to say, through the labours

[1] *Luke* ii. 31.   [2] *Gen.* iii. 16.

which the woman undergoes in child-birth, and in the bringing up of children in the faith and in a good Christian life; by the merit whereof she will be saved."[1]

CHAPTER III.

4 One that ruleth well his own house, having his children in subjection with all chastity.
5 But if a man know not how to rule his own house, how shall he take care of the church of God?

The Virgin Mother had her Child, Almighty God made Man, subject to her.[2] May we not ask: If she knew how to rule well the holy house of Nazareth, and to have her Lord subject to her, is she not worthy and well able to take care of the Church of God, and shall not its members be subject to her?

9 Holding the mystery of faith in a pure conscience.

Thus did Mary: nay, she bore "the Author and Finisher of faith" in her virginal womb.

11 The women chaste.

Following the example of the Virgin of virgins.

13 For they that have ministered well, shall purchase to themselves a good degree, and much confidence in the faith which is in Christ Jesus.

What degree of glory, then, has not Mary purchased for herself: who, though the Mother of God, took her place, rather, as the Lord's handmaid, and, after His example, came not to be ministered unto but to minister.——Correspondingly great, too, must be the confidence of her access to her Divine Son.

14 These things I write to thee, hoping that I shall come to thee shortly.
15 But if I tarry long, that thou mayest know how thou oughtest to behave thyself in the house of God, which is the church of the living God, the pillar and ground of the truth.
16 And evidently great is the mystery of godliness, which was manifested in the flesh, was justified in the spirit, appeared unto

---

[1] Cornelius a Lapide, *in loc.*   [2] *Luke* ii. 51.

angels, hath been preached unto the gentiles, is believed in the world, is taken up in glory.

S. Timothy needed instruction how to behave as Bishop in the Church: for the Church has to deal with and make known the great mystery of godliness, the Incarnation. But Mary needed a still higher wisdom to know how to bear herself to the Incarnate God Himself. Her Epistle and teaching was the Holy Ghost.[1]——Evidently great is the mystery of Mary, the true Virgin Mother of God—ever indissolubly united, as she is, to the great mystery of godliness, the Eternal Word Incarnate; since through and of her He was made man, manifested in the flesh and given to mankind. Evidently great is the mystery of Mary, who was overshadowed, filled, justified, and sanctified by the Holy Ghost; whom the Angel, appearing as the ambassador from on high, saluted as closely united to God: whose spirit exulted in God alone; who was to be celebrated, *Virgo prædicanda*, as the Blessed one by all generations; whose glorious life illumines all the churches; who after death was taken up into heaven and crowned in presence of angels and saints with exceeding glory.

CHAPTER IV.

10 We hope in the living God, who is the Saviour of all men, especially of the faithful.

And most especially is He the Saviour of Mary, the first-fruits and Mother of the faithful, *Beata quæ credidisti*; redeemed and saved, as she was, in most perfect and singular manner from ever coming under the dominion of Satan, or contracting any stain of sin. Mary therefore in a singular manner and beyond all others hoped and rejoiced in the living God—to whom, indeed, she herself gave His human life—as *her* Saviour: "Exultavit spiritus meus in Deo salutari meo."

12 Be thou an example of the faithful in word, in conversation, in charity, in faith, in chastity.

[1] See S. Chrys. *Hom. in S. Ignat.* n. 2.

14 Neglect not the grace that is in thee.
15 Meditate upon these things, be wholly in these things: that thy profiting may be manifested to all.
16 Take heed to thyself and to doctrine: be earnest in them. For in doing this thou shalt both save thyself and them that hear thee.

If S. Timothy, by the merits of his works and example, could thus save others; how much more may not Mary save us? Since she exemplified all these virtues so much more brightly than S. Timothy, viz., holy conversation, charity, faith, chastity, correspondence to grace, meditation, example. To be convinced of this it is enough to gather together the passages in the Gospels which speak of Mary, to mark well the traits of her life and character therein contained, then to fill up the sketch by devout meditation and reflection, and lastly to compare all this with what early tradition says of her in the Holy Fathers, specially S. Ambrose.

CHAPTER V.

3 Honour widows, that are widows indeed.
5 But she that is a widow indeed, and desolate, let her trust in God, and continue in supplications and prayers night and day.
6 For she that liveth in pleasures, is dead while she is living.
7 And this give in charge, that they may be blameless.
8 But if any man have not care of his own, and especially of his house, he hath denied the faith, and is worse than an infidel.
9 Let a widow be chosen of no less than threescore years of age, who hath been the wife of one husband.
10 Having testimony for her good works, if she have brought up children, if she have received to harbour, if she have washed the saints' feet, if she have ministered to them that suffer tribulation, if she have diligently followed every good work.

And shall we not honour Mary, so long a widow from the death of S. Joseph; a widow indeed, and desolate, after the death of Jesus Christ? Did she not trust in God, and continue in prayer?[1] Mary must surely have been *the widow indeed*, present, implicitly at least, in the Apostle's mind; the type and model of all holy widows. What testimony of her good works must have been in the Church at the time he wrote. She had brought up her Child—and what a Child!

---

[1] *Acts* i. 10.

Moreover, all Christians had been commended by Him as children to her maternal care. She had received to harbour the afflicted, such as Mary Magdalene. She had washed saints' feet, nay, the feet of the Saint of saints, in His infancy and childhood, and when His body was taken down from the Cross and placed in her arms. She had, as tradition tells us, during the years that remained to her on earth diligently followed every good work.

"A triple good," says S. Antoninus, "attaches to holy widowhood. 1. *Liberty for contemplation* (v. 5). Hence we read of the widow Anna, the prophetess, that 'she departed not from the temple, by fastings and prayers serving God night and day.'[1] 2. *Mortification of the flesh*; for the Apostle says (v. 6) that the widow 'that liveth in pleasures, is dead while she is living.' Hence the holy widows Judith and Anna practised fasting. 3. *Exercise of works of piety and mercy* (v. 10). Thus the widow of Sarepta supported Elias with food to sustain his life. Now all these things were beyond comparison in the Blessed Virgin Mary; for not only did she observe the fasts prescribed by the Law, but S. Ambrose says that she added others besides; she was wholly given to prayer and contemplation; out of her poverty she nourished Christ who was a mendicant and poor."[2]

But if any man, etc. (v. 8). Mary, then, will not neglect those of her household, that is, who are in her confraternities and wear her livery.

THE SECOND EPISTLE OF S. PAUL
TO
TIMOTHY.

CHAPTER I.

14 Keep the good thing committed to thy trust by the Holy Ghost, who dwelleth in us.

[1] *Luke* ii. 36, 37.   [2] *P.* iv. *tit.* 15, *c.* 24, § 3.

The good thing committed to Mary's trust by the Holy Ghost was nothing less than the Son of God.

CHAPTER II.

10 Therefore I endure all things for the sake of the elect, that they also may obtain the salvation, which is in Christ Jesus, with heavenly glory.
11 A faithful saying: for if we be dead with him we shall live also with him.
12 If we suffer, we shall also reign with him.

Much more might Mary say that all she endured in her dolours was for the sake of the elect; and far more availing for their salvation were the sufferings of Mary than those of S. Paul. Having suffered and died indeed with Jesus Christ her Divine Son, she now lives and reigns with Him the nearest to Him in glory. It is meet that she who is Regina martyrum, should be Regina cœli.

20 But in a great house there are not only vessels of gold and of silver, but also of wood and of earth: and some indeed unto honour, but some unto dishonour.
21 If any man therefore shall cleanse himself from these, he shall be a vessel unto honour, sanctified and profitable to the Lord, prepared unto every good work.

In the great house of God's Church, the holy immaculate Virgin Mary is prized, and constantly invoked by the faithful, as Vas spirituale, Vas honorabile, Vas insigne devotionis.

CHAPTER IV.

6 The time of my dissolution is at hand.
7 I have fought a good fight, I have finished my course, I have kept the faith.
8 As to the rest, there is laid up for me a crown of justice, which the Lord the just judge will render to me in that day: and not only to me, but to them also that love his coming.

If such was the Apostle's confidence, what must have been that of Mary when the time of her dissolution was at hand, as she looked back at the course of her life upon earth, and all that she had done and suffered for God. What her joy at the assured reward, the bright crown which she saw awaiting her.

She, like the Apostle, thought not of herself alone, but also of all her children who love her Divine Son, and of the glory which they would one day share with herself.——As the love she had for the coming of her Lord surpassed that of all others, so does the crown of justice that He awarded to her exceed that of all others in glory.

THE EPISTLE OF S. PAUL
TO
TITUS.

CHAPTER I.

4 To Titus my beloved son, according to the common faith, grace and peace from God the Father, and from Christ Jesus our Saviour.

If S. Paul calls Titus his son, is not Mary our Mother?

CHAPTER II.

4 That they may teach the young women to be wise, to love their husbands, to love their children,
5 To be discreet, chaste, sober, having a care of the house, gentle, obedient to their husbands, that the word of God be not blasphemed.

Here is another assemblage of virtues which the tradition of the faithful has ever associated with the Virgin Mother, especially, and in the highest degree. Hence she is invoked as Sedes sapientiæ, Virgo prudentissima, Mater castissima, O clemens, O pia, O dulcis Virgo Maria.

> Virgo singularis,
> Inter omnes mitis,
> Nos culpis solutos
> Mites fac et castos.

11 For the grace of God our Saviour hath appeared to all men.
13 Looking for the blessed hope and coming of the glory of the great God and our Saviour Jesus Christ.

"*For the grace of God our Saviour hath appeared* . . . See how this man of God is speaking from God, and attests by a preaching most evident that the grace of God appeared from Mary. And lest, perchance, thou shouldst say, that it was not from Mary that God appeared, he at once added the name of Saviour, for the very purpose that thou mightest believe that He who was born of Mary is God, whom thou canst not deny to have been born a Saviour, according to what is written: 'For this day is born to you a Saviour.'[1] O admirable Master, Blessed Paul, verily given by God to the Gentiles . . . *The great God and our Saviour Jesus Christ:* It is not allowed to say, Christ was born from Mary, and yet not God; for the Apostle proclaims: God. It is not allowed to say, Jesus was born of Mary, and not God; for the Apostle testifies: God. It is not allowed to say, a Saviour is born, and not God; for the Apostle affirms: God."[2]

We quote these words of Cassian, not on account of their testimony to the Divinity of Jesus Christ, and to Mary's Divine Maternity, but because they clearly show how obvious it was to that holy Father, that S. Paul in his teaching about Jesus Christ, had the Blessed Virgin His Mother present to his mind.

THE EPISTLE OF S. PAUL
TO
PHILEMON.

10 My son whom I have begotten in my bonds.

Much more, and in a more excellent sense, did Mary become our Mother through her Dolours.

[1] *Luke* ii. 11.
Cassian, *De Incarn. Christi*, Lib. ii. c. 4.

THE EPISTLE OF S. PAUL

TO THE

HEBREWS.

CHAPTER I.

3 Who being the brightness of his glory, and the figure of his substance, and upholding all things by the word of his power, making purgation of sins, sitteth on the right hand of the majesty on high

4 Being made so much better than the angels, as he hath inherited a more excellent name than they.

5 For to which of the angels hath he said at any time, Thou art my Son, to-day have I begotten thee? And again, I will be to him a Father, and he shall be to me a Son?

6 And again, when he bringeth in the first begotten into the world, he saith: And let all the angels of God adore him.

7 And to the angels indeed he saith: He that maketh his angels spirits, and his ministers a flame of fire.

8 But to the Son: Thy throne, O God, is for ever and ever: a sceptre of justice is the sceptre of thy kingdom.

9 Thou hast loved justice, and hated iniquity: therefore, God, thy God, hath anointed thee with the oil of gladness above thy fellows.

10 And: Thou in the beginning, O Lord, didst found the earth: and the works of thy hands are the heavens.

11 They shall perish, but thou shalt continue: and they shall all grow old as a garment.

12 And as a vesture shalt thou change them, and they shall be changed: but thou art the self-same, and thy years shall not fail.

13 But to which of the angels said he at any time: Sit on my right hand, until I make thy enemies thy footstool.

14 Are they not all ministering spirits, sent to minister for them, who shall receive the inheritance of salvation?

Is Mary the brightness of her Son's glory; or, is Jesus the brightness of His Mother's glory? Both. Here we may apply to Jesus and Mary those words of the Apostle: "The Man is the image and glory of God, but the Woman is the glory of the Man. For the Man is not of the Woman, but the Woman of the Man: for the Man was not created for the Woman, but the Woman for the Man. But yet neither is the Man without the Woman, nor the Woman without the Man."[1] Besides if S. Paul could write to his disciples: "You have

---

[1] 1 *Cor.* xi. 7-11.

known us in part that we are your glory, as you also are ours in the day of our Lord Jesus Christ,"[1] could not the Son of God say to his Mother: I am thy glory, as thou also art Mine? But O what a glory for Mary, to possess Him, to be able to boast of as her very own, the Blessed Fruit of her womb, Him Who is the brightness of His Father's glory! No wonder that she was seen "clothed with the Sun."[2]

S. Ephrem, especially, speaks frequently of Jesus being the glory of Mary, thus: "With everything didst Thou adorn her, Thou ornament of Thy Mother."——"Because He put His Mother's garment on, she clothed her body with His glory." ——"Thy Mother put on in her virginity the garment of Glory that sufficeth for all."[3]

Mary's Son *sitteth on the right hand of the Majesty on high*. Of this the Angel told the Blessed Virgin at the moment when the Son of God was about to take flesh of her, in order *to make purgation of sins:* "He shall be great and shall be called the Son of the Most High . . . and of His kingdom there shall be no end."[4] Gabriel had spoken, indeed, of "the throne of David His father;" but Mary knew the words of David: "The Lord said to My Lord: Sit Thou on My right hand." Mary also has her throne *at the right hand of Jesus*. James and John had coveted that place, but they forgot His Mother's claims.

The Apostle contends that Jesus Christ is so much better and greater than the angels, in that He has inherited a far more excellent name than they, that is to say, of Son of God. By parity of reason, though of course on other grounds—not by virtue of hypostatic union and of right, but by grace—Mary is greater and higher than the angels, on account of *the so much more excellent name* which belongs to her, viz., that of Mother of the Son of God, in virtue of her Divine Maternity: "Of whom was born Jesus." To which of the angels could He say at any time: Thou art My Mother, to-day was I born

---

[1] 2 *Cor.* i. 11. [2] *Apoc.* xii. 1.
[3] *Rhythm* viii., Morris p. 41; *R.* xii. p. 51; *R.* xii. p. 53.
[4] *Luke* i. 32.

of thee?[1] And again: I will be to her a Son, and she shall be to Me a Mother? And again: Let the Son of God be subject to Mary?——If the Son has His throne for ever and ever, is anointed King, and exalted above all creation at the right hand of the Eternal Father, His enemies being made His footstool, where shall be the place for Mary, the Mother of this Divine Son, of this anointed King—for her who gave Him that Humanity which is thus exalted in His Divine Person? David shall tell us where, in the very passage to which S. Paul here refers: "The Queen stood on thy right hand in gilded clothing; surrounded with variety . . . her beauty the King shall greatly desire . . . All the glory of the King's daughter is within, in golden borders, clothed round with varieties . . . After her shall virgins be brought to the King . . . her neighbours shall be brought."[2] S. John also will tell us of her in her glory, as "a woman clothed with the sun, and the moon under her feet, and on her head a crown of twelve stars."[3]——Verily is the glory of Mary exalted above that of all the Angels; for *are they not all ministering spirits, sent to minister for them who shall receive the inheritance of salvation;* and is she not the true Mother of Him, Who is the head of all principality and power, the Redeemer and the Author of salvation? We should here bear in mind that when the Eternal Father *brought in the First-begotten into the world* at His birth in the stable of Bethlehem, *and all the angels of God adored Him*, Mary, His Mother was there. How profoundly must they then have venerated her. This is S. Bonaventure's thought. "But if," says a devout writer commenting on it, "those blessed spirits paid veneration to Mary whilst she was still on earth, what honour think you, do they

---

[1] "The Maker of all things, and the Father of ages He saith that He hath *to-day* begotten; that by attaching a term indicative of time to the season of His Generation, the words may bring before one not the Existence before the ages, but the Generation in time by the Flesh for man's salvation" (S. Greg. Nyss. i. p. 386 d).——"One saith, As for this Child, this day was His birth (*Is.* ix. 6; *Ps.* ii. 7): and another, The Ancient of Days, and the Elder of all the Creation" (*Dan.* vii. 6; *Eccles.* i. 4.)—S. Ephrem, *Rhythm against the Jews.* Morris, p. 67.

[2] *Ps.* xliv. 9-16.   [3] *Apoc.* xii. 1.

render to her now that she holds the first place in heaven after God, in splendour of unimaginable glory on her throne at the right hand of her most dearly beloved Son?"[1]

CHAPTER II.

3 How shall we escape if we neglect so great salvation? which having begun to be declared by the Lord, was confirmed unto us by them that heard him.

Since the fact of having heard the word of Jesus Christ was the ground of authority which *gave it confirmation*. What confirmation must Mary not have given; for who was there who heard, who knew Him as she did?

5 For God hath not subjected unto angels the world to come, whereof we speak.

But to Mary "the Father of the world to come"[2] was really subject. Mary had over Him the rights of a mother. It is little to say of her that she is above the Angels, and the rest of creation. For what, after all, is it to be Queen of Angels and all creation, compared with being Mother of God, the Maker and Lord of Angels, and the whole creation? What honour, short of that which belongs to God alone, can be too great for us to pay to her whom God has thus honoured?

9 But we see Jesus, who was made a little lower than the angels, for the suffering of death, crowned with glory and honour: that, through the grace of God, he might taste death for all.
10 For it became him, for whom are all things, and by whom are all things, who had brought many children into glory, to perfect the author of their salvation, by his passion.

Mary, too, who is of all the most closely allied with Jesus, though lower than the Angels by nature, is crowned with surpassing glory and honour.—It was meet that she who had the chief share with Jesus in the work of our salvation, and is our spiritual mother, should be made perfect, by having the chief share in His Passion.

---

[1] **Alexius a Salo,** *De art. amandi Deip.* c. i.   [2] *Isa.* ix. 6.

11 For both he that sanctifieth, and they that are sanctified, are all of one. For which cause he is not ashamed to call them brethren.

Jesus Christ and His faithful *are all of One*, that is, of One God and Father. Hence Jesus Christ is our Brother. Again, they with Him are all of One, that is, of One Mother, the Blessed Virgin Mary. We have here another ground for claiming Him as our Brother.

14 Therefore because the children are partakers of flesh and blood, he also himself in like manner hath been partaker of the same: that, through death, he might destroy him who had the empire of death, that is to say, the devil:
15 And might deliver them, who through the fear of death were all their life-time subject to servitude.

Here, implicitly, but emphatically, the Apostle refers to Mary. For well did he know that it was of Mary alone Jesus Christ received that same flesh and blood, through which by death, He triumphed over Satan and wrought our redemption.

16 For no where doth he take hold of the angels: but of the seed of Abraham he taketh hold.
17 Wherefore it behoved him in all things to be made like unto his brethren.

Of the seed of Abraham He took hold in His Incarnation, generally and remotely: but of Mary He took hold, in particular and immediately. Through Abraham, says the Apostle, we are made brethren of Jesus Christ: and Abraham is our father. How much more, then, through Mary; and how much more is she our Mother. For of her pure blood alone did He take hold, and therefrom derived His own most precious Blood, by which we were redeemed from death and received our life.

18 For in that, wherein he himself hath suffered and been tempted, he is able to succour them also that are tempted.

In a true sense we might apply these words of S. Paul to Mary, who, on our account, had the greatest share in all the sufferings of her Divine Son. How well might she use the language of the old poet: *Haud ignara mali miseris succurrere disco.*

"There is not one amongst all the Saints," says S. Antoninus, "who can ever feel for us in our miseries, both corporal and spiritual, like this woman, the Blessed Virgin Mary."[1]

CHAPTER III.

5 And Moses indeed was faithful in all his house as a servant, for a testimony of those things which were to be said:
6 But Christ as the Son in his own house: which house are we, if we hold fast the confidence and glory of hope unto the end.

Mary was faithful as the Mother and Mistress in her own house. And what a house and family was that over which she presided! Do we not here see a claim for Mary's dignity, and for her pre-eminence over all the choirs of Angels and Saints in heaven? And may we not trust that faithful Virgin to care for, as Lady and Mother, the house of Christ her Son on earth, His Holy Church, to which we are called; and to take care of ourselves in particular, if only we hold fast, by true devotion to her, the *confidence and glory of hope*, which we have in her protection, unto the end?

"It was just—according to what the Apostle says in his Epistle to the Hebrews, regarding *Moses as a faithful servant in his house*, and *Christ as an only Son ruling in His house*—that His own Mother should by her virtues and glory preside over the whole family, next after Himself in the same house. As, therefore, to her belongs the name, peerless and unique, high above all others, after God, of Mother of God; so peerless and unique, high above all others after God, here on earth and in heaven, is the grace and glory of the same Mother of God."[2]

CHAPTER IV.

1 Let us fear therefore lest the promise being left of entering into his rest, any of you should be thought to be wanting.
2 For unto us also it hath been declared, in like manner as unto them. But the word of hearing did not profit them, not being mixed with faith of those things they heard.

---

[1] *P.* iv., *tit.* xv. *cap.* 2.
[2] Petrus Venerab. *L.* iii. *Ep.* 7. *Bib. Max. t.* 22, *p.* 901.

3 For we, who have believed, shall enter into rest; as he said.
9 There remaineth therefore a day of rest for the people of God.
11 Let us hasten therefore to enter into that rest.

The Holy Ghost has more than once borne testimony to Mary that she believed, and kept the Divine word in her heart to her profit. She is emphatically pronounced blessed for her faith. Is not, then, her super-eminent faith blessed with a corresponding share of *the rest of Paradise?* If there remaineth a rest for the people of God, how much more for the Mother of God—for her who whilst on earth so ardently aspired and hastened to enter into that rest: "In all these I sought rest ... in the holy city likewise I rested ... and my abode is in the full assembly of the saints."[1]

12 For the word of God is living and effectual, and more piercing than any two-edged sword; and reaching unto the division of the soul and the spirit, of the joints also and the marrow, and is a discerner of the thoughts and intents of the heart.
13 Neither is there any creature invisible in his sight; but all things are naked and open to his eyes, to whom our speech is.

There is much similarity of ideas in these words of the Apostle and those of Simeon to Mary: "And thy own soul a sword shall pierce, that out of many hearts thoughts may be revealed."[2] The word of God that Mary then heard was to her indeed living and effectual, and as a two-edged sword pierced her soul, revealing to her many diverse thoughts both of sorrow and joy. The living Incarnate Word of God Himself, proved to be to her also such a sword in His Passion and Death.[3] In commenting upon Simeon's words, S. Ambrose, S. Augustine, S. Bede, and other Fathers interpret these words of S. Paul in the same sense, and apply them to our Lady.

"God," says S. Antoninus, "may be said to be by His presence in all things, because He knows all the most secret things of creation: *All things are naked and open to His eyes.* But He was by His presence in the Blessed Virgin, not only

---

[1] *Ecclus.* xxiv. 11-16. See the Breviary Office for the Feast of the Assumption, 15th August.
[2] *Luke* ii. 35.   [3] See *supra, Eph.* vi. 17

because He saw all things that were secret in her, her thoughts and affections, with the eye of cognition; but also because He approved all her acts interior and exterior, with the eye of approbation."[1]

14 Having therefore a great high-priest that hath passed into the heavens, Jesus the Son of God: let us hold fast our confession.
15 For we have not a high-priest, who cannot have compassion on our infirmities: but one tempted in all things like as we are, without sin.
16 Let us go therefore with confidence to the throne of grace: that we may obtain mercy, and find grace in seasonable aid.

We might apply these words regarding our Divine Redeemer to Mary, in a sense they could not attach to any other: Having therefore an advocate passed into heaven, Mary the Mother of God, given to be our Mother also—one full of mercy and compassion, who herself suffered and was tempted in all things as we are, yet without sin—let us go with confidence to her throne of grace, for she is full of grace, that we may obtain mercy and grace, through her intercession, and seasonable aid.

CHAPTER V.

4 Neither doth any man take the honour to himself, but he that is called by God, as Aaron was.
5 So Christ also did not glorify himself, that he might be made a high-priest: but he that said unto him: Thou art my Son, this day have I begotten thee.
6 As he saith also in another place: Thou art a priest for ever, according to the order of Melchisedech.
7 Who in the days of his flesh, with a strong cry and tears, offering up prayers and supplications to him that was able to save him from death, was heard for his reverence.
8 And whereas indeed he was the Son of God, he learned obedience by the things which he suffered.
9 And being consummated, he became, to all that obey him, the cause of eternal salvation.

Neither did Mary ever think to take the honour to herself, or to glorify herself, that she should be the Mother of God, but He who sent unto her: "Behold thou shalt conceive in

---

[1] *P.* iv *tit.* 15, *cap.* 21.

thy womb, and shalt bring forth a Son, and thou shalt call His Name Jesus—the Son of God."[1] From Mary, let us bear in mind, it was that Christ received the essential constituent elements of His priesthood; to wit, that Sacred Humanity, whereby as *a Priest for ever after the order of Melchisedech*, He continually offers up in His holy Church His Body and Blood, under the appearance of bread and wine.

"Mary too," says B. Albertus Magnus, " when she prays to her Son for us, is heard *for her reverence*, that is to say, for the reverence which is due to her as His own Mother."

We may also say of Mary, that whereas indeed she was the Mother of God, she *learned obedience by the things which she suffered;* an obedience most like to that of Jesus Christ, in whose sufferings she had the greatest share, since the same sword that caused His Passion pierced at the same time her own heart. It is, so to say, quite a commonplace amongst the earliest Fathers, that as Eve was by her disobedience the cause of our ruin, so Mary by her obedience obtained our salvation.

CHAPTER VI.

10 For God is not unjust, that he should forget your work, and the love which you have shewn in his name, you who have ministered, and do minister to the saints.

Mary ministered not to Saints alone, and in the name of Jesus, but to Himself in person, the Lord and King of Saints, the most beloved Only-begotten Son of God, as a Mother to her own Son. What a showing forth of work and love to Jesus was the whole life of Mary. Is He unjust that He should forget her and all that she did for Him on earth? Does He not reward her proportionately with glory now in Heaven?

CHAPTER VII.

1 For this Melchisedech, king of Salem, priest of the most high God, who met Abraham returning from the slaughter of the kings, 6 Blessed him that had the promises.

Melchisedech, the type of Jesus Christ our great High-

---

[1] *Luke* i. 31-35.

priest, blessed the patriarch Abraham, who, remotely, *had the promises*, viz., that through his seed, that is, Jesus Christ, all the nations of the earth should be blessed. What, then, must be the blessing that our Lord Jesus Christ, the true Melchisedech, bestowed upon Mary, to whom the promises were actually fulfilled, by herself being His own Mother.

14 For it is evident that our Lord sprung out of Juda.

It is clear that the Apostle has here Mary in his mind, though he is silent with regard to her personally. How could it be *evident* to S. Paul and to those for whom he writes, *that our Lord sprung out of Juda*, unless with the actual thought of our Lord's Mother, "Mary of whom was born Jesus"? Hence we see that the silence about Mary in the Epistles cannot be brought forward any way as an index of the little share and place she had in the mind and estimation of the sacred writers.

26 For it was fitting that we should have such a high priest, holy, innocent, undefiled, separated from sinners, and made higher than the heavens.

If Mary, from whom Jesus Christ derived His human nature, viz., that flesh and blood which were to be essential constituent elements of His perfect priesthood, had been once a sinner, subject to the curse of original sin, then He would not have been, as the Apostle affirms He was, *a high priest separated from sinners*. Mary was, therefore, entirely sinless and immaculate. *This too was fitting.*[1]

"A learned author observes that, according to S. Paul, it was fitting that our Blessed Redeemer should not only be separated from sin, but also from sinners; according to the explanation of S. Thomas, who says that 'it was necessary that He, who came to take away sins, should be separated from sinners, as to the fault under which Adam lay.'[2] But how could Jesus Christ be said to be separated from sinners, if He had a Mother who was a sinner? S. Ambrose says that 'Christ chose this vessel into which He was about to descend,

---

[1] See 2 *Cor.* vii. 1, *supra*.   [2] 3 *p. q.* iv. *art.* 6, *ad.* 2m.

not of earth, but from heaven; and He consecrated it a temple of purity.[1] The Saint alludes to the text of S. Paul: 'The first man was of the earth, earthly: the second man from heaven, heavenly.'[2] The Saint calls the Divine Mother 'a heavenly vessel,' not because Mary was not earthly by nature, as heretics have dreamt, but because she was heavenly by grace; she was as superior to the angels of heaven in sanctity and purity, as it was becoming that she should be, in whose womb a King of Glory was to dwell. This agrees with that which S. John the Baptist revealed to S. Bridget, saying, 'It was not becoming that the King of Glory should repose otherwise than in a chosen vessel exceeding all men and angels in purity.'[3] And to this we may add that which the Eternal Father Himself said to the same Saint: 'Mary was a clean and an unclean vessel: clean, for she was all fair; but unclean, because she was born of sinners; though she was conceived without sin.'[4] And remark these last words, 'Mary was conceived without sin, that the Divine Son might be born of her without sin.' Not that Jesus Christ could have contracted sin, but that He might not be reproached with even having a Mother infected with it, who would consequently have been the slave of the devil."[5]

CHAPTER IX.

2. For there was a tabernacle made the first, wherein were the candlesticks, and the table, and the setting forth of loaves, which is called the Holy.

3 And after the secondveil, the tabernacle, which is called the Holy of Holies:

4 Having a golden censer, and the ark of the testament covered about on every part with gold, in which was a golden pot that had manna, and the rod of Aaron that had blossomed, and the tables of the testament.

11 But Christ, being come an high-priest of the good things to come, by a greater and more perfect tabernacle not made with hand, that is, not of this creation:

---

[1] *De Inst. Virg.* c. 5.   [2] 1 *Cor.* xv. 47.   [3] *Rev.* lib. i. c. 31.
[4] *Ib.* l. v.   *Exp. Rev.* xiii.
[5] S. Alph. Lig. *Disc. on Mary's Immac. Concept. Glories of Mary*, p. 250, 1

12 Neither by the blood of goats, or of calves, but by his own blood, entered once into the Holies, having obtained eternal redemption.

24 For Jesus is not entered into the Holies made with hands, the patterns of the true: but into heaven itself, that he may appear now in the presence of God for us.

In the writings of the Fathers and in the language of Catholic devotion most of the particulars here enumerated are applied mystically to the Blessed Virgin.

"'When the ark was lifted up, Moses said : Arise, O Lord, and let thy enemies be scattered.'[1] Thus was Jericho conquered. Thus also the Philistines; 'for the ark of God was there.'[2] It is well known that this ark was a figure of Mary. Cornelius a Lapide says, 'In time of danger Christians should fly to the Most Blessed Virgin, who contained Christ as manna in the ark of her womb,[3] and brought Him forth to be the food and salvation of the world.'"[4]

"O burning bush unconsumed, open meadow, and *blossoming rod of Aaron!*" exclaims S. Ephrem, "for thou truly wert the rod, and thy Son the flower; since from the root of David and Solomon budded forth Christ, our Creator, Almighty God and Lord, the alone Most High. Of Him Who is God and Man art thou Mother, Virgin before birth, Virgin in birth, and Virgin after birth."[5] The same Saint says elsewhere : "A King's palace she was by Thee, O Son of the King, and *a Holy of Holies* by Thee, O High priest."[6]

And S. Germanus : "Thou art *the tabernacle not made with hands*, but made by God, into which only God the Word and first High priest entered in once at the end of ages,[7] secretly to accomplish in thee sacred mysteries."[8]

"By *the tables of the Testament*," says Blessed Albert the Great, "are signified the perfect knowledge of the Old and

---

[1] *Numb.* x. 35.   [2] *Kings* xiv.18.
[3] *A golden pot that had manna* : see S. Basil of Saleucia, *supra*, Rom. ix. 23.
[4] S. Alph. Lig., *Glories of Mary*, p. 113.
[5] *De laud. Gen. Dei Maria. Opp. Gr. t.* iii. p. 575. See *supra*, Rom. xv. 12.
[6] *De Natal. Dom.* xii. *Opp. Syr. t.* ii. Morris, p. 53.
[7] See v.v. 7, 11, 25, 26 ; iv. 14 ; viii. 2.   [8] *In Nativ. S. Deip.*

New Law which Mary had fully, because the Author of the Scriptures dwelt in her: hence S. Jerome says that she was most excellently versed in the Scriptures as is clear from her own words: Sicut locutus est ad patres nostros;[1] and also from what we read: 'Mary kept all these words, pondering them in her heart;'[2] so that she afterwards taught the Apostles, and was instructress of the New Testament. For since in Mary was the whole by prefigurement, she may be truly said to have had a full knowledge of both Laws; and this is signified by the union in the ark, of Deuteronomy and the tables of the Testament."[3]

"In Mary," says S. Antoninus, "was the treasure of wisdom,[4] signified by the Law laid up in the ark. For no pure creature had so great knowledge of divine things and such as pertain to salvation as Mary; hence she was the instructress of the Apostles and Evangelists, to teach them concerning the mysteries of Christ. And no wonder that she had an immense treasure of wisdom since in her reposed Christ in whom are all the treasures of the wisdom and knowledge of God in fulness. And he, says S. Ambrose, who knows Christ, knows the treasure of wisdom and knowledge. There was also in the ark *the rod*, which signifies power and dominion. For Mary is Queen of heaven, and Mistress (Domina) of the angels. Now as the ark was considered as what was most precious in the tabernacle of old, so also Mary is held to be that which is most precious and holy in the tabernacle of the Church."[5]

"Christ, our High priest," says Armandus de Bello-visu, "entered once into the Holy of Holies, that is, the Virgin's womb, when He took to Himself blood for the expiation of our sins. Hence it is said, *Christ being come a high priest . . . not by the blood of goats or of calves,* for then He would not have been of our race; *but by His own blood,* that is to say, by

---

[1] *Luke* i. 55.   [2] *Ib.* ii. 19, 51.   [3] *De laud. B.M.V.* cap. 1.
[4] *Wisd.* vii. 14.   [5] *P.* iv. *tit.* xv. *cap.* xiv. § 4.

assuming our human blood, *entered once into the Holies*, that is, the Virgin."¹

"As our Lord Jesus Christ *entered into heaven itself, that He may appear now in the presence of God for us;* so the Mother of God assumed to heaven, appears in the presence of her Son, as the bow in the clouds, the token of divine clemency, and shows to Him her breasts, whereby she ceases not to invoke His mercy in behalf of us sinners. Hence in the prayer called *the Secret* of the Mass for the Vigil of the Assumption, the Church supplicating to be heard through the prayers of the Mother of God, utters these words concerning her: *Since for this cause Thou hast translated her from this present world, that before Thee she may intercede with confidence for our sins.*"²

CHAPTER X.

5 Wherefore when he cometh into the world, he saith: Sacrifice and oblation thou wouldest not: but a body thou hast fitted to me:
19 Having therefore, brethren, a confidence in the entering into the Holies by the blood of Christ;
20 A new and living way which he hath dedicated for us through the veil, that is to say, his flesh.
21 And a high-priest over the house of God.

There is here no direct reference to Mary, and to the share which she had in giving that Body, of Flesh and Blood, whereby Christ became at once our High-priest and Sacrifice. But the thought of Mary could not have been absent from the Apostle's mind, illumined so fully as he was to see the whole mysteries of which he wrote in all their truth and bearings.

CHAPTER XI.

11 By faith also Sara herself, being barren, received strength to conceive seed, even past the time of age; because she believed that he was faithful who had promised,
12 For which cause there sprung even from one (and him as good as dead) as the stars of heaven in multitude, and as the sand which is by the sea-shore innumerable.
17 By faith Abraham, when he was tried, offered Isaac: and he that had received the promises, offered up his only-begotten son;

---

¹ Ap. *Sum. Aur. de B.M.V.* Tom. ii. p. 1532.   ² Adam. Brower., *Ibid.*

18 (To whom it was said: In Isaac shall thy seed be called).
19 Accounting that God is able to raise up even from the dead. Whereupon also he received him for a parable.

"If," says S. Alphonsus, "the sacrifice of Abraham by which he offered his son Isaac was so pleasing to the Divine Majesty, that as a reward God promised to multiply his descendants as the stars of heaven: 'Because thou hast done this thing, and hast not spared thy only-begotten son for My sake, I will bless thee, and I will multiply thy seed as the stars of heaven:[1] we must certainly believe that the more noble sacrifice which the great Mother of God made to Him of her Jesus, was far more agreeable to Him; and therefore, that He has granted, that through her prayers the number of the elect should be multiplied; that is to say, increased by the number of her fortunate children; for she considers and protects all her devout clients as such."[2]

"'So also,' says S. Bonaventure, 'we can say of Mary, that she has so loved us, as to give her only-begotten Son for us.' . . . If Abraham had such fortitude as to be ready to sacrifice with his own hands the life of his son, with far greater fortitude would Mary (far more holy and obedient than Abraham) have sacrificed the life of hers."[3]

38 Of whom the world was not worthy; wandering in deserts, in mountains, and in dens, and in caves of the earth.
39 And all these being approved by the testimony of faith, received not the promise;
40 God providing some better thing for us, that they should not be perfected without us.

Jesus and Mary were above all others those *of whom the world was not worthy*, and were at the same time, of all the most despised, and had most to suffer. "He came to His own, and His own received Him not."[4] Of Himself He said: "The foxes have holes, and the birds of the air nests; but the Son

---

[1] *Gen.* xxii. 16, 17. See *supra, Rom.* iv. 3, 16-25; ix. 8, 9; *Gal.* iii. 6-9, 14, 16, 18, 22, 26-29; iv. 22-31; and *infra, James* ii. 21-23.
[2] *Discourse on the Purification. Glories of Mary*, p. 344.
[3] *Ib.* pp. 32, 3.   [4] *John* i. 11.

of Man hath not where to lay His head."[1] Mary shared in all His contempt and misery. She had to betake herself to the cold stable-cave at Bethlehem in mid-winter to give Him birth; in her flight with Him to Egypt to take refuge in dens and caves amongst the mountains, and to wander hither and thither through the inhospitable desert, and to dwell with Him homeless in a strange land. When expressing their contempt for Jesus, the Jews coupled her name with His, saying: "Is not this the carpenter's son? is not his mother called Mary?"[2]

"If Paul says of the other saints, *Of whom the world was not worthy*, what shall we say of the Mother of God, who outshines all the Martyrs, as much as does the sun the stars?"[3]

But Mary, being above all others *approved by the testimony of faith, received the promise*, even her God to be her Son, through whom *some better thing has been provided for us, that we may be perfected* not wanting in any grace.

CHAPTER XII.

22 But you are come to Mount Sion, and to the city of the living God, the heavenly Jerusalem, and to the company of many thousands. of angels,
23 And to the church of the first-born, who are written in the heavens, and to God the judge of all, and to the spirits of the just. made perfect.
24 And to Jesus the mediator of the new testament, and to the sprinkling of blood which speaketh better than that of Abel.

Mary is in truth the holy city and habitation of the living God, Who dwelt in her chaste womb for nine months. As Mother of God she is exalted higher far in the heavens than His myriads of Angels. She is, of all the elect, the first-born, next after her Divine Son—*Primogenitus a mortuis*—the first of creatures written in God's decrees.[4] If we are brought nigh to God, to Jesus the Mediator of the New Testament, to the Angels, and to the spirits of the just, we are, in a special manner, brought nigh to Mary, our own earth-born daughter,.

---

[1] *Matt.* viii. 20; *Luke* ix. 58.   [2] *Matt.* xiii. 55; *Mark* vi. 3; *John* vi. 42.
[3] S. Basil of Seleucia. *Orat.* x. *de Annunt.*
[4] See *Note, James* i. 18, *infra.*

the glory of our race: through whom we obtained for us Jesus our Mediator, from whom He received that precious Blood which pleads so powerfully in our behalf. If already we are brought nigh to the Angels who are of a different nature from ourselves, Mary in heaven is not estranged from us here on earth—from us for whom she was made what she is.——But Mary, now in glory, to whom is she herself brought nigh? and how nigh? What is her proximity now to Jesus and to God? Is she less near than she was when on earth? *Dominus tecum.* For we should note that this present approach, this actual proximity of ours, is the climax of all the glorious privileges here enumerated by the Apostle, as belonging to us Christians in the Communion of Saints: *You are come*, he says. What then must be the climax for Mary, for her who was ever with God, for her to whom Jesus Christ first came; of whom He was and is; through whom He came to all others, and all others come to Him?

28 Therefore, receiving an immovable kingdom, we have grace whereby let us serve, pleasing God, with fear and reverence.

This is all realised in Mary: "Hail, full of grace." "Behold the handmaid of the Lord." "Thou hast found grace with God." "He hath regarded the humility of His handmaiden." "His mercy is on them that fear Him." "Holy is His Name."

CHAPTER XIII.

12 Wherefore Jesus also, that he might sanctify the people by his own blood, suffered without the gate.
13 Let us go forth therefore to him without the camp, bearing his reproach.

Where Jesus suffered, there was Mary: "Now there stood by the Cross of Jesus His Mother."[1] *She went forth to Him without the camp, bearing His reproach.* Let us follow Mary; she is our example.

15 By him therefore let us offer the sacrifice of praise always to God, that is to say, the fruit of lips confessing to his name.
16 And do not forget to do good, and to impart; for by such sacrifices God's favour is obtained.

[1] *John* xix. 25.

By Jesus, present in her virginal womb, Mary offered to God the sacrifice of praise, confessing to His Name, when she poured forth her Canticle, "My soul doth magnify the Lord. . . . Holy is His Name. . . ." Her offering of praise was not alone the fruit of her lips, but Jesus Himself, "the blessed fruit of her womb."

We need but to recall the scenes of the Visitation, and the Wedding-feast at Cana, to see that Mary *forgot not to do good and to impart* to others of the gifts and graces which she had herself received, and that the acts which she there did, were sacrifices acceptable and well-pleasing to God, since it was through her mediation that He then wrought such great marvels.

20 And may the God of peace, who brought again from the dead the great pastor of the sheep, our Lord Jesus Christ, in the blood of the everlasting testament,
21 Fit you in all goodness, that you may do his will; doing in you that which is well pleasing in his sight, through Jesus Christ; to whom is glory for ever and ever. Amen.

The God of peace, in reconciling the world to Himself, filled Mary with grace *to do His will—Fiat mihi secundum verbum tuum*—and wrought in her that which was well pleasing in His sight, so that she became the Mother of the great Pastor of the sheep, our Lord Jesus Christ, who shed His Blood for our redemption, and rose again from the dead for our justification.

24 Salute . . . all the saints.

Ave, Regina cœlorum,
Ave Domina Angelorum;
Salve radix, salve porta
Ex qua mundo lux est orta.

Gaude, Virgo gloriosa;
Super omnes speciosa;
Vale O valde decora,
Et pro nobis Christum exora.

THE CATHOLIC EPISTLE

OF

S. JAMES THE APOSTLE.

CHAPTER I.

3 Knowing that the trying of your faith worketh patience.
4 And patience hath a perfect work; that you may be perfect and entire, failing in nothing.

Mary, next to Jesus Christ her Son, had the most to suffer, and was most exercised in patience. In her, *patience had a perfect work*, as she stood by the Cross assisting at the death of her Son. As He was made perfect through suffering, so too was Mary through her patience made *perfect and entire, failing in nothing.*

"*Patience*," says S. Antoninus, "*hath a perfect work*, when one is not excited on account of adversity, but one bears it when it comes with equanimity. For this there are the examples of the Saints, who, though just, had many things to suffer, but did so most patiently. Now the most blessed Virgin had no lack of adversities, as neither had her Son; but when a few days after the birth of her Babe He was sought for to be slain, she had to fly into Egypt, and there remain for seven years amongst idolators, and strangers; and when at the age of twelve He remained behind in the temple, without her knowledge, she sought Him for three days, not without sorrow, but without anger, and such sadness as to absorb or obscure reason. She was likewise most patient in the persecutions of her Son; and hence is said of her: 'As the lily among thorns, so is my love among the daughters.'[1] Neither the lily, nor the rose loses its beauty and fragrance amongst thorns, so neither did Mary lose the sweet odour of patience amongst tribulations."[2]

---

[1] *Cant.* ii. 2.　　　　[2] *P. iv. tit.* 15, *c.* 26, § 1.

9 But let the brother of low condition glory in his exaltation:
10 And the rich, in his being low.

Mary, in her lowly-mindedness as the handmaid of the Lord, gloried in her exaltation: *Et exultavit spiritus meus . . . quia fecit mihi magna qui potens est.* Again, Mary, though so rich in grace, and possessed of Him " in whom are hid all the treasures of wisdom and knowledge," gloried, rather, in her low estate, which God had deigned to regard: *Quia respexit humilitatem ancillæ suæ.*"

12 Blessed is the man that endureth temptation; for when he hath been proved, he shall receive the crown of life, which God hath promised to them that love him.

Mary, the blessed amongst women, had pre-eminently this blessedness of which the Apostle here speaks. For who was ever tried, who ever endured as she? Having been well proved, the crown of life that she has received surpasses that of all others in glory; since she loved God with a love exceeding far that of all others, and loved Him both as her God, and as her Son.

17 Every best gift, and every perfect gift, is from above, coming down from the Father of lights, with whom there is no change, nor shadow of alteration.
18 For of his own will hath he begotten us by the word of truth, that we might be some beginning of his creature.

The Gift of gifts, the best and the most perfect of all others, was given by the Father of lights to Mary, even that of His Only-begotten co-equal Son. Mary was in a peculiar, and far higher sense than others, the chosen daughter of the Eternal Father. And not only was she *begotten by the word of truth, and was the beginning of His creation,*[1] but she herself conceived and gave birth to the Divine Incarnate Word of truth.

---

[1] " Ego ab ore Altissimi prodivi primogenita ante omnem creaturam." " Ab initio creata sum," etc. *Ecclus.* xxiv. 5. 14. " Dominus possedit me in initio viarum suarum, antequam quidquam faceret a principio," etc. *Parab. Salom.* viii. 22. Words spoken of Eternal Wisdom, but applied by the Holy Church to the Blessed Virgin in the Breviary Lections for our Lady's Feasts.

"No grace," says S. Bernardine of Sienna, "comes down from heaven save through Mary. Such is the hierarchical order of the effusion of heavenly graces. They come from God into the blessed soul of Christ: *Every best gift, and every perfect gift, is from above, coming down from the Father of lights.* They then descend into the soul of the Virgin: into the Seraphim and Cherubim, and the other angelic orders: into the soul of the Saints, lastly on the Church militant."[1]

19 And let every man be swift to hear, but slow to speak, and slow to anger.
21 Wherefore . . . with meekness receive the ingrafted word, which is able to save your souls.
22 But be ye doers of the word, and not hearers only, deceiving your own selves.
23 For if a man be a hearer of the word, and not a doer, he shall be compared to a man beholding his own countenance in a glass.
24 For he beheld himself, and went his way, and presently forgot what manner of man he was.
25 But he that hath looked into the perfect law of liberty, and hath continued therein, not becoming a forgetful hearer, but a doer of the work; this man shall be blessed in his deed.
26 And if any man think himself to be religious, not bridling his tongue, but deceiving his own heart, this man's religion is vain.
27 Religion clean and undefiled before God and the Father, is this: to visit the fatherless and widows in their tribulation: and to keep one's self unspotted from this world.

If we study the portrait of the Blessed Virgin, as sketched in the Gospel narrative, and her character, as unvarying tradition has impressed it in the minds and hearts of the faithful, we shall find shining brightly in her all those virtuous traits which the Apostle here commends. She was most prudent in her speech, sweet and gentle in her bearing: she received with meekness the divine word, keeping and pondering over it in her heart, listening to it with humble attention from the lips of all whoever they might be, whether the Archangel Gabriel or Elizabeth, Shepherds or Sages, Simeon or Anna; welcoming it though it might deeply wound her heart.—— Mary was not a hearer only but a faithful doer of the word, and was blessed in her deed. She shewed to all a

---

[1] *Serm. de glorios. nom. Mariæ.* art. 3. c. 2.

perfect model of religion, clean and undefiled, before God and the Father, by her holy life of spotless purity, and her works of charity and mercy towards others : of these the Visitation, and her mediation at Cana are typical instances, and wil suggest to us how many were the services she rendered to those in need and distress, whilst following our Lord in His public ministry, and, after His Ascension, in the infant Church during the years she still remained on earth.[1]

CHAPTER II.

1 My brethren, have not the faith of our Lord Jesus Christ of glory with respect of persons.

2 For if there shall come into your assembly a man having a golden ring, in fine apparel, and there shall come in also a poor man in mean attire,

3 And you have respect to him that is clothed with the fine apparel, and shall say to him : Sit thou here well; but say to the poor man : Stand thou there, or sit under my footstool :

4 Do you not judge within yourselves, and are become judges of unjust thoughts?

The faith of our Lord Jesus Christ that Mary had, was free from all such respect of persons. She knew that He, the Lord of glory, was meek and humble of heart, that He scatters the proud and lofty-minded, and exalts the humble. Her heart was most like to His own. She knew how to receive the poor, rude, and simple shepherds, with a like sweet grace, courtesy and charity, as she did the rich and royal Magi.

"And deem not," says S. Ambrose, "the words of the shepherds to be despised as though of little worth. For from the shepherds Mary gathers faith. From the shepherds a people is congregated for the worship of God. They were, too, in admiration, all who heard what was said to them by the shepherds. But Mary kept all these words, pondering

---

[1] Hence Mary is styled by the Church, and invoked by the faithful, as Virgo prudentissima, Vas spirituale, Vas insigne devotionis—and as Mater misericordiæ, dulcedo et spes nostra, O clemens, O pia, O dulcis Virgo Maria, Mater amabilis, Virgo clemens, Causa nostræ lætitiæ, Salus infirmorum, Refugium peccatorum, Consolatrix afflictorum, Auxilium Christianorum.

them over in her heart. Let us learn the chastity in all things of holy Mary, who no less pure in speech than in body, pondered over the arguments of faith in her heart."[1]

5 Hearken, my dearest brethren: hath not God chosen the poor in this world, rich in faith, and heirs of the kingdom which God hath promised to them that love him.

What choice did God ever make like to His choice of Mary to be His Mother—the model, type and crown of all His elections? Poor indeed in this world she was, for she gave birth to her Divine Child in a stable. But *rich in faith*— blessed in believing—surpassing all others in the wealth of her love to God, she was on earth the first heir of the promise. What, then, is her right amongst the heirs of the heavenly kingdom? Surely, as she so excelled in all that gives aught of claim in God's kingdom on earth, her right is to be Queen over all in His kingdom above. *Regina cœli, lœtare, Alleluia!*

21 Was not Abraham our father justified by works, offering up Isaac his son upon the altar?
22 Seest thou, that faith did co-operate with his works; and by works faith was made perfect?
23 And the scripture was fulfilled, saying: Abraham believed God, and it was reputed to him to justice, and he was called the friend of God.

Abraham, to whom the promise was made, became through his faith, the father of the faithful. Mary, to whom first the promise was actually fulfilled, became, by her excelling faith, in a far higher sense than Abraham is their father, the Mother of the faithful. Like Abraham, Mary also was justified by works: of which in either case the principal was that of offering a sacrifice. But what a difference in the sacrifice of one and the other. Abraham offered up in will, though not in effect, the sacrifice of Isaac his son—Mary offered up, not only in will, but also in effect, Jesus Christ her only Son, Whom she loved incomparably more than Abraham loved Isaac, on the altar of the Cross. Isaac was a type of Jesus Christ the Lamb slain from the foundation of the world;

---

[1] *Lib.* ii. *in Luc. c.* ii. *circa med.*

and Abraham's offering was but a figure of the sacrifice which Mary made.

"O Lady," says S. Anselm, "what fountains of tears burst forth from thy most modest eyes, as thou didst behold thy only Son, so holy and innocent, before thee scourged, bound, bruised, His flesh torn by wicked men. And yet so conformed wert thou to the Divine Will, as to be most eager for the salvation of mankind, that (I am bold to say it), had there been no one found to crucify thy Son, thou wouldst have thyself placed Him on the Cross, if so the salvation of men and the will of God required it. For we are not to believe that there was less perfection and obedience towards God in Mary, than in Abraham, who offered to God his own son as a sacrifice to be slain, and bound with his own hands."

Seest thou not how faith did cooperate with her works; and by her works which corresponded in excellence to her faith— *her faith was made perfect? And the Scripture was fulfilled, saying,* "Blessed art thou that hast believed, because those things shall be accomplished, that were spoken to thee by the Lord."[1] Thus faith obtained for Mary a complete triumph over Satan, God's enemy, who had brought to ruin our first mother Eve; and it *was reputed to her for justice,* and she was called, and was indeed, *the friend of God*,[2] even His own beloved Mother.

CHAPTER III.

17 But the wisdom, that is from above, first indeed is chaste, then peaceable, modest, easy to be persuaded, consenting to the good, full of mercy and good fruits, without judging, without dissimulation.

18 And the fruit of justice is sown in peace, to them that make peace.

Here we have a beautiful description of Mary, who is called by the Church, *Sedes Sapientiæ*, as her character has been impressed on the mind of the faithful and traced by tradition.

---

[1] *Luke* i. 45.   [2] "Amica mea." *Cant.* ii. 2.

CHAPTER IV.

6 But he giveth greater grace. Wherefore he saith: God resisteth the proud, and giveth grace to the humble.
7 Be subject therefore to God, but resist the devil, and he will fly from you.
8 Draw nigh to God, and he will draw nigh to you.
10 Be humbled in the sight of the Lord, and he will exalt you.

Who so humble as Mary, who so subject to God as she? *Ecce ancilla Domini*—To her then God gave *His greatest grace*.

"To be the Mother of God," says S. Bonaventure, "is the *greatest grace* that can be conferred on a pure creature. God could make a greater world, God could make a greater heaven: a greater Mother than Mother of God, God could not make."[1]

"The last grace of Mary's perfection," says S. Antoninus, "was that which prepared her for the Conception of the Son of God: and this preparation was by means of *profound humility*."[2]

It was indeed her own triumphs of humility that she was recounting, when thus she magnified God: "He hath scattered the proud in the conceit of their hearts. He hath put down the mighty from their seat, and hath exalted the humble." Through her humility and consequent excelling grace, she so effectually resisted and vanquished the devil, and still forces him to flee from her children who strive to imitate her humility and invoke her aid.

Approach to God on our part through His attracting grace is the condition of His approach to and union with us. How wondrously perfect, then, must have been Mary's *drawing nigh to God*, before He became so wondrously united to her. Thus must she have been prepared in order to become a worthy Mother of His Son. The height of Mary's exaltation corresponded to the depth of her humility. *Respexit humilitatem ancillæ suæ*, etc.

CHAPTER V.

7 Be patient therefore, brethren, until the coming of the Lord. Behold, the husbandman waiteth for the precious fruit of the earth: patiently bearing till he receive the early and latter rain.

---

[1] *Spec. B. M. V.* Lect. x. [2] *P.* iv. *tit.* xv. *c.* 6, *n.* 2.

8 Be you therefore also patient, and strengthen your hearts: for the coming of the Lord is at hand.

How patiently did Mary wait while the years of her sojourning were prolonged, until the coming of her beloved Lord, when she should receive the precious fruit of her labours, the recompense of her sufferings. As she had waited with persevering, calm, confident prayer for the coming of the Paraclete; so also, *strengthening her heart*, did she wait for the coming of her Divine Son to take her home to Himself.

11 Behold, we account them blessed who have endured.

Mary the blessed amongst women has the first and chief part in this as in every other blessedness: for who ever endured as that Mother of sorrows?

16 Pray one for another, that you may be saved. For the continual prayer of a just man availeth much.

17 Elias was a man passible like unto us: and with prayer he prayed that it might not rain upon the earth, and it rained not for three years and six months.

18 And he prayed again: and the heaven gave rain, and the earth brought forth her fruit.

As Jesus Christ anticipated the time for His first miracle—whereby He manifested His glory and His disciples believed in Him—at the prayer of His Mother; so too Mary's prayers hastened the time of His coming; when *the heaven gave rain, and the earth brought forth her fruit*—Rorate cœli desuper, et nubes pluant Justum. Aperiatur terra, et germinet Salvatorem. Benedicat nos Deus, Deus noster, benedicat nos Deus. Terra dedit fructum suum——And still are Mary's prayers of efficacious avail with her Son to obtain us grace, *that we may be saved.*

"If the Gentiles at Jerusalem," writes Cardinal Newman, "sought Philip, because he was an Apostle, when they desired access to Jesus, and Philip spoke to Andrew, as still more closely in our Lord's confidence, and then both came to Him, is it strange that the Mother should have power with the Son, distinct in kind from that of the purest Angel, and the most triumphant Saint?"[1]

[1] *Sermons to Mixed Congregations—The Glories of Mary for the sake of her Son.*

THE FIRST EPISTLE

OF

S. PETER THE APOSTLE.

CHAPTER I.

3 Blessed be the God and Father of our Lord Jesus Christ, who according to his great mercy hath regenerated us unto a lively hope, by the resurrection of Jesus Christ from the dead,

4 Unto an inheritance incorruptible, and undefiled, and that cannot fade, reserved in heaven for you.

5 Who, by the power of God, are kept by faith unto salvation, ready to be revealed in the last time.

6 Wherein you shall greatly rejoice, if now you must be for a little time made sorrowful in divers temptations:

7 That the trial of your faith (much more precious than gold which is tried by the fire) may be found unto praise and glory and honour at the appearing of Jesus Christ.

The liveliness of Mary's hope, as also the surpassing glory of the heavenly inheritance reserved for her, was proportioned to the greatness of her sanctity, and dignity as Mother of God. ——So, too, was her rejoicing, when she beheld again her divine Son risen from the tomb on Easter morning, in proportion to her sorrowing at the foot of the Cross: whilst her joy now in Paradise is according to the intensity of her dolours on earth. What, then, will be *her praise and glory and honour at the appearing of Jesus Christ, since the trial of her faith was so great and precious?*

8 Whom having not seen, you love: in whom also now, though you see him not, you believe: and believing shall rejoice with joy unspeakable and glorified.

How much more ardently, then (S. Peter would seem to say), would you love Him had you seen Him. Indirectly, the having seen Jesus Christ is here set forth as a means and source of divine charity. Who saw Jesus as did His Mother Mary? Who, seeing Him, loved Him as she?

10 Of which salvation the prophets have inquired and diligently searched, who prophesied of the grace to come in you.
11 Searching what or what manner of time the spirit of Christ in them did signify: when it foretold those sufferings that are in Christ, and the glories that should follow.

Many of those things concerning the salvation to be wrought by Jesus Christ, which the prophets inquired and searched into, and foretold, they did not themselves adequately understand—*v.g.*, the fulness of the grace to come, the precise time, the signification of the Spirit of Christ, all His sufferings and glories. These were all perfectly revealed to Mary, on whom the Spirit of God was poured without measure; who lived and conversed so many years with Him alone, who herself shared so intimately both in His sufferings, and in His glories.

12 To whom it was revealed, that not to themselves, but to you they ministered those things which are now declared to you by them that have preached the gospel to you, the Holy Ghost being sent down from heaven, on whom the angels desire to look.
13 Wherefore having the loins of your mind girt up, being sober, trust perfectly in the grace which is offered you in the revelation of Jesus Christ.

The Gospel. What Gospel? How many things must have been contained in the Gospel here referred to, wherewith those to whom the Apostle writes are supposed to be well acquainted, which he takes for granted as well known, and yet are not even alluded to in this Epistle. And if not in this, why should they be mentioned in any other, or, indeed, in all the Epistles put together? *The Gospel, the revelation,* or preaching forth *of Jesus Christ,* here spoken of by S. Peter, was not in writing at all, but was oral.——It was impossible to set forth the Person and Nature of Our Lord Jesus Christ, without at the same time speaking of and setting forth Mary, His blessed Virgin Mother. The Apostles must surely have spoken much of her, from whom they themselves had learned so much of Him.

23 Being born again not of corruptible seed, but incorruptible, by he word of God who liveth and remaineth for ever.
25 But the word of the Lord endureth for ever. And this is the word which by the gospel hath been preached unto you.

That *word of God* by which they were born again, is not contained in this Epistle, nor adequately and fully in any one, nor in all of the Epistles taken together, nor is it so contained in any of the Four Gospels, nor in all of them: nor, indeed, in the entire New Testament. But even though it were thus contained, still that word whereby they were actually born again must have been independent of the written Books of the New Testament, since these had not for the most part reached those converts to whom S. Peter writes. That word was oral; yet *it endureth for ever, the word of God incorruptible* in the mind of the Church. That same word was full and entire, the whole Gospel. And as it contained the doctrines of the Blessed Trinity, and of the Incarnation, which are not to be found explicitly set forth with all their bearings and developments in the written Word: so too that same Word contained the full explicit teaching of truth about Mary in all its bearings and consequences, though these may not be found in the written Word.

CHAPTER II.

12 Having your conversation good among the Gentiles: that whereas they speak against you as evil-doers, they may, by the works, which they shall behold in you, glorify God in the day of visitation.

13 Be ye subject therefore to every human creature for God's sake: whether it be to the king as excelling.

"In the midst of an evil and perverse people," writes S. Antoninus, "the Blessed Virgin Mary above all others had her conversation so innocent and edifying, that her glorious life illumines all the Churches; for she omitted nothing that ought to be done, did nothing that ought not to be done, took part with no one in his wrong-doing, communicated not to anyone what good of hers might not be shared in, gave to no one bad example in anything, was scandalised by no one's evil act. Hence, says S. Ambrose, 'In Mary you have clear examples of probity, to know what you should avoid, and what you should choose.'" [1]

[1] *P.* iv. *tit.* 15, *cap.* 18, § 5.

Mary gave the most perfect example of such subjection, after that of Jesus Christ Himself, in her submission to her holy Spouse Joseph, to the Roman Emperor Augustus, and to the tyrant Herod.

20 For what glory is it, if committing sin, and being buffeted for it, you endure? But if doing well you suffer patiently; this is thanksworthy before God.
21 For unto this are you called: because Christ also suffered for us, leaving you an example that you should follow his steps.

How glorious for herself, and thanksworthy before God was Mary's enduring patience. She suffered patiently with her Jesus, and after Him the most of all others: not for any sin of her own—for she had none—but for us. Thus did Mary leave us a perfect example of *suffering patiently in well-doing*. Moreover, literally, she followed in Christ's steps on His way to Calvary.

CHAPTER III.

1 In like manner also let wives be subject to their husbands: that if any believe not the word, they may be won without the word, by the conversation of the wives.
2 Considering your chaste conversation with fear.
3 Whose adorning let it not be the outward plaiting of the hair, or the wearing of gold, or the putting on of apparel:
4 But the hidden man of the heart in the incorruptibility of a quiet and a meek spirit, which is rich in the sight of God.
5 For after this manner heretofore the holy women also, who trusted in God, adorned themselves, being in subjection to their own husbands.

If we think of Mary, as sketched forth in the Gospel, as handed down by tradition, and as her character is impressed in the minds of the faithful—we shall find that all that the Apostle here recommends meets in her, as the great ideal model of all holy women, the bright mirror to which all should look, and wherein they may find all virtues and perfections.

22 Who is on the right hand of God, swallowing down death, that we might be made heirs of life everlasting: being gone into heaven, the angels and powers and virtues being made subject to him.

The Apostle speaks thus of Jesus Christ as Man. Where, then, is the place of her in heaven from whom He received this His triumphant Manhood? In making the angelic choirs subject to His glorified Humanity, where does He set His own Mother Mary, to whom He Himself was on earth subject? Will He not in the glory of heaven make the angels and powers and virtues subject to her?[1]

CHAPTER IV.

10 As every man hath received grace, ministering the same one to another: as good stewards of the manifold grace of God.

Mary having found grace with God, and being full of grace, ministered it to others, as the Gospel tells us, at the Visitation. She had power with her Divine Son, and she used her influence for others, as at the Marriage-feast at Cana. We may trust her for ourselves also, if only we ask her; and she will not be wanting to us: for that *Faithful Virgin* is a good steward of the manifold grace of God.

13 But if you partake of the sufferings of Christ, rejoice that when his glory shall be revealed, you may also be glad with exceeding joy.

See what is said above, *James* i. 12; 1 *Pet.* i. 6, 9.

CHAPTER V.

1 The ancients therefore that are among you, I beseech, who am myself also an ancient, and a witness of the sufferings of Christ: as also a partaker of that glory which is to be revealed in time to come.

S. Peter rests his claim to exhort and persuade on his being an ancient, and a witness of the Passion and death of Jesus Christ. This was a ground for his authority, and for respect and attention being shown to him. And yet we know that during the Passion he followed afar off, denied his Lord, and fled to a distance through fear. How much greater consideration and honour, then, should be shown to Mary, simply on

---

[1] See *supra*, *Heb.* i. 5.

the ground of her being a witness of the same Passion and death of Jesus Christ—to her, who, not an ancient as S. Peter, but Christ's own Mother, stood the three hours long watching her Son's agony with intrepid faith and love at the foot of the Cross, deterred neither by fear, nor human respect, nor her own bitter anguish.——Again, S. Peter claims to be heard and to persuade on the ground of his being a partaker of the future glory. But how much greater is Mary's claim on us here also, inasmuch as her share in glory, on account of her exceeding merits and dignity, must far surpass that of all the other Saints.

7 Casting all your care upon him, for he hath care of you.
8 Be sober and watch: because your adversary the devil, as a roaring lion, goeth about seeking whom he may devour.

On the grief that Mary felt at the doubt of her holy spouse Joseph, Fr. Barradas says: "The Virgin was silent, but had the greatest confidence in God, casting the care of her honour on Him, according to the words of S. Peter: *Casting all your care upon Him, for He hath care of you;* and of the Psalmist: 'Cast thy care upon the Lord, and He shall sustain thee; He shall not suffer the just to waver for ever.'[1] God lets not the just waver for ever: but the Virgin He did not allow to waver even for a moment. Her spouse wavered: the Virgin stood unmoved, stayed by the anchor of divine confidence: and, as Mount Sion, was settled on the foundation of firm hope; as is said in *Psalm* cxxiv. 1, 'They that trust in the Lord shall be as Mount Sion,' etc."[2]

Innocent III., after quoting this verse (8) of S. Peter, says: "Whoever, then, feels any assault from his enemies, whether from the world, the flesh, or the devil, let him look to her who is 'terrible as an army set in array,'[3] let him supplicate Mary, that she will, by means of her Son, 'send him help from the sanctuary, and defend him out of Sion.'"[4]

---

[1] *Ps.* liv. 23.
[2] *Tom.* i. *l.* viii. *c.* 7; ap. Morales, *l.* iv. *tr.* 6.
[3] *Cant.* vi. 9.
[4] *Ps.* xix. 3. *Serm. de Assump.*

THE SECOND EPISTLE

OF

S. PETER THE APOSTLE.

CHAPTER I.

16 For we have not followed cunningly-devised fables, when we made known to you the power and presence of our Lord Jesus Christ: but having been made eye-witness of his majesty.

17 For he received from God the Father, honour and glory: this voice coming down to him from the excellent glory: This is my beloved Son, in whom I have pleased myself, hear ye him.

18 And this voice we heard brought from heaven, when we were with him in the holy mount.

The Apostle again grounds his claims to be believed, as to all that he taught about the divinity of our Lord Jesus Christ, on his having been himself with Him, and on what he had himself seen and heard. But how much was there of our Lord's life known only to Mary who dwelt with Him alone for thirty years. How many mysteries were there of which she alone was eye-witness, and wherein she alone had part. Some of these she made known to the Apostles and Evangelists, and through them, especially through S. Luke, they are revealed to us. But how many still remain concealed in the consciousness of Mary's soul.

CHAPTER III.

15 And account the long-suffering of our Lord, salvation; as also our most dear brother Paul, according to the wisdom given him, hath written to you:

16 As also in all his epistles, speaking in them of these things; in which are certain things hard to be understood, which the unlearned and unstable wrest, as they do also the other scriptures, to their own destruction.

17 You therefore, brethren, knowing these things before: take heed, lest being led aside by the error of the unwise, you fall from your own steadfastness.

18 But grow in grace, and in the knowledge of our Lord and Saviour Jesus Christ. To him be glory both now and unto the day of eternity. Amen.

S. Peter says that in all the Epistles of S. Paul, as well as in the rest of Holy Scripture, *there are certain things hard to be understood*, which, without sure guidance and explanation, may be easily taken in a perverse sense. He does not tell us what these hard things are, much less does he give the true sense of them, or explain them in this or in his former Epistle. Nor do any of the other sacred writers of the New Testament do this in their Gospels or Epistles. Hence, clearly, the right rule for interpreting Scripture is not contained in the written word. And yet the Apostle bids Christians *take heed, remain steadfast, and grow in the knowledge of our Lord Jesus Christ*. Of what, then, must they take heed? The Apostle had before laid down as a first principle, which the faithful should well understand, that all that the sacred penmen wrote was under the inspiration of the Holy Ghost; and that consequently Holy Scripture is of no mere private interpretation; but, to be known in its true sense, it must have a like infallible authority to explain it.[1] Hence S. Peter here bids those whom he addresses beware of their own private judgment of Holy Scripture, as well as the mere private judgment of others on its sense, lest they should be led aside into error and folly. To what, then, does he bid them remain steadfast? To the teaching that had been orally preached to them by the Church. And how must they grow in the knowledge of our Lord Jesus Christ? Especially by continuing to listen with docile faith and attention to the instructions thus orally delivered to them, and to the explanations of those hard passages in the written word, that should be thus given to them by the teaching Church, which has the promise of the ever-abiding assistance of the Holy Ghost. All that the Church teaches with regard to the Blessed Virgin Mary is here included. The silence about Mary in the written word is to some one of those *hard things*, which by many is perverted to wrong conclusions, and to their own spiritual loss.

[1] 2 *Pet.* i. 20, 21

THE FIRST EPISTLE

OF

S. JOHN THE APOSTLE.

CHAPTER I.

1 That which was from the beginning, which we have heard, which we have seen with our eyes, which we have looked upon, and our hands have handled, of the word of life:
2 For the life was manifested; and we have seen and do bear witness, and declare unto you the life eternal, which was with the Father, and hath appeared to us:
3 That which we have seen and have heard, we declare unto you, that you also may have fellowship with us, and our fellowship may be with the Father, and with his Son Jesus Christ

This was S. John's ground for dignity, authority, communication of grace to others, and fellowship with the Father, and with His Son Jesus Christ; viz., that he had himself heard, and seen, and looked upon with his own eyes, and handled with his own hands the Incarnate Word of God.[1] Think of Nazareth, and Bethlehem, and Jerusalem, and Egypt, and Nazareth and Jerusalem again—and say whether Mary had not enjoyed these privileges more intimately and abundantly, unspeakably far, than the Apostle, and whether her dignity in this respect does not immeasurably surpass that of S. John. If on this title Christians might have fellowship with the Father and with His Son Jesus Christ, how much more through Mary.

8 If we say that we have no sin, we deceive ourselves, and the truth is not in us.

"The holy Mary," writes S. Augustine, "lived without any sin. No other of the Saints was without sin. He (Pelagius) goes on to make mention of those 'who are recounted not only not to have sinned, but also to have lived justly, Abel, Enoch,

---

[1] See *infra*, Note B, p. 279.

Melchisedech, Abraham, Isaac, Jacob, Josue, . . . Joseph to whom the Virgin Mary was espoused, and John.' He adds women also, 'Debbora, . . . Elisabeth, and Mary the Mother of our Lord and Saviour,' whom, he says, 'piety necessarily obliges us to confess to have been without sin.' Except, then, the holy Virgin Mary, concerning whom, for the Lord's honour, I will have no question raised at all, in treating of sins,—for we know that more grace[1] was conferred on her to be victorious over sin from every quarter,[2] from the fact that she merited to conceive, and give birth to Him, Who, it is certain, had no sin. This Virgin, therefore, excepted; could we gather together, and ask all those holy men and women, whether when they lived here on earth, they were without sin, what, think we, they would answer? Would it be what this man says, or what the Apostle John says? I ask you—however great the excellence of their sanctity whilst in the body—if they could be questioned, would they not cry out with one voice, *If we say we have no sin, we deceive ourselves, and the truth is not in us.*"[3]

CHAPTER II.

1 My little children, these things I write to you, that you may not sin. But if any man sin, we have an advocate with the Father, Jesus Christ the just.

"*We have an Advocate with the Father, Jesus Christ the just,* 'Who also maketh intercession for us,' says S. Paul.[4] But because He is not only our Advocate, but also appointed to be Judge of the living and of the dead,'[5] and so will examine into everything, and will leave no sin unpunished; human weakness, and especially a sinner—since the just is scarcely secure before Him[6]—might perhaps, not bear to approach to Him as Advocate. And consequently God most loving has

---

[1] Or, according to the other reading: "For, how do we know what was the greater grace conferred on her . . . who merited," etc.?
[2] Or, "for the entire conquest of sin," *ad vincendum omni ex parte peccatum.*
[3] S. August., *De Natura et Gratia,* cap. 36. See *supra, Rom.* iii. 23.
[4] *Rom.* viii. 34.   [5] *Acts* x. 42.   [6] 1 *Pet.* iv. 18.

provided us with an advocate in Mary who is all mild and sweet. Nothing harsh is found in her, never did a hard word come forth from her." [1]

5 But he that keepeth his word, in him in very deed the charity of God is perfected; and by this we know that we are in him.

In Mary then, in very deed, *was the charity of God perfected*. For of her emphatically the Holy Ghost records: "His Mother kept all these (His) words in her heart." [2] Again the Angel assures her from God that she is united to Him—*Dominus tecum*. Hence to Mary above all others belongs that supreme blessedness pronounced by her Divine Son, on those who hear the Word of God and keep it. By this we know that she, in a sense beyond all others, is in Him.

20 But you have the unction from the Holy one, and know all things.

Who had the unction from the Holy One as Mary, upon whom the Holy Ghost came, and whom the power of the Most High overshadowed; of whom was born the Holy One; with whom the Holy One lived and conversed so many years; on whom the Holy Ghost descended again in His fulness on the day of Pentecost? What, then, must have been the fulness of Mary's knowledge.

CHAPTER III.

1 Behold what manner of charity the Father hath bestowed upon us, that we should be called, and should be the sons of God. Therefore the world knoweth not us, because it knew not him.
2 Dearly beloved, we are now the sons of God; and it hath not yet appeared what we shall be. We know, that, when he shall appear, we shall be like to him: because we shall see him as he is.
3 And every one that hath this hope in him, sanctifieth himself, as he also is holy.

O charity in manner yet more admirable, bestowed upon Mary, that she should not only be the elect one, blessed above others amongst all God's daughters, but moreover be called,

---

[1] S. Antoninus, *p.* iv. *tit.* 15, *c.* 14, § 7.
[2] *Luke* ii. 52, and v. 19. See *supra, Rom.* ii. 13.

and really be His own beloved Mother!—a charity wherein we are made to share, in that we also have His Mother for our Mother, and are called, and in truth are, the children of Mary. May we not well say: Behold what manner of charity our Lord Jesus Christ from the Cross hath bestowed upon us, that we should be called by Him, and should be the children of Mary His own most holy Mother, and that thus He should become our own Brother. We need not wonder that *the world knows not* but rejects Mary—her dignity, her holiness and her power; and that it opposes her servants and children, and sets itself against the practice of devotion to her.

If such will be the manifestation of all the children of God, what will be the glorious manifestation of His chosen one, of Mary His own most perfect Mother?——As we are unable to conceive the blessedness of Mary's assured hope of the beatific vision, so neither can we comprehend the sanctification by which she prepared herself for it.

8 He that committeth sin is of the devil: for the devil sinneth from the beginning. For this purpose, the Son of God appeared, that he might destroy the works of the devil.
9 Whosoever is born of God, committeth not sin: for his seed abideth in him, and he cannot sin, because he is born of God.
10 In this the children of God are manifest and the children of the devil.
13 Wonder not, brethren, if the world hate you.

The Apostle here takes us back to *the beginning*, and evidently refers to the primeval prophecy and promise contained in *Genesis*:[1] "I will put enmities between thee (the serpent) and the woman, and thy seed and her seed: she shall crush thy head, and thou shalt lie in wait for her heel." Whether it is there said that the Woman (Mary, the Second Eve), or her Seed, that is Jesus Christ her Son—and in and by Him all His true members, the faithful—should destroy the power of the devil, is immaterial.——We see that what there is called "the seed of the woman" is here by S. John called *the children of God*, those *born of God*. Hence we may learn that it is one

---

[1] *Gen*. iii. 15.

and the same thing to be children of God, and children of Mary. We must not wonder, then, that *the world*, that is, the seed of the serpent, who are the children of error, *should hate* the children of God and Mary; since it had been prophesied long before, even from the beginning: "I will put enmities between thy seed and her seed."

16 In this we have known the charity of God, because he hath laid down his life for us: and we ought to lay down our lives for the brethren.

Mary was ready a thousand times to lay down her life for her children, had such been the will of God. She did in effect, what cost her far more. She was transfixed in her heart with the wounds of her Divine Son. The same sword which pierced Him pierced her maternal soul through and through. Mary at the foot of the Cross laid down for us a life dearer far than her own.

21 Dearly beloved, if our heart do not reprehend us, we have confidence towards God:
22 And whatsoever we shall ask, we shall receive of him: because we keep his commandments, and do those things which are pleasing in his sight.
23 And this is his commandment, that we should believe in the name of his Son Jesus Christ: and love one another, as he hath given commandment unto us.
24 And he that keepeth his commandments, abideth in him, and he in him. And in this we know that he abideth in us, by the Spirit which he hath given us.

If the prayers of good Christians in the grace of God are thus powerful, what must be the exceeding power with God of the prayers of Mary His Mother, who possessed, as the Spirit of truth expressly testifies, in such an excellent degree all the conditions here mentioned for favour and acceptance in His sight.——Mary had *confidence towards God*, so that when her petition to her Divine Son was seemingly refused, she still with confidence pressed her suit.[1] *She kept God's Word.*[2] She did what was *pleasing in His sight.* "Thou hast found grace with God."[3] She was *strong in faith.* "Blessed art thou that

---

[1] *John* ii. 3-5.   [2] *Luke* ii. 52.   [3] *Ib.* i. 30.

hast believed."[1] She *abounded in fraternal charity*, so that Jesus from the Cross gave her to us, His beloved ones, to be our Mother, giving her at the same time a Mother's heart and a Mother's love.[2] *She abode in God.* "The Lord is with thee." She knew and had full assurance of her union with Him *by the Spirit*, which *was given to her*.[3]

CHAPTER IV.

1 Dearly beloved, believe not every spirit, but try the spirits if they be of God: because many false prophets are gone out into the world.
2 By this is the spirit of God known. Every spirit which confesseth that Jesus Christ is come in the flesh, is of God:
3 And every spirit that dissolveth Jesus, is not of God: and this is Antich.ist.[4]

"*Believe not every spirit, but try the spirits if they be of God;* 'for Satan himself transformeth himself into an angel of light,'[5] to be adored. . . . 'The spiritual man judgeth all things,'[6] says S. Paul, that is, discerns what should be done from what should not be done, and the fictitious from the true. Because, then, Mary was spiritual above all others she had beyond all others the discernment of spirits. When S. Anthony on seeing in spirit the whole world full of snares closely set together cried out, Oh, who shall escape these snares? the answer was, *Humility alone*. The Blessed Virgin was incomparably more humble than all others; and therefore through this grace of discernment of spirits, escaped all deceits. The evil spirit is wont to tempt to spiritual pride, but the Blessed Mary never had any movement of pride. The Apostle Paul says of himself, 'We are not ignorant of his (that is, the devil's) devices.' But since Mary is more than Paul, much less was she ignorant, but had greater discernment, and was never deceived by him."[7]

---

[1] *Ib.* i. 45.   [2] *John* xix. 26.
[3] *Luke* i. 28, 35. See *Acts* i. 14; ii. 1, 4; 1 *John* iv. 12, 13.
[4] The Apostle again denounces in his Second Epistle (v.v. 7-11) the heresy of which he here speaks.
[5] 2 *Cor.* xi. 14.   [6] 1 *Cor.* ii. 15.   [7] S. Antoninus, *p.* iv. *tit.* 15, *cap.* 19, § 7.

The very essential ideal of everything that is most opposed to Jesus Christ is Antichrist, and the spirit of Antichrist. On the contrary, the most perfect ideal of all that is *for* Jesus Christ, is Mary, and her spirit, which breathes in the souls of the faithful devotion to her. For Mary is the living testimony and pledge in the Church on earth, and in heaven to Angels and Saints for all eternity of the truth of the Incarnation, that God is indeed become Man. Take away Mary and *Jesus Christ is dissolved.* Whoever entertains wrong thoughts and ideas of her will hold error, explicitly or implicitly, with regard to Our Lord Jesus Christ. Let devotion to Mary droop, and Catholic Faith will soon grow weak, or die. Mary is still the guardian of her Divine Son, as she is of us her children. The experience of ages has proved this. Hence the Church sings: *Gaude Maria Virgo, cunctas hæreses sola interemisti in universo mundo. Dignare me laudare te Virgo sacrata. Da mihi virtutem contra hostes tuos.* The Spirit of Mary is the Spirit of Christ, the Spirit of God.

21 And this commandment we have from God, that he who loveth God, love also his brother.

"As there never was, and never will be," writes S. Alphonsus, "anyone who loved God as much as Mary loved Him, so there never was, and never will be, anyone who loved her neighbour as much as she did. Father Cornelius a Lapide, on these words of the Canticles: 'King Solomon hath made him a litter of the wood of Libanus . . . the midst he covered with charity for the daughters of Jerusalem,'[1] says that 'this litter was Mary's womb, in which the Incarnate Word dwelt, filling it with charity for the daughters of Jerusalem; for Christ, who is love itself, inspired the Blessed Virgin with charity in its highest degree, that she might succour all who had recourse to her. So great was Mary's charity when on earth, that she succoured the needy without even being asked, as was the case at the marriage-feast of Cana, when she told her Son that family's distress, ' They have no wine,'[2] and

---

[1] *Cant.* iii. 9, 10. [2] *John* ii. 3.

asked him to work a miracle. Oh, with what speed did she fly when there was question of relieving her neighbour! When she went to the house of Elizabeth to fulfil an office of charity: 'She went into the hill country with haste.'[1] She could not, however, more fully display the greatness of her charity than she did in the offering which she made of her Son to death for our salvation. On this subject S. Bonaventure says, 'Mary so loved the world as to give her only-begotten Son.' Hence S. Anselm exclaims, 'O blessed amongst women, thy purity surpasses that of the angels, and thy compassion that of the saints.'[2] 'Nor has this love of Mary for us,' says S. Bonaventure, 'diminished, now that she is in heaven, but it has increased, for now she better sees the miseries of man.' And therefore the Saint goes on to say: 'Great was the mercy of Mary towards the wretched when she was still in exile on earth; but far greater is it now that she reigns in heaven.'"[3]

THE CATHOLIC EPISTLE
OF
S. JUDE THE APOSTLE.

3 I was under a necessity to write unto you: to beseech you to contend earnestly for the faith once delivered to the saints.

This faith was delivered by oral teaching. We may see in this short Epistle several points of divine revelation which are not mentioned anywhere else in holy writ, and must have been transmitted by tradition. So too is it with much of the explicit teaching on the Blessed Virgin. S. Jude supposes this faith to be known by those to whom he writes. He alludes, at the same time (v.v. 17, 18), to Epistles of Apostles, whence they derived their knowledge on some particular matter, thus in 1 *Tim.* iv. 1-3; 2 *Tim.* iii. 1-5; 2 *Pet.* iii. 3, 4. Hence we see the late date of this Epistle.

[1] *Luke* i. 39.   [2] *Invoc. B. V. et Filii.*
[3] *Spec. B. V. M.* lect. x. *Glories of Mary*, p. 448, 9.

The very essential ideal of everything that is most opposed to Jesus Christ is Antichrist, and the spirit of Antichrist. On the contrary, the most perfect ideal of all that is *for* Jesus Christ, is Mary, and her spirit, which breathes in the souls of the faithful devotion to her. For Mary is the living testimony and pledge in the Church on earth, and in heaven to Angels and Saints for all eternity of the truth of the Incarnation, that God is indeed become Man. Take away Mary and *Jesus Christ is dissolved.* Whoever entertains wrong thoughts and ideas of her will hold error, explicitly or implicitly, with regard to Our Lord Jesus Christ. Let devotion to Mary droop, and Catholic Faith will soon grow weak, or die. Mary is still the guardian of her Divine Son, as she is of us her children. The experience of ages has proved this. Hence the Church sings: *Gaude Maria Virgo, cunctas hæreses sola interemisti in universo mundo. Dignare me laudare te Virgo sacrata. Da mihi virtutem contra hostes tuos.* The Spirit of Mary is the Spirit of Christ, the Spirit of God.

21 And this commandment we have from God, that he who loveth God, love also his brother.

"As there never was, and never will be," writes S. Alphonsus, "anyone who loved God as much as Mary loved Him, so there never was, and never will be, anyone who loved her neighbour as much as she did. Father Cornelius a Lapide, on these words of the Canticles: 'King Solomon hath made him a litter of the wood of Libanus ... the midst he covered with charity for the daughters of Jerusalem,'[1] says that 'this litter was Mary's womb, in which the Incarnate Word dwelt, filling it with charity for the daughters of Jerusalem; for Christ, who is love itself, inspired the Blessed Virgin with charity in its highest degree, that she might succour all who had recourse to her. So great was Mary's charity when on earth, that she succoured the needy without even being asked, as was the case at the marriage-feast of Cana, when she told her Son that family's distress, 'They have no wine,'[2] and

---

[1] *Cant.* iii. 9, 10.   [2] *John* ii. 3.

asked him to work a miracle. Oh, with what speed did she fly when there was question of relieving her neighbour! When she went to the house of Elizabeth to fulfil an office of charity: 'She went into the hill country with haste.'[1] She could not, however, more fully display the greatness of her charity than she did in the offering which she made of her Son to death for our salvation. On this subject S. Bonaventure says, 'Mary so loved the world as to give her only-begotten Son.' Hence S. Anselm exclaims, ' O blessed amongst women, thy purity surpasses that of the angels, and thy compassion that of the saints.'[2] 'Nor has this love of Mary for us,' says S. Bonaventure, 'diminished, now that she is in heaven, but it has increased, for now she better sees the miseries of man.' And therefore the Saint goes on to say: ' Great was the mercy of Mary towards the wretched when she was still in exile on earth; but far greater is it now that she reigns in heaven.'"[3]

THE CATHOLIC EPISTLE

OF

S. JUDE THE APOSTLE.

3 I was under a necessity to write unto you: to beseech you to contend earnestly for the faith once delivered to the saints.

This faith was delivered by oral teaching. We may see in this short Epistle several points of divine revelation which are not mentioned anywhere else in holy writ, and must have been transmitted by tradition. So too is it with much of the explicit teaching on the Blessed Virgin. S. Jude supposes this faith to be known by those to whom he writes. He alludes, at the same time (v.v. 17, 18), to Epistles of Apostles, whence they derived their knowledge on some particular matter, thus in 1 Tim. iv. 1-3; 2 Tim. iii. 1-5; 2 Pet. iii. 3, 4. Hence we see the late date of this Epistle.

[1] *Luke* i. 39.   [2] *Invoc. B. V. et Filii.*
[3] *Spec. B. V. M.* lect. x. *Glories of Mary*, p. 448, 9.

THE APOCALYPSE OF S. JOHN THE APOSTLE.

The *Apocalypse*, if not an Epistle, is one of the Apostolic writings. And as written by an Apostle who himself wrote Epistles, it claims a place in our inquiry. Many Fathers and Catholic writers have interpreted much of the figurative language in the *Apocalypse*, of the Blessed Virgin, or have applied it to her. We shall choose here only three passages, for our comments.

CHAPTER II.

7 To him, that overcometh, I will give to eat of the tree of life, which is in the paradise of my God.

"The earthly paradise," says Blessed Albert the Great, "is the one of old in which the Lord God placed man whom He had created.[1] The heavenly paradise, here spoken of, is that wherein He formed the Second Adam, the Incarnate Word, Our Lord Jesus Christ. Mary is this paradise, this garden of delights; the principal tree whereof is the tree of life, viz., Jesus Christ, Who is well called the Tree of life, because its fruit, that is, the Eucharist, is the antidote of death. But this fruit belongs only to those who conquer their vices: 'to him that overcometh.'"[2]——S. Gregory Thaumaturgus had said before: "Mary is the ever-blooming paradise of incorruptibility, wherein is planted the tree that giveth life, and provideth all the fruits of immortality."[3]

28 I will give him the morning star.

Mary is well compared to the morning star—and is so styled by the Holy Church, *Stella Matutina*—as surpassing the other stars in brightness, and as shining before day-break and the rising of the Sun. Thus did Mary precede and usher in the rising of Jesus Christ, the Sun of Justice, and His Gospel-day.

[1] *Gen.* ii. 8-15; iii. 23, 24.   [2] B. Albert. Magn., Lib. xii.
[3] Orat. I. *De Annunt.*

CHAPTER XII.

1 And a great sign appeared in heaven: A woman clothed with the sun, and the moon under her feet, and on her head a crown of twelve stars:
2 And being with child, she cried travailing in birth, and was in pain to be delivered.
3 And there was seen another sign in heaven: and behold a great red dragon, having seven heads, and ten horns: and on his heads seven diadems:
4 And his tail drew the third part of the stars of heaven, and cast them to the earth: and the dragon stood before the woman who was ready to be delivered; that, when she should be delivered, he might devour her son.
5 And she brought forth a man-child, who was to rule all nations with an iron rod: and her son was taken up to God, and to his throne.
6 And the woman fled into the wilderness, where she had a place prepared by God, that there they should feed her a thousand two hundred sixty days.
7 And there was a great battle in heaven, Michael and his angels fought with the dragon, and the dragon fought and his angels:
8 And they prevailed not, neither was their place found any more in heaven.
9 And that great dragon was cast out, that old serpent, who is called the devil and satan, who seduceth the whole world; and he was cast unto the earth, and his angels were thrown down with him.
10 And I heard a loud voice in heaven, saying: Now is come salvation, and strength, and the kingdom of our God, and the power of his CHRIST.
13 And when the dragon saw that he was cast unto the earth, he persecuted the woman, who brought forth the man-child:
17 And the dragon was angry against the woman: and went to make war with the rest of her seed, who keep the commandments of God, and have the testimony of Jesus Christ.

Amongst much that is obscure in the vision here described some points stand out as quite clear:—

1. That the Man-child, spoken of as born of the Woman, who was to rule the nations,[1] and was taken up to God, and to His throne, is, in the primary sense, no other than Jesus Christ, the Incarnate Word: and consequently that the Woman is Mary His Mother. 2. That she is here seen by S. John crowned with exceeding glory in heaven. 3. That the dragon is identical with the Serpent of *Genesis*, the devil who seduced our first parents to sin. 4. That the war de-

[1] *Ps.* ii. 9.

Angels: and yet though so highly excelling in purity she partook of our lump: for what is it that David saith of the Lord's conception? *He shall descend as rain upon a fleece, and as a drop which droppeth upon the earth;* meaning by *earth* the Holy Mother of the Lord, in that she was consubstantial with us earthly beings. But let Eutyches, his impious dogma touching the Mother of God and the Lord's Incarnation, be cast forth out of the divine precincts. And that she was clothed with the sun, and had the moon under her feet, Habakkuk is a sufficient voucher in those words of his: *The sun was lifted up, and the moon stood still in her order,* meaning the Sun of Righteousness, Christ the Saviour, who by the preaching of the Gospel was exalted and set aloft: while the moon, that is, the Jews' Synagogue, no longer received after Christ's manifestation any accession by proselytes from the Gentiles. . . . With this too what Gabriel said to the Virgin harmoniseth: *The power of the Most High shall overshadow thee:* for to have a covering cast about one (to be clothed), is all one with being overshadowed. Others again, of whom is S. Methodius[1] of Patara, adapt the vision to holy Church as considering that this passage does not go well with the Lord's Birth, because He had been brought forth such a long while before it. The Church then is clad with the Sun of Righteousness, and also has the light of the law, that nightly-shining moon.'—The fact, however, that two views of the passage existed, shows that it admitted a twofold application.——S. Epiphanius inclines to applying it to S. Mary,[2] while S. Austin says that 'the Woman signifies Mary, who, being spotless, brought forth our spotless Head. Who herself also showed forth in herself a figure of holy Church, so that as she in bringing forth a Son remained a Virgin, so the Church also should during the whole of time be bringing forth His members and yet not lose her virgin estate.'[3] This view of S. Mary, as the type of the

---

[1] *Conviv. Virg.* viii. 7.   [2] *Hær.* 78, n. 11.
[3] *De Trad. Symb. ad Cat.* iv. 1.

Church, seems absolutely necessary to reconcile the two interpretations."[1]

"Mary," writes a devout author, "is indeed *a great sign* of grace and glory, of merit and reward. Great, because a Virgin; greater, because a Mother; greatest, because Mother of God, beyond which there is no creature greatness. To whom did this great sign appear? To the whole Church: to the Church triumphant by spiritual vision: to the Church militant, that believes this, by faith."[2]

"Mary," says S. Bonaventure, "is that one, greater than whom God could not make: God could make a greater world, God could make a greater heaven: a greater mother than Mother of God, God could not make."[3]

S. Thomas asks, "Whether God could make better all that He has made?" and answers that "He could, with the exception of three things, viz., Christ, the Blessed Virgin, and our beatitude. For the humanity of Christ, he says, from its being united to God; created beatitude, from its being the fruition of God; and the Blessed Virgin, from her being Mother of God, have a kind of infinite dignity, from the infinite good which is God; and, regarded in this light, nothing can be made better than them, just as nothing can be better than God."[4]

"In what heaven was it that Mary appeared?" asks Daniel Agricola. "Heaven," he answers, "is threefold: the *aerial*, wherein the birds fly: the *sidereal*, wherein the stars shine: and the *empyrean*, wherein the angels praise God. In none of these three: since, beyond doubt, the Blessed Virgin has been exalted above all the choirs of Angels. But in a heaven still higher, if such there be; or in the higher part of the empyrean, where is the throne of the Divine Majesty, which is called the heaven of the Most Holy Trinity. For we can conceive of nought higher in heaven than where Mary sits, as is believed,

---

[1] Morris, *Select Works of S. Ephrem*, p. 85.
[2] Dan. Agricola, ap. *Sum. Aur. B. M. V.*
[3] *In Speculo B. Virginis*, cap. 8.   [4] 1 P. *qu.* 25, *art.* 8, *ad* 4.

on a throne of majesty at the right hand of her Son, as was prefigured in the mother of Solomon."[1]

Why is the Blessed Virgin Mary said to be *clothed with the sun*?

1. "With reason," says Blessed Albert the Great, "is Mary said to be clothed with the sun, since she appears wholly immersed in that inaccessible light:[2] not reflecting merely the divine fire, but covered with it on every side, and encompassed with its splendour. Thou hast become, O Lady, to Him, one so familiar (familiaris); thou clothest Him, and art clothed by Him: thou clothest Him with the substance of flesh, and He clothes thee with the glory of His Majesty."[3]

2. "Mary was thus clothed with the sun, when the Sun of Justice came down to take His abode in her."[4]

3. "All the planets," says S. Antoninus, "receive their light from the sun, and so all the Saints receive the light of glory from Christ, who is the Sun of Justice. 'Of His fulness we all have received, and grace for grace,'[5] that is, the perfected grace of glory, for sanctifying grace which was had in the present life. Now, *the Woman*, the Blessed Virgin Mary herself, the Star of the Sea, receives light from the Sun; and yet she is not here said to be illumined by the Sun, but clothed with the Sun itself; thereby to show her most exceeding reward; that, as nothing is more close and united to the body than its clothing, so nothing approaches more nearly to the glory of Christ, than the glory and recompense of the Blessed Virgin Mary. Fitly too; that as she clothed the Sun Himself in this world—the Son of God with her flesh, according to Ezechiel,[6] 'I will cover the sun with a cloud,'—so He should clothe her in heaven with the Sun of exceeding glory."[7]

"In thee," writes S. Bernard, "abides Christ, the Sun, and thou in Him; and thou clothest Him, and art clothed by Him. Thou clothest Him with the substance of flesh, and

---

[1] 3 *Kings* ii. 19.
[2] 1 *Tim.* vi. 16.
[3] See the passages quoted from Ephrem, *Heb.* i. 3. *supra.*
[4] B. Jacob. de Voragine.
[5] *John* i. 16.
[6] *Ezech.* xxxii. 7.
[7] *P.* iv. *tit.* 15. *cap.* 20. § 1.

He clothes thee with the glory of His Majesty. Thou clothest the Sun with a cloud, and thyself art clothed with the Sun."[1]

4. "*Clothed with the Sun*, that is, with an immortal body. 'All the glory of the King's daughter is from within,'[2] referring to the glory of the soul. 'Surrounded with variety,' referring to corporal endowments, which redound from within, from the soul to the body. In this way, from the redundancy of prudence, results brightness in Mary's body; from the redundancy of fortitude, impassibility; from the redundancy of temperance, subtility; from the redundancy of justice, which penetrated all her powers, results agility."[3]

5. "*Clothed with the sun*, that is, with a glorious body, which is called the sun on account of four gifts which the bodies of the elect will have, and which answer to four properties of the sun. For the sun shines with utmost brightness, agility, and subtility. Thus, as soon as it has begun to rise in the East in one hemisphere, its light strikes the Western heavens of the same hemisphere, and in a moment it penetrates the most distant parts of the earth, overcoming the solidity of glass and crystal. Impassibility, also, because the sun alone knows not failure, nor corruption; for neither does water soften it, nor stench corrupt it, nor fire burn it, nor sword rend it, nor glass resist it; and so it is impassible. To say then, *a Woman clothed with the sun*, means with a glorified body, possessed of those four endowments which are remarked in the sun. For, in Mary's Assumption, the Sun, whom she had clothed with the glorious diadem of flesh, as we read in the Canticles[4]—when the Word of God was made flesh in her—the Son to repay His Mother, caused her to shine forth with His own glorious brightness."[5]

6. "As the sun," says S. Bernard, "arises alike upon the good and evil, so Mary does not examine past deserts, but shows herself easily entreated, and, most clement to all, with unbounded affection pities and succours the needs of all."

---

[1] Serm. *de Verb. Apocalyps.*   [2] *Ps.* xliv. 14.
[3] B. Jacob. de Voragine.   [4] *Cant.* iii. 11.   [5] Dan. Agricola.

"The Blessed Virgin is made all to all, to all she opens her bosom of mercy, that everyone may receive of its fulness: the captive redemption, the sick cure, the sad consolation, the sinner pardon, the just grace, the angels gladness; in fine, the whole Trinity glory, the Person of the Son the substance of human flesh; so that no one should be hid from her heat. Bethinketh thee that she is *the Woman clothed with the sun?* She who, as it were, clothed another sun with herself. In the sun is both heat and abiding splendour. In the moon splendour only, and *that* altogether changeable and uncertain, never remaining in the same state. Justly, therefore, is Mary said to be clothed with the sun, since she penetrated, beyond what might seem credible, into the most profound abyss of Divine Wisdom. By that same fire the Prophet's lips are purified,[1] by that fire the Seraphim are enkindled. But far otherwise did Mary merit, not as though once for all to be touched, but rather to be covered all over, encompassed, and, as it were, embraced by the fire itself. Of most dazzling brightness, verily, but also of most burning heat, is this Woman's clothing, whereof everything is visibly so surpassingly illumined, that nothing may be thought of in her, I say not, darksome, but even obscure, or less lucid; nor anything, not to say tepid, but that is not most fervent."[2]

7. "Mary is said to be *clothed with the sun*, because she was free from the darkness of any sin," says Cardinal Hugo.——

"*Clothed with the sun*, that is, whilst Mary lived here on earth, flames of most ardent love to God, as garments, ever wrapt round her body and soul. Or, we may say, that the sun wherewith she is said to be clothed, is the Eternal Word, the Sun of Justice, our Lord Jesus Christ; and that when she bore Him in her virginal womb, He filled, not her soul only with so great splendour, but also her whole body, from the sole of the foot, even to the head. We may say, moreover, that she was clothed with the sun, from the fulness of glory which she obtained in heaven; by the splendour of which all

---

[1] Dan Agricola, vi. 6, 7. [2] S. Bernard, *loc. cit.*

the mansions of paradise are lit up, and all its inhabitants are beyond measure delighted."[1]

"Did Mary," asks Blessed Albert the Great, "receive greater glory in the Assumption, when her whole flesh was clothed with the Sun; or at the Conception of her Son, when she embraced the entire Sun of Justice in her flesh, according to the words of Jeremias, *A woman shall compass a Man?*[2]—— It would seem more glorious," he replies, "to receive a King as guest, than to be the King's guest. Mary's glory was more hidden, when she received the King; accordingly then 'all the glory of the King's daughter was from within.'[3] Her other glory was more manifest when she was received by the King with regal magnificence. The one was more secret, the other more public and solemn."

What is signified by *the moon under the Blessed Virgin's feet?*
1. That Mary is superior to all defect, frailty and corruption.——2. The moon from its changeableness signifies the world, wherein some are at times in full prosperity which soon declines and passes away, which wanes with some, and is lost to others. The Blessed Virgin despised the world, and worldly prosperity; and hence appeared with the moon under her feet.——3. The moon from its eclipses signifies defect: Mary alone was without any sin.——4. The moon signifies the Church, which is under the protection of the Mother of God, and is ever prostrate before her throne, seeking her intercession.

What is signified by *the crown of twelve stars* on the Blessed Virgin's head?

According to S. Bernard: Twelve privileges of Mary, on account of which she is also called Full of grace. Four of these belong to heaven: Four to her body: Four to her soul.
——As stars there shine *from heaven*, Mary's Conception and Birth, the Angelic salutation, the coming upon her of the Holy Ghost, her ineffable Conception of the Son of God.—— In her *body* shine forth, her peerless Virginity, her fecundity

[1] Alexius a Salo. [2] Jer. xxxi. 22. [3] Ps. xliv.
[4] De laud. B. Virg. § 12, n. 3.

without corruption, her pregnancy without burden, her Childbearing without pain.——From her *soul* shine forth, the gentle meekness of her modesty, the devotion of her humility, the magnanimity of her faith, her spirit of martyrdom.

It is also said that the twelve stars signify the nine Choirs of Angels and the three Orders of Saints, viz., Martyrs, Confessors, and Virgins.——And again, twelve virtues, comprised under the four Cardinal Virtues, which adorned Mary's life on earth, and now shine forth gloriously in heaven like so many stars: thus: *Prudence:* 1. in her memory as to the past; 2. in her understanding as to the present; 3. in her foresight as to the future.——*Temperance:* 1. Abstinence in her palate; 2. Continence from luxury; 3. Modesty in speech. ——*Fortitude:* 1. Magnanimity in difficulties; 2. Equanimity in adversity; 3. Longanimity in enduring protracted suffering, and in waiting for deferred reward.——*Justice:* 1. Reverend submission to superiors; 2. Benevolence towards equals: 3. Clemency to inferiors.

"The Assumption of Mary," writes Ludolph of Saxony, "was figured forth of old to John in the Island of Patmos. For he saw a certain wondrous woman in heaven, who was clothed with the sun; thus Mary went up to heaven environed by the divinity. The moon was seen to be under her feet; whereby is denoted Mary's perpetual stability: whereas the moon which is unstable, and remains not long full, signifies the world and all things of earth. Mary, despising these unstable things, trod them under her feet, and aspired to heaven, where all things are stable. The woman had, moreover, on her head a crown composed of twelve stars. The crown, which is used as a mark of honour, signifies the honour which worthily befits the glorious Virgin. By the twelve stars are understood the Apostles, who, it is said, were all present at Mary's departure. To the Woman were given wings to fly: by which is signified her Assumption to heaven, both of body and soul."[1]

[1] *Vita Christi,* pars ii. cap. 86, 5.

Note A.

"There is in reality," writes Auguste Nicolas, referring to *Eph.* iii. 14, 15, "one only paternity, that of God. It was an act of this paternity that brought forth the universe out of nothingness: And not less is God Father in the *reproduction* of the creatures that He first made, for He it is who gave them this power of reproduction. He might have created each successive individual, as He created the first one; instead whereof, He created in them species; whilst His own paternity operates over that of His creatures, which is but the instrument. Hence He is the paternity of fathers, and the maternity of mothers. . . . This the mother of the Machabees admirably expressed, when stripping herself, so to say, of her own maternity to restore it to God, and refer to Him the gratitude and confidence of her children whom she was encouraging to martyrdom, she said to them: 'I know not how you were formed in my womb: for I neither gave you breath, nor soul, nor life, neither did I frame the limbs of every one of you. But the Creator of the world that formed the nativity of man, and that found out the origin of all, He will restore to you again in His mercy, both breath and life, as now you despise yourselves for the sake of His laws.'[1]

"But here is not all the paternity of God. This is a *creative* paternity, which is paternity inasmuch as it gives life, but is not so, in that it does not give it of its own substance, nor engender it, nor reproduce itself. This latter paternity is evidently more perfect than the former: and those creatures to whom God has given it, would consequently have received from God more than He Himself possesses, had He been deprived of it, and thus *all* paternity would not descend from the Father, before whom we bend the knee, or would only descend from Him to exalt itself against His own infecundity. Shall God who makes fathers, not be Himself Father? 'Shall not I, that make others to bring forth children, Myself bring forth? saith the Lord. Shall I, that give generation to others, be barren? saith the Lord thy God.'[2] This may not be; and God is Father of another paternity, a *generative* paternity. By His creative paternity, He *makes*, He creates life in the world: by His generative paternity, He engenders life in a being which is the fruit of His own substance—His Wisdom, His Word, of whom the generation is eternal, and by whom, and to the image of whom, He has made and preserves life in all things: *Genitum, non factum, consubstantialem Patri, per quem omnia facta sunt.* Thus in wondrous manner are these two paternities, generative and creative, connected together. By His generative paternity God is eternally Father of the Word who springs unceasingly from His bosom; and by this same Word creating life in the world, He acquires a creative paternity, that is, so to say, a springing forth from His generative paternity.

"Again, there is a third paternity of God, which attaches to the creative paternity and to the generative paternity; and this is His

---

[1] 2 *Mac.* vii. 22, 23.   [2] *Is.* lxvi. 9.

adoptive paternity, whereby we are made children of God in Jesus Christ. In the order of creation and nature, we are God's children, inasmuch as He has given us life—as to the rest of creatures—and has given it us to His own image and likeness by a special privilege; but we are not God's children, in the sense of being engendered by Him, sharing in His divine life, having part in His felicity, being heirs of His kingdom, and enjoying all the rights of natural and legitimate filiation. In this sense God has but one Son, *Only-begotten*, *Unigenitus*, Who is the Word. And just as by this *uncreated* Word, we have been created to the life of all creation, so by this same Word *incarnate*, Jesus Christ, we are raised from this condition of creatures to the dignity of children of God, as He is Himself; that is to say, we are begotten, not properly and strictly speaking, but by way of adoption, and, O prodigy of grace! identically, as to the effects, with all other adoptive filiation: in such sort that the Only-begotten (*Unigenitus*) Son of God becomes the *First-begotten* (*Primogenitus*) in relation to us, His brethren, His co-heirs, making us but one with Him, and by Him with God—ourselves Gods in some sort as He: *Ego dixi: Dei estis*.[1]

"Such are the three paternities of God, generative, creative, adoptive. The last is interlinked with the two others, and completes their design: for it raises the outflow of God's paternity in creation to the height of its source, and makes it in some sort return thither by virtue of the grace of Jesus Christ, 'which becomes in him who receives it a fountain of water springing up into everlasting life.'[2]

"Now the Blessed Virgin is in close relation with this threefold fecundity of God; she co-operates therewith; and may consequently be called in an eminent manner, the Spouse of the Heavenly Father, *of Whom is all paternity.*

"The Blessed Virgin has no share of co-operation in the generative fecundity of God, as regards His eternal generation of His Word, but as regards His generation of Him in time. I say that she co-operated as regards His generation in time: for the Son of God, we know, became Incarnate in the Virgin's womb. In this temporal generation He had no father, as in His eternal generation He had no mother; but this not in one and the same sense: for in an absolute sense He had no mother in His eternal generation, whilst only in a relative sense is it true to say that in His temporal generation He had no father, in the sense, viz., of human paternity that would infringe on virginity. Since, for that matter, in His temporal generation, He continued to have for Father Him Who begets Him eternally, that is to say, unceasingly, not by a paternity that passes away, but one that is continuous, of which the temporal generation in Mary's womb is, consequently, but an extension, if I may so say, and a continuation. In a word, Mary is not Mother of the Son of God as God is His Father, by any power of her own, but as the Angel announced to her, 'by the power of the Most High Who overshadowed her.'

"S. Hilary, Origen, S. Cyril, S. Ambrose, and S. Athanasius

---

[1] *Ps.* lxxxi. 6; *John* x. 34.   [2] *John* iv. 14.

teach the same, by referring to the temporal birth of the Word from the womb of Mary the words of the Psalmist cited by S. Paul: *Filius meus es tu: Ego hodie genuite.* 'Thou art My Son, to-day I have begotten Thee,'[1] that is to say, in time. It is also most especially to this temporal generation that the words quoted above from Isaias refer.[2] "Bossuet, commenting on *Ps.* ii. 7, says: 'It is no subversion of S. Paul's sense to refer the word *hodie, to-day*, to the temporal birth of the Son of God from the womb of the Blessed Virgin; and the same Apostle is not inconsistent with himself when in the *Acts*, he transfers its application to the Resurrection of Jesus Christ. For what really are this birth and this resurrection, but a continuation of His eternal generation, and, so to say a sort of progress and extension? Surely, when the Holy Ghost came upon Mary and the power of the Most High overshadowed her, the Heavenly Father did nought else but pour forth His Only Son from His own bosom wherein He bore Him into the bosom of Mary, and thus begat Him in a new way; whence the Angel infers: "And therefore also the Holy which shall be born of thee shall be called the Son of God." Son, consequently, not adopted, but own and proper; so that this Holy, who is God and Man, was one only natural Son of God. For the same reason He Himself expressed His twofold birth by one single word, saying: "I came forth from the Father, and am come into the world:"[4]—the same, from His Father eternally, and from man temporally, come forth, and come into the world: whereon S. Hilary says: "Having come from the Father because He came forth from God, this coming forth from God is His birth, properly speaking."[5] Not that anything is wanting to His eternal birth, but that remaining the same, by His advent into the world, He becomes by extension Man, and Son of Man.'[6]

"Thus the temporal birth of the Son of God is but an extension of His eternal birth. Consequently, Mary is His Mother by an extension of God's paternity, that is, of His generative paternity. The maternity of our own mothers is, as we have seen, also an extension of God's paternity, but of His creative paternity—the original matter, so to speak, of which is nothingness—as it is in the rest of creation. Besides, this is not an immediate paternity; for it is exercised over the generations of our fathers. But the paternity with which Mary is associated is that proper Paternity of God, whereof the substance is God Himself, begetting from all eternity a Son like to Himself; a Paternity unique, personal, admitting none other to its participation, and which drawn from the infinite depths of Being, is its perpetual and immanent act. Thus it is by the immediate power of this same act of the generative Paternity of God that Mary is Mother, with a Maternity unique in time, as this Paternity is unique in eternity, and which associated immediately with this Paternity, without intermediation of any other, forms a Maternity divine and virginal. It is through means of this august Maternity that the generative Paternity of God has come forth in

[1] *Ps.* ii. 7; *Acts* xiii. 33; *Heb.* i. 5; v. 5.   [2] *Is.* lxvi. 9.
[3] *Luke* i. 35.   [4] *John* xvi. 28.   [5] *De Trinit.* l. ix. n. 30.
[6] *Supplenda in Psalmos*, in *Ps.* ii. 7.

time, and revealed itself in sight of men. Of both the fruit is one and the same, viz., the Word; of God alone the Son in eternity; of God and of Mary—her alone—in time: so that in Mary's giving Him thus to the world, conjointly with the Eternal Father, we may say with Cardinal Berulle, that she is the Mother in solidarity, so to speak, of Him, of whom He is eternally the Father, and that they two together have for their own one only Son.

"'After that, O Mary,' writes Bossuet, 'had I the intelligence of an Angel, and of the most sublime hierarchy, my conceptions would be too mean to comprehend that union most perfect of the Eternal Father with thee. Associating thee to His eternal generation, He has made thee Mother of one same Son with Himself. He has willed thee to be the Mother of His Only Son, and Himself to be the Father of thine. O prodigy! O abyss of Charity! What mind would not lose itself in contemplating the incomprehensible complacencies that He had for thee, since thou touchest Him so nearly by this Son thou hast in common with Him, the inviolable knot of your holy alliance, the pledge of your mutual affections, which you have lovingly given the one to the other: He full of impassible deity, thou clothed, in obedience to Him, with mortal flesh.'[1]

"Thus sublimely, holily, and in a way altogether above all human conceptions, we may say that Mary is the Spouse of the Father considered in His highest, that is, His generative paternity.

"But Mary is also associated with His adoptive paternity; as is evident.

"Jesus Christ, the Only Son of God and of Mary, is, because He is Son by nature, the First-born, regarded as Head of the elect, His brethren, His members and His co-heirs by adoption. And this filiation by adoption is not a mere consequence, but is the proper end of the Incarnation of the Word. Mary gave birth to the Son of God in time, only to give children to God in eternity, and to make Him Father of the elect. Thus is it through Mary, that God is Father not only of the Word Incarnate, but also of the whole race of Christians. This adoptive paternity of God is grafted on His generative paternity, and the title of Spouse which belongs to Mary from her relation to this latter, must consequently extend to His adoptive paternity.

"Nay, it must extend also to the creative paternity of God.

"As we have already established in our first book, the divine plan of creation must all be referred to Jesus Christ. God has created heaven and earth, angels and men, together with all that exists, only as an accompaniment of Jesus Christ, the one chief end of His works, who ordered their whole arrangement. Christ in this sense, is the reason of all, *propter quem omnia*. It hence follows, that in giving to the world, conjointly with the Heavenly Father, the Son of God, Mary gave the creative reason of the world. And she gave it knowingly and willingly, since in this august marriage of God with human nature, the consent of the holy Virgin was asked. Across, then, the four thousand years which divide the Creation from the Incarnation, and which are nothing to Him, 'with whom one day is as a thousand years, and a thousand years as one day,'[2] we must look for some

[1] 3me *Serm. sur la Nativ. de la Ste. Vierge.* Point 2.   [2] 2 *Pet.* iii. 8.

connection between the *Fiat* of God who created heaven and earth, and the *Fiat* of Mary who conceived their Lord and Heir; between the Spirit of God, Who moved over the abyss whence were to come forth the world and nature, and the same Spirit Who came upon Mary, as upon another abyss of voluntary nothingness and humility, from whence has come forth the world of grace. Thus under the inspiration of one same plan, the creative paternity, the generative paternity, and the adoptive paternity of God were manifested, and Mary, associated immediately, as she was, with the most august of these paternities, was associated also with the two others."[1]

Note B.

"Inspiration must not be assumed to dispense with the ordinary means of acquiring knowledge, such as inquiry of eye-witnesses, when a fact is to be ascertained. If S. Luke, who has told us the most about our Lord's infancy and childhood, had said nothing whatever to lead us to think he used diligent inquiry to come at the facts, still we might fairly have assumed that he did use such inquiry. But as it is, he expressly tells us, that the reason why he wrote on the subject, was because he had accurately followed up all the circumstances from the first;[2] and he says, it seemed good to him *also* to do so, though others who had heard from those who had been eye-witnesses and ministers of the Word from the beginning, had written Gospels. Now what eye-witness of the Word from the beginning but Mary, there was to consult, it is not very easy to say. S. Joseph was certainly dead before the Crucifixion, as he would else have been the proper person to have entrusted Mary to. S. Luke therefore had recourse to our Lady for information. . . .

"Again, S. John, who beyond all doubt was acquainted with the Blessed Virgin, had opportunities of hearing from her of the Conception, *i.e.*, *that which was from the beginning;* of the Visitation and Nativity, *i.e.*, *that which we have heard;* and of knowing the Personal appearance of Jesus, *i.e.*, *that which we have seen with our eyes;* and the miracles, transfiguration, agony, and passion, *i.e.*, what we have been spectators of: *which we have looked upon;* and the Resurrection, *i.e.*, what we have felt with our hands concerning the Word of life: *and our hands have handled of the Word of life.* . . . It certainly seems as if S. John was here going through the different events of our Lord's life from first to last, and encouraging the disciples to trust to ear-witnesses and eye-witnesses for the truths he had preached to them. But this is less certain than the passage of S. Luke. Nevertheless, what from S. Luke is certain of one Evangelist, that we may feel next to certain was the case with all. But if the Evangelists depended upon the Blessed Virgin for their information, and there is consequently no reason to make a miraculous, where a natural source is at hand, then she could make her own terms.

"The Magnificat shows us what sort of Gospel Mary would dictate, viz., one in which all her own privileges were kept as much out of sight, and all that tended to humble herself in men's eyes put as

---

[1] *La Vierge Marie*, etc., t. i. pp. 308-316. 1869.
[2] παρηκολουθηκότι ἄνωθεν πᾶσιν ἀκριβῶς, *Luke* i. 1-4.

much forward, as possible. Hence we see why things that seem at first sight to be disparaging to her are inserted; humility, even in ordinary saints, rejoices in having such things put forward. A blind obedience to Mary's will then, will account for the little that the Evangelists say of her, quite as well, to say the least, as the supposition that they thought but little of her. It is worth remarking, that the Gospel written last of all contains in our view of the matter two things regarding Mary; one is, that the first miracle is done in obedience to her, and the other is, that *after* Jesus had made John her son, John always introduces himself as 'that disciple whom Jesus loved.' We will say nothing here of allusions to her in the *Apocalypse*, as 'Ark of the Covenant,' or, the Tabernacle which was blasphemed, or as 'a woman clothed with the sun.'[1] When the pressure of Mary's humility is removed, S. John begins to disclose her prerogatives with her Son, even after he had commenced his ministry. S. John does this after her departure, even at the sacrifice of his own humility.

"Now if anyone replies to this, that if the veneration and worship of the Virgin was of as great consequence as it has been represented in this book to be, it pertained to the Providence of God to see that a thing so important was fully declared in His revelation to man; we answer, that we most fully admit. Nevertheless, revelation consists of Scripture *and* Tradition, the written *and* the living oracles of God, and hence whoever will be saved must hold fast the traditions delivered to the saints once for all. But if Scripture is deficient upon the point of Mary's privileges, nobody will be therefore safe for neglecting to profit by them: for Scripture takes good care to inform you, that there is another source to draw the waters of salvation from: 'Stand fast,' says S. Paul, 'and hold the traditions which you have learned, whether by word, or by our Epistle.'[2] Hence if the Epistles say nothing about our Lady, the traditions learnt by word might have said a great deal about her. S. Paul might have taught his disciples to call her 'Blessed,' by epistle; but he does not do so. He might have taught that John was made her son at the Crucifixion, by epistle; but he does not do so. He might have told them, when recommending obedience and respect to parents, that Jesus was subject to Mary at Nazareth, did a miracle to please her at Cana, and thought of her in His torments on the Cross, by epistle; but he does not do so. Yet there would have been nothing 'unscriptural' in all this: a pious Protestant might have said it. Nay, it would have been 'unscriptural' to omit it, unless he had also given them traditions by word to hold fast.

"The silence of the New Testament then may be explained, by remembering that Christians learn their religion by tradition: the Apostles learnt from Mary, and the first Christians from the Apostles. This is the case with the silence of Scripture, even when it is not overstated: but it may be overstated. The same is the case with the silence of tradition: it is in part overstated, in part it may be explained."[3]

[1] *Apoc.* xi. 19; xii. 1; xiii. 6.   [2] *Thess.* ii. 14.
[3] *Jesus the Son of Mary*, etc. By the Rev. John Brande Morris, M.A. 1851. Vol. ii. p. 147-151.

LIST OF AUTHORS,
QUOTED OR REFERRED TO ON THE PAGES INDICATED.

A.

Ægidius Romanus, Cardinal, a disciple of S. Thomas Aquinas, very devout to the B. Virgin ; Prior General of the Order of the Hermits of S. Augustine, died **1316**, 117.

Albert, B., the Great, Archbishop of Ratisbon, **1194-1280**, 131, 142, 230, 233, 264, 270, 273.

Alexius Segala a Salo, an Italian, O.S.F., renowned for his preaching, learning, and piety. He wrote, **1608**, his treatise, *Ars singularis amandi et colendi B.V. Mariam*, 224, 272.

Alphonsus Liguori, S., Doctor, Bishop of S. Agatha of the Goths, **1696-1787**, 90, 110, 206, 231, 233, 236, 262.

Ambrose, S., Doctor, Bishop of Milan, **340-397**, 39, 102, 117, 121, 127, 144, 155, 169, 172, 179, 191, 194, 195, 207, 213, 217, 218, 228, 231, 234, 243, 250, 276.

Anselm, S., Doctor, Archbishop of Canterbury, **1033-1109**, 39, 155, 205, 245, 263.

Antoninus, S., Archbishop of Florence, **1389-1459**, 103, 106, 143, 152, 160, 161, 195, 199, 201, 218, 227, 228, 234, 240, 246, 250, 257, 261, 270.

Aretas, Andrew, Archbishop of Cæsarea in Cappadocia ; the first ecclesiastical author who has left a commentary on the Apocalypse. He most probably lived at the latest before the latter part of the V. century. There was another Aretas, successor to the former in the same See, who also wrote a commentary on the Apocalypse very much in the line of his predecessor. Some critics place him at the close of the V. century or in the VI. Others considerably later, 267.

Armandus de Bello-visu, O. P., born in Provence, Lector Sacri Palatii in the time of John XXII. ; died about **1334**, 234.

Athanasius, S., Doctor, Patriarch of Alexandria, **297-373**, 276.

Augustine, S., Doctor, Bishop of Hippo, **354-430**, 89, 98, *Int. Opp.* 110, 119, 135, 139, 140, 145, 149, 151, 153, 166, 167, 168, 174, 175, 193, 199, 228, 268.

B.

Barradas, Sebastian, S. J., Portuguese, **1543-1615**, 253.

Basil, of Seleucia, S., Bishop, cl. **448**, 120, 237.

Bede, S., the Venerable, Abbot, O. S. B., Anglo-Saxon, **671-735**, 228.

Bernard, S., Doctor, Abbot of Clairvaux, **1091-1153**, 101, 123, 137, 141, 169, 187, 270, 271, 272, 273, 274.

Bernardine of Sienna, S., O. S. F., **1380-1444**, 88, 89, 206, 242.

Berulle, Cardinal, **1575-1629**, 278.

Bonaventure, S., Doctor, O. S. F., Cardinal, Bishop of Albano, **1221-1274**, 154, 224, 236, 246, 263, 269.

Bossuet, Bishop of Meaux, **1629-1704**, 277, 278.

Bridget, S., **1302-1373**, 232.

Brower, Adam, Dutch writer of the present century, 235.

C.

Cajetan, Cardinal, Archbishop of Palermo, General O. P., **1469-1534**, 177.

Canus, Melchior, O. P., Spaniard, **1524-1560**, 33.

Cassian, Abbot, native of Egypt, or Scythia according to some, **355-430**, 220.

Chrysostom, S. John, Doctor, Archishop of Constantinople, **347-407**, 22, 53-55, 60-2, 125, 216.

Cornelius a Lapide, S. J., **1566-1637**, 151, 214, 233, 262.

Cyril of Alexandria, Patriarch, Doctor, died **444**, 276.

Cyril, S., of Jerusalem, Bishop, Doctor, **315-386**, 127.

D.

Daniel Agricola, of the Order of Friars Minor, wrote at the beginning of the XVI. century, 197, 200, 269, 271.

D'Argentan, Capuchin, of the present century, 170.

E.

Ephrem, S., Deacon of the Church of Edessa, and probably Priest, born at the end of the III. or at the beginning of the IV. century ; died **379**, 105, 106, 125, 145, 164, 165, 180, 223, 224, 233, 267.

Epiphanius, S., Doctor, Archbishop of Salamis, 149, 153, 193, 268

Estius, Professor at Louvain and Douay, of which latter he was Chancellor, died **1613,** 176.

Eusebius of Emisa, Bishop, native of Edessa, **295-359,** some few of his works in Greek have survived, 147.

F.

Franzelin, Cardinal, S. J., of the present century, 71.

G.

Germanus, S., Patriarch of Constantinople, 13th century, 233.

Gerson, Chancellor of the University of Paris, **1363-1429,** 174.

Gregory, S., Thaumaturgus, Bishop of Neo-Cæsarea, from **240** until **270,** 264.

Gregory, S., of Nyssa, Bishop, **331-395,** 224.

Guerric, Canon and Professor at the Cathedral School of Tournay, entered the Cistercian Order at Clairvaux, **1131,** made by S. Bernard Abbot of Igny, **1138,** died **1157,** 165.

H.

Hilary, S., Bishop of Poictiers, Doctor, died about **368,** 276, 277.

Hugo, Cardinal, O. P., XIII. century, 155, 272.

I.

Ignatius, S., Martyr, Bishop of Antioch, martyred **107**, 63, 135.
Ildephonsus, S., Archbishop of Toledo, **607-667**, 101, 200.
Innocent III., Pope, **1198-1216**, 253.
Irenæus, S., Bishop of Lyons, from **177** until his martyrdom, **202**, 170.
Isidore, Archbishop of Thessalonica, cl. **1401**, 205.
Isidore, S., Bishop of Seville, **560-636**, 169.

J.

Jacobus de Voragine, B., O. P., Archbishop of Genoa, died **1298**, beatified by Pius VII., 198, 209, 270, 271.
Jeanjacquot, S. J., of the present century, 153.
Jerome, S., Doctor, **331-420**, 63, 127, 149. 154, *Int. Opp. ibid.*, 163, 194, 206, 234.
John Damascene, S., Monk, died **780**, 160.
Justin, S., Martyr, **100-166**, 170.

L.

Ludolph of Saxony, born about **1280**, entered **1300** the Dominican Order, after some 30 years passed to that of the Carthusians at Strasburg, where he became Prior, 274.
Lyra, Nicholas of, entered into the Order of S. Francis, **1291**, Professor of Theology at Paris, died there as Provincial, **1340**, 154.

M.

Melia, of the present century, 151.
Methodius, S., of Patara, Bishop of Tyre, martyred **312**, 268.
Morales, S. J., wrote **1610**, 32, 134, 154, 169, 174, 205, 206.
Morris, John Brande, of the present century, 267-9, 279-80.

N.

Newman, Cardinal, 140, 247, 266, 267.
Nilus, S., Abbot, V. century, 149.
Nicolas, Auguste, of the present century, 275-9.

O.

Origen, **185-254**, 63, 64, 276.
Osorius, Jerome, of Lisbon, **1506-1580**, 158.

P.

Patrick, S., Apostle of Ireland, **373-493**, 112.
Peter, the Venerable, Abbot of Cluny, contemporary of S. Bernard, died **1156**, 227.
Prudentius, Latin Christian Poet, Spaniard, **348-413**, 168.

R.

Rupert, Abbot of Deutz, O. S. B., XI. century, 39, 155.
Richard of S. Lawrence, 120.

S.

Sedulius, Latin poet, IV. century, 98.
Sophronius, S., Bishop of Jerusalem, died **637**, 89, 206.
Suarez, S. J., **1548-1617**, 33, 38-40.
Sulpicius Severus, Priest of Agen, died at Marseilles about **403**, *Int. Opp.*, 187.

T.

Tauler, John, O. P. **1290-1361**, 185.
Tertullian, born at Carthage **150**, converted **185**, Priest **192**, died between **220** and **240**, 170.
Theophylact, Archbishop of Achris, XI. century, 214.
Thomas of Aquin, S., Doctor, O. P., **1226-1274**, 88, 89, 147, 148, 149, 174, 176, 231, 269.
Thomas, S., of Villanova, Hermit of S. Augustine, Archbishop of Valence, **1488-1555**, 66.

ANALYTICAL INDEX OF SUBJECTS.

MARY, MOTHER OF GOD—HER SUBLIME DIGNITY.—*Rom.* i. 1-5; viii. 14-17; ix. 4, 5. 2 *Cor.* i. 14; viii. 9, 23. *Gal.* iv. 1, 2, 4-7. *Eph.* i. 19-23; ii. 18-22; iii. 1-3; iv. 8-10. *Philip.* i. 21. *Col.* i. 15-19; ii. 3, 9, 10. 2 *Thess.* i. 10, 12. 1 *Tim.* iii. 9, 14, 16. 2 *Tim.* i. 14; ii. 12; iv. 8. *Tit.* ii. 11, 13. *Heb.* i. 3-14; ii. 5, 9, 14-16; iii. 5, 6; v. 4-9; vii. 14; ix. 11, 12, 24; x. 5, 19-21; xii. 22-24. 1 *Pet.* iii. 22. 1 *John* iii. 1-3; iv. 2, 3.

MARY'S PREDESTINATION AND VOCATION.—*Rom.* i. 1-5, 14; viii. 28-30; ix. 23. 1 *Cor.* i. 4-9, 24-31. *Gal.* i. 15, 16. *Eph.* i. 1-12. *Philip.* i. 6. 2 *Thess.* ii. 12, 13. *James* ii. 5.

MARY'S PLENITUDE OF GRACES AND PRIVILEGES CORRESPONDING TO HER ELECTION.—*Rom.* v. 2, 17; viii. 28-32; xi. 33-36; xii. 6; xiv. 17, 18; xv. 15-17; xvi. 20. 1 *Cor.* i. 4-9, 24-30; ii. 9-16; vi. 15, 19, 20. 2 *Cor.* iii. 6-9; iv. 15. *Eph.* i. i-12; iv. 7-13; v. 30; vi. 24. *Philip.* i. 10, 11; iv. 1, 7. 1 *Thess.* v. 23. 2 *Thess.* i. 11, 12; ii. 3, 4. 2 *Tim.* i. 14; ii. 20, 21. *Heb.* xii. 28; xiii. 20, 21. *James* i. 17, 18; iv. 6-10.

MARY'S FULNESS OF THE HOLY GHOST, AND SPIRIT OF ADOPTION.— *Rom.* v. 17; viii. 14-17. 1 *Cor.* ii. 9-16; iii. 16, 17; vi. 19. *Gal.* iv. 4-7. *Eph.* iii. 16, 19. *James* i. 18. 1 *John* ii. 20; iii. 24.

MARY'S SINLESSNESS AND IMMACULATE CONCEPTION.—*Rom.* iii. 23; viii. 10, 11; xvi. 20. 1 *Cor.* i. 9; x. 31. 2 *Cor.* vi. 14-18. *Gal.* iv. 22-31. *Eph.* i. 3-5. *Philip.* i. 6. *Col.* i. 21, 22. 1 *Thess.* v. 23. 1 *Tim.* iv. 10. *Heb.* vii. 26. 1 *John* i. 8; iii. 8.

ANALYTICAL INDEX OF SUBJECTS. 287

MARY'S SANCTITY, UNION WITH GOD, CONFORMITY TO HIS WILL, AND LIKENESS TO JESUS CHRIST.—*Rom.* viii. 29, xii. 1, 2; xiv. 8. 1 *Cor.* iii. 16, 17; x. 31; xv. 47. 2 *Cor.* iii. 18; vi. 1. *Philip.* i. 20-24; ii. 5-8; iv. i. 1 *Thess.* v. 23; 2 *Thess.* ii. 3, 4. *Heb.* iv. 13; xii. 22-24; xiii. 20, 21. 1 *John* ii. 5; iii. 21-24.

MARY'S GRATUITOUS GIFTS ("GRATIÆ GRATIS DATÆ").—1 *Cor.* xii. 4-11. 1 *John* iv. 1.

MARY'S PLACE AND OFFICE IN CHRIST'S MYSTICAL BODY THE CHURCH: ANALOGY BETWEEN MARY AND THE CHURCH.—*Rom.* x. 15; xii. 4-6; xv. 29. 1 *Cor.* iii. 9; iv. 1; vi. 15-20; xi. 3, 7-12; xv. 28. 2 *Cor.* iii. 6-9; xi. 2, 3. *Gal.* iv. 4-7. *Eph.* ii. 18-23; iv. 11-13; v. 29, 32. *Col.* ii. 19. 1 *Tim.* iii. 4, 5, 14-16. 2 *Tim.* i. 14; ii, 20, 21. *Heb.* iii. 5, 6.

HER RELATION TO THE PRIESTHOOD OF JESUS CHRIST.—*Heb.* v. 4-7; vii. 26; ix. 12; x. 5, 19, 20, 21.

MARY'S POWER OF INTERCESSION AND COMMUNICATING GRACE AND SANCTIFICATION.—*Rom.* i. 9-12, 14; viii. 26, 27; x. 15; xv. 15-17, 29-33: xvi. 1-16. 1 *Cor.* iv. 1, 2. 2 *Cor.* i. 10, 11. *Eph.* iii. 12-19; vi. 18, 19. *Philip.* i. 3-5, 9-11, 19. *Col.* i. 25-28; iv. 12. 2 *Thess.* iii. 1. 1 *Tim.* ii. 1-6; iii. 13; iv. 16. 2 *Tim.* ii. 10. *Heb.* iv. 14-16; v. 4-9; ix. 11, 12, 24; xii. 20-24. *James* i. 17; v. 16-18. 1 *Pet.* iv. 10; v. 8. 1 *John* i. 1-3; ii. 1; iii. 21-24; iv. 21.

MARY THE SECOND EVE.—*Rom.* xvi. 20. 1 *Cor.* xi. 3, 7-12; xv. 22; 2 *Cor.* xi. 2, 3. 1 *Tim.* ii. 15. *Heb.* v. 8, 9. 1 *John* iii. 1-3. *Apoc.* xii. 1-17.

MARY'S CO-OPERATION IN THE WORK OF REDEMPTION.—*Rom.* viii. 32; xi. 33-36; xvi. 1-16. 1 *Cor.* iii. 9; xi. 3, 7-12; xv. 22. 2 *Cor.* i. 1-7; vi. i. *Col.* i. 24-27. 1 *Tim.* ii. 15; iv. 16. 2 *Tim.* ii. 10, 12. *Heb.* ii. 9, 10; ix. 11, 12, 24.

MARY OUR MOTHER.—*Rom.* iv. 16-18; viii. 32; ix. 8, 9; xv. 15-17; xvi. 1, 2. 1 *Cor.* iv. 14-16; xii. 26, 27. 2 *Cor.* vi. 11-13. *Gal.* iii. 6-9, 26, 29; iv. 4-7, 19, 20, 22-31. *Eph.* iii. 15. *Note* A, p. 275. *Eph.* iv. 11-13; v. 8, 29, 30. *Col.* ii. 1, 5; iv. 18. 1 *Thess.* ii. 7, 8, 11. *Tit.* i. 4. *Philemon* 10. *Heb.* ii. 11, 16, 17. *James* ii. 21. 1 *John* iii. 1-3, 8-10, 13.

MARY'S MERCY AND COMPASSION—HER ZEAL FOR SOULS.—*Rom.* i. 14; ix. 1-3; x. 10; xii. 19. 1 *Cor.* x. 33. *Gal.* iv. 19, 20. *Philip.* i. 7-11. *Col.* ii. 1, 5; iv. 12. 1 *Thess.* i. 7, 8, 11, 17-20. 1 *Tim.* v. 8. 2 *Tim.* iv. 6-8. *Heb.* ii. 18; iv. 14, 16. 1 *John* iv. 21.

MARY'S SHARE IN THE PASSION OF HER SON—HER DOLOURS—HER PATIENCE.—*Rom.* v, 3, 4; vi. 5, 8; viii. 17-19, 35-39; ix. 2, 3, 32, 33; xii. 12. 1 *Cor.* xii. 26. 2 *Cor.* i. 3-7; iv. 10, 11; vi. 4-10. *Gal.* ii. 19, 20; iii. 1; vi. 2, 14, 17. *Eph.* iii. 18; v. 29, 30; vi. 17. *Philip.* i. 29; iii. 10, 11; iv. 1. *Col.* iv. 18. 2 *Tim.* ii. 10-12. *Heb.* ii. 9, 10, 18; iv. 12; v. 8, 9; xi. 38-40; xiii. 12, 13. *James* i. 3, 4, 12; ii. 21-23; v. 7, 8, 11. 1 *Pet.* i. 6, 8; ii. 20, 21; iv. 13; v. 1. 1 *John* iii. 16.

MARY'S JOYS.—*Rom.* v. 2, 3; xii. 12; xv. 13. 1 *Cor.* xi. 26. 2 *Cor.* i. 3-7; ix. 6. *James* i. 9, 10. 1 *Pet.* i. 1-7; iv. 13.

MARY THE GLORY OF HER SON, AND THE SON THE GLORY OF HIS MOTHER.—*Rom.* xiii. 14. 1 *Cor.* xi. 3, 7-12. *Philip.* i. 20. 2 *Thess.* i. 10-12. *Heb.* i. 1.

MARY, AFTER HER SON, THE FIRST-FRUITS OF THE ELECT; ABOVE ALL ANGELS AND SAINTS IN SANCTITY AND DIGNITY.—*Rom.* viii. 29; xvi. 5. 1 *Cor.* xv. 23, 41. *Eph.* i. 19, 23; ii. 18-52; iv. 3-10. *Col.* ii. 19. 2 *Thess.* ii. 12, 13. 1 *Tim.* iv. 10. *Heb.* i. 3-11; iii. 5, 6; xi. 38; xii. 22-24. *James* i. 18.

MARY'S CLAIMS ON OUR HONOUR, PRAISE, SALUTATION, LOVE, GRATITUDE, AND INVOCATION.—*Rom.* ii. 10, 29; viii. 26, 27; x. 15; xii. 14, 15; xiii. 7, 8, 14, 15; xiv. 18; xv, 15-17, 30-32; xvi. 1-16. 1 *Cor.* ix. 1. 2 *Cor.* iv. 5; viii. 23; ix. 6. *Gal.* i. 24; vi. 8. *Eph.* v. 29, 30; vi. 1. *Philip.* i. 20; ii. 1, 29, 30; iv. 21. *Col.* iii. 20; iv. 12, 18. 2 *Thess.* i. 4; ii. 12, 13; iii. 1. 1 *Tim.* v. 3, 5-10. 2 *Tim.* ii. 20, 21. *Heb.* iii. 5, 6; v. 4-9; xiii. 16, 24. 1 *Pet.* v. 1.

MARY, OUR SWEETNESS, HOPE, JOY, CROWN, AND GLORY—IN GLORIFYING HER, WE GLORIFY GOD.—*Rom.* i. 1-16. 2 *Cor.* i. 14; iv. 15; x. 17, 18. *Gal.* i. 24. *Eph.* v. 1, 2. *Philip.* i. 9, 11; ii. 1; iv. 1. 1 *Thess.* ii. 19, 20. 2 *Thess.* i. 4, 12.

DEVOTION TO MARY, THE MARK OF THE TRUE FAITHFUL.—2 *Thess.* ii. 3, 4. 1 *John* iii. 1-3; iv. 2, 3.

MARY'S SUBLIME WISDOM AND KNOWLEDGE—HER MAGNIFICAT.—
Rom. xv. 14. 1 *Cor.* i. 27-31; ii. 7-10, 12, 16; iv. 7; ix. 7; xii. 8-11. 2 *Cor.* iv. 6; x. 4, 5, 17, 18. *Gal.* ii. 20; iii. 6-18; vi. 14. *Eph.* i. 17, 18; iii. 4, 5, 14-19; v. 18-20, 24; vi. 17. *Philip.* ii. 5. *Col.* ii. 3, 9, 10; iii. 15-17; v. 26. 1 *Tim.* iii. 15; iv. 10. *Heb.* ix. 2; xiii. 15. *James* i. 9, 10; iii. 17, 18; iv. 6-8, 10. 1 *John* ii. 20.

HER DISCERNMENT OF THE HOLY EUCHARIST.—1 *Cor.* xi. 29.

MARY'S INTIMATE CONVERSE WITH JESUS CHRIST DURING HIS LIFE ON EARTH—FROM HER THE APOSTLES AND EVANGELISTS LEARNT MANY THINGS OF HIM, THAT WERE CONTAINED IN THEIR ORAL TEACHING, AND IN THEIR WRITINGS.—*Rom.* viii. 29; xv. 14. 1 *Cor.* ii. 16; 2 *Cor.* iii. 18; iv. 6. *Heb.* ii. 3; ix. 2. 1 *Pet.* i. 8, 10-12, 23, 25; vi. 1. 2 *Pet.* i. 16-18; iii. 15-18. 1 *John* 1-3. *Note* B, p. 279. *Jude* 3.

HER SHARE IN THE POVERTY OF JESUS CHRIST.—2 *Cor.* viii. 9.

MARY AN IDEAL OF ALL VIRTUES.—1 *Cor.* xiii. 4-8. 2 *Cor.* vi. 3-10. *Gal.* v. 22-25. *Philip.* iv. 3-9. *Col.* ii. 19. 1 *Tim.* i. 5; ii. 9-12; iv. 12-16. *Tit.* ii. 4, 5. *James* i. 19-27; iii. 17, 18. 1 *John* iii. 21-24.

MARY A MODEL FOR OUR IMITATION.—1 *Cor.* iv. 16; ix. 22; xi. 1. *Eph.* v. 1, 2. *Philip.* iii. 17; iv. 4-9. *Col.* iii. 17. 2 *Thess.* iii. 9. 1 *Tim.* i. 5; iv. 12. *James* i. 19-27. 1 *Pet.* i. 12.

MARY'S FAITH, HOPE, AND CHARITY.—*Rom.* iv. 3, 16-25; v. 1-5; viii. 28, 35-39; xii. 12; xiv. 8; xv. 13, 14. 1 *Cor.* xi. 29. *Gal.* iii. 6-9. *Eph.* iii. 17-19; vi. 24. *Philip.* i. 21, 23, 29. 1 *Tim.* i. 5; iii. 9; iv. 10. *Heb.* iv. 2, 3; xi. 11, 12, 17-19. *James* i. 12; ii. 1-5, 21-23. 1 *Pet.* i. 1-8; v. 7. 1 *John* ii. v.; iv. 21.

MARY'S HUMILITY AND OBEDIENCE.—*Rom.* xii. 10, 11, 16; xiii. 1; xiv. 18. 1 *Cor.* i. 24-31; xi. 3. 2 *Cor.* x. 4, 5. *Eph.* v. 23, 24; vi. 1. *Philip.* ii. 5-8. *Col.* iii. 20. 2 *Thess.* ii. 3, 4. 1 *Tim.* iii. 3. *Heb.* xii. 28. *James* i. 9, 10, 21-25; ii. 1-4; iv. 6-10. 1 *Pet.* ii. 13. 1 *John* iv. 1.

MARY'S KINDNESS AND CONDESCENSION.—*Rom.* xii. 10, 13; xiv. 1; xv. 2. 1 *Cor.* ix. 22; xiii. 4-8. *Gal.* v. 13. 1 *Thess.* ii. 7, 8, 11. 1 *Tim.* v. 10. *Heb.* xiii. 16. *James* i. 19, 21, 27; ii. 1-5; 1 *John* iv. 21.

MARY'S SPIRIT OF SACRIFICE.—*Rom.* viii. 32; ix. 1-3; xii. 1. 2 *Cor.* v. 16. *Gal.* i. 16. *Eph.* v. 1, 2. *Heb.* xi. 11, 12, 17-19; xiii. 15, 16. *James* ii. 21-23. 1 *John* iii. 16.

MARY'S MEDITATION, SILENCE, AND PRAYER, THANKSGIVING, REVERENCE, STUDY OF JESUS CHRIST.—*Rom.* ii. 29; viii. 29; xii. 11, 12, 16; xiv. 17, *Col.* ii. 15-17. 1 *Tim.* ii. 11, 12; iv. 15; v. 5. *Heb.* xii. 28. *James* i. 21-25.

MARY'S KEEPING GOD'S WORD.—*Rom.* ii. 13, 29. *Heb.* iv. 2. *James* i. 21-25. 1 *John* ii. 5; iii. 21-24.

MARY A MODEL FOR CHRISTIAN WOMEN.—1 *Tim.* ii. 9-12, 15; iii. 11. *Tit.* ii. 4, 5. 1 *Pet.* iii. 1-5.

MARY THE SPOUSE OF JOSEPH.—2 *Cor.* xi. 2, 3. *Gal.* iv. 1, 2. *Eph.* v. 22-24, 31, 32. *Col.* iii. 18. 1 *Pet.* v. 7.

MARY HAD JESUS CHRIST SUBJECT TO HER.—*Gal.* iv. 1, 2. *Eph.* vi. 1. *Col.* iii. 20. 1 *Tim.* iii. 4, 5; v. 10. *Heb.* i. 3-11; ii. 5; iii. 5, 6; vi. 10.

MARY AS VIRGIN.—1 *Cor.* vii. 25, 34-40. 2 *Cor.* xi. 2, 3. *Eph.* v. 32. 1 *Tim.* iii. 4.

HER VIRGINITY HIDDEN FROM THE DEVILS.—1 *Cor.* ii. 7, 8.

MARY AS WIDOW—HER LIFE AFTER THE ASCENSION.—*Rom.* xv. 14. 2 *Cor.* v. 6-9. *Philip.* i. 22-24; iii. 20. *Col.* iii. 1-3. 1 *Tim.* v. 3, 5-10. 2 *Tim.* iv. 6-8. *Heb.* iv. 3-9, 11. *James* i. 27; v. 7, 8.

PROPHECIES, PROMISES, AND TYPES FULFILLED IN MARY.—*Rom.* iv. 3, 16-25; ix. 4, 5, 8, 9, 23, 32, 35; xii. 1, 2; xv. 12. *Gal.* iii. 6-9, 14, 16, 18, 22, 26-29; iv. 22-31. *Heb.* vii. 1, 6, 14; ix. 2-4, 11, 12, 24; xi. 11, 12, 17-19, 39, 40. *James* ii. 23. 1 *Pet.* i. 10-12, *Apoc.* ii. 7, 28; xii. 1-17.

MARY'S OUTWARD PRIVILEGES OF ANCESTRY AND KIN.—*Rom.* ix. 3-5. 1 *Cor.* i. 24-31 ; ix. 5. *Gal.* i. 19. *Heb.* vii. 14.

MARY'S ASSUMPTION.—*Rom.* viii. 10, 11. 1 *Cor.* i. 8, 9. *Philip.* i. 6 ; iii. 21. *Heb.* ix. 11, 12, 24. *Apoc.* xii. 1-17.

MARY'S GLORY AND RECOMPENSE.—*Rom.* ii. 6, 7 ; v. 17 ; vi. 8 ; viii. 17, 19, 30; ix. 23. 1 *Cor.* ii. 9 ; xv. 23, 41. 2 *Cor.* iv. 17 ; v. 8 ; ix. 6. *Gal.* vi. 8. *Eph.* iv. 8-10. *Philip.* ii. 9-11 ; iii. 9. *Col.* iii. 4. 2 *Thess.* i. 10-12. 1 *Tim.* iii. 13 ; iv. 6-8. 2 *Tim.* ii. 10-12 ; *Heb.* i. 3-11 ; iv. 1-3, 9, 11 ; vi. 10 ; xii. 22-24. *James* i. 12; ii. 5 ; 1 *Pet.* i. 1-17; v. 1. 1 *John* iii. 1-3. *Apoc.* xii. 1-17.

www.ingramcontent.com/pod-product-compliance
Lightning Source LLC
Chambersburg PA
CBHW032046230426
43672CB00009B/1493